The Globalization of Foreign Aid

Why do aid agencies from wealthy donor countries with diverse domestic political and economic contexts arrive at very similar positions on a wide array of aid policies and priorities? This book suggests that this homogenization of policy represents the effects of common processes of globalization manifest in the aid sector. Drawing on both quantitative and qualitative analysis of policy adoption, the book argues that we need to examine macro-level globalizing influences at the same time as understanding the micro-level social processes at work within aid agencies, in order to adequately explain the so-called 'emerging global consensus' that constitutes the globalization of aid.

The book explores how global influences on aid agencies in Canada, Sweden, and the United States are mediated through micro-level processes. Using a mixed-methods approach, the book combines cross-national statistical analysis at the global level with two comparative case studies which look at the adoption of common policy priorities in the fields of gender and security. *The Globalization of Foreign Aid* will be useful to researchers of foreign aid, development, international relations and globalization, as well as to the aid policy community.

Liam Swiss is Associate Professor of Sociology at Memorial University of Newfoundland in St. John's, Canada.

Routledge Global Cooperation Series

This series develops innovative approaches to understanding, explaining and answering one of the most pressing questions of our time – how can cooperation in a culturally diverse world of nine billion people succeed?

   We are rapidly approaching our planet's limits, with trends such as advancing climate change and the destruction of biological diversity jeopardising our natural life support systems. Accelerated globalisation processes lead to an ever growing interconnectedness of markets, states, societies, and individuals. Many of today's problems cannot be solved by nation states alone. Intensified cooperation at the local, national, international, and global level is needed to tackle current and looming global crises.

Series editors:

Tobias Debiel, Claus Leggewie and Dirk Messner are Co-Directors of the Käte Hamburger Kolleg/Centre for Global Cooperation Research, University of Duisburg-Essen, Germany. Their research areas are, among others, Global Governance, Climate Change, Peacebuilding and Cultural Diversity of Global Citizenship. The three Co-Directors are, at the same time, based in their home institutions, which participate in the Centre, namely the German Development Institute/Deutsches Institut für Entwicklungspolitik (DIE, Messner) in Bonn, the Institute for Development and Peace (INEF, Debiel) in Duisburg and the Institute for Advanced Study in the Humanities (KWI, Leggewie, former Director, now retired) in Essen.

www.routledge.com/Routledge-Global-Cooperation-Series/book-series/RGC

Titles:

Integrating Sustainable Development in International Investment Law
Normative Incompatibility, System Integration and
Governance Implications
Manjiao Chi

Moral Agency and the Politics of Responsibility
Challenging Complexity
*Edited by Cornelia Ulbert, Peter Finkenbusch, Elena Sondermann
and Tobias Debiel*

Public Participation in African Constitutionalism
Edited by Tania Abbiate, Markus Böckenförde and Veronica Federico

Region-Making and Cross-Border Cooperation
New Evidence from Four Continents
Edited by Elisabetta Nadalutti and Otto Kallscheuer

"This long-awaited book provides a compelling account of why foreign aid donors engage in herd behaviour and how the process plays out in specific cases. In it, Liam Swiss makes a very insightful and nuanced contribution to the literature on foreign aid and policy diffusion."

— Stephen Brown, School of Political Studies,
University of Ottawa, Canada

"Based on sustained personal and professional experience, Liam Swiss provides a meticulous analysis of the many forces that produce convergence in international development policy, norms and priorities. Swiss manages the rare combination of compelling detail, clarity, and theoretical innovation."

— Emma Mawdsley, Reader in Human Geography,
University of Cambridge, UK

"Combining mixed-methods research with his insights as a former international aid worker, Swiss offers a compelling explanation of how donors get stuck in inflexible approaches to development. This books gives us a glimpse into both the dark side of global consensus, and how to break free of it."

— Elizabeth Heger Boyle, Professor of Sociology,
University of Minnesota, USA

"This book is an indispensable contribution to our understanding of how aid works. Swiss deftly explores the challenges faced by the development industry today and blazes new trails into the global politics of bilateral assistance. I know of no other comparative study of aid agencies that takes a sociological approach as sophisticated as this."

— Jeffrey T. Jackson, Associate Professor of Sociology,
University of Mississippi, USA, and author of The Globalizers:
Development Workers in Action

The Globalization of Foreign Aid

Developing Consensus

Liam Swiss

Routledge
Taylor & Francis Group

LONDON AND NEW YORK

Centre for
**Global
Cooperation
Research**

SPONSORED BY THE

Federal Ministry
of Education
and Research

First published 2018
by Routledge
2 Park Square, Milton Park, Abingdon, Oxon OX14 4RN

and by Routledge
711 Third Avenue, New York, NY 10017

Routledge is an imprint of the Taylor & Francis Group, an informa business

© 2018 Liam Swiss

British Library Cataloguing-in-Publication Data
A catalogue record for this book is available from the British Library

Library of Congress Cataloging-in-Publication Data
A catalog record for this book has been requested

ISBN: 978-1-138-56984-3 (hbk)
ISBN: 978-0-203-70404-2 (ebk)
ISBN: 978-1-138-56985-0 (pbk)

Typeset in Times New Roman
by Out of House Publishing

Printed and bound by CPI Group (UK) Ltd, Croydon, CR0 4YY

To Nicole, Noel, and Evie

Contents

List of figures and tables

Figures

Tables

Acknowledgements

Given this book is about how the individual power and agency of development workers shapes the globalization of foreign aid policy, the research was only possible through the willingness of development workers and donor officials in Canada, Sweden, and the United States to talk to me about their work and experiences. I am greatly indebted to their tolerance and support of the research process, and apologetic for the time it has taken for me to tell their story. In addition, my field-work in Sweden was helped immeasurably by the wonderful Petersson-Hökeberg family, who opened their homes and provided great assistance to my efforts during my stay.

I am grateful for the financial support of the Social Sciences and Humanities Research Council of Canada during this project's initial stages, and of the Käte Hamburger Kolleg/Centre for Global Cooperation Research at the Universität Duisburg-Essen, where I was a Senior Fellow at the time of its completion.

Special thanks are due to Kathleen Fallon, who as my mentor for many years enthusiastically ushered me through many drafts of the project that became this book. She encouraged me to be more daring in my claims and generously supported my research efforts even when it was not in keeping with her focus. Undoubtedly, she now knows more about bilateral foreign aid than she ever thought or hoped she might. I have also benefited greatly from her collaborative approach to research on other projects and her willingness to take me under her wing. It is her mentorship that most helped professionalize me as a researcher and taught me important lessons about when to say 'no' and when to celebrate small victories.

I also appreciate the guidance of other mentors and colleagues who have contributed to this research: Stephen Brown, Andrew Dawson, Mark Stoddart, Wes Longhofer, Karen Stanbridge, and others have all strengthened this project in one way or another.

Finally, the people deserving of the most thanks are Noel, Evangeline, and Nicole. My children, Noel and Evangeline, have done more to contribute to my work in the past ten years than either knows. Their assessment that my book 'sounds boring for kids' but that they plan to read it when they are adults is a promise I aim to hold them to. My wife, Nicole, has been the picture of support and understanding throughout this entire project; always challenging me and ensuring I do not take myself too seriously. In return, I promise I will not ask her to read it – even though she is already an adult.

LS
Duisburg, Germany
June 2017

List of abbreviations

ADB	Asian Development Bank
AWID	Association for Women's Rights in Development
CAD	Canadian Dollar
CCIC	Council for International Cooperation
CDPF	Country Development Programming Frameworks
CEDAW	Convention on the Elimination of All Forms of Discrimination Against Women
CIDA	Canadian International Development Agency
CMM	Conflict Management and Mitigation
CPDC	Conflict Peace and Development Cooperation
CPP	Conflict Prevention Pools
CRS	Creditor Reporting System
CSO	Civil Society Organizations
CUSO	Canadian University Service Overseas
DAC	Development Assistance Committee
DANIDA	Danish International Development Agency
DDR	Disarmament Demobilization Reintegration
DFAIT	Department of Foreign Affairs and International Trade (Canada)
DFID	Department for International Development (UK)
DND	Department of National Defence (Canada)
EAO	External Aid Office (Canada)
EU	European Union
GAD	Gender and Development
GNI	Gross National Income
GNP	Gross National Product
GOS	Government of Sweden
GPSF	Global Peace and Security Fund
GPSP	Global Peace and Security Program
HIPC	Highly Indebted Poor Country
IBRD	International Bank for Reconstruction and Development
ICPD	International Conference on Population and Development
IDA	International Development Association
IGO	Inter Governmental Organizations

IGWG	Interagency Gender Working Group (US)
ILO	International Labour Organization
INGO	International Non-Governmental Organization
MCC	Millennium Challenge Corporation
MDG	Millennium Development Goals
MFA	Ministry of Foreign Affairs
NGO	Non-Governmental Organization
ODA	Official Development Assistance
OECD	Organisation for Economic Co-operation and Development
PGD	Policy for Global Development (Sweden)
PRSP	Poverty Reduction Strategy Paper
PRT	Provincial Reconstruction Teams
PVO	Private Voluntary Organizations
SAREC	Swedish Agency for Research Cooperation
SEK	Swedish Kronor
Sida	Swedish International Development Cooperation Agency
SIDA	Swedish International Development Agency
SSR	Security Sector Reform
START	Stabilization and Reconstruction Task Force
SWAP	Sector Wide Approaches
UNDP	United Nations Development Programme
UNFPA	United Nations Population Fund
UNICEF	United Nations Children's Fund
USAID	United States Agency for International Development
USD	United States Dollar
VOLAG	Voluntary Agencies
WAD	Women and Development
WID	Women in Development
WINGO	Women's International Non-Governmental Organization

About the author

Liam Swiss is Associate Professor of Sociology at Memorial University of Newfoundland in St. John's, Canada. His research examines the role of foreign aid in international norm diffusion, violence against aid workers, the politics of Canadian aid policy, and the causes and effects of women's political representation in the Global South. His research has appeared in journals such as the *American Sociological Review, Social Forces, Social Science Research,* and *World Development*. He is a past-President of the Canadian Association for the Study of International Development. Before pursuing his doctorate, he worked at the Canadian International Development Agency on Canada's aid programme to Pakistan and the South Asia region.

Part I
Emerging global consensus?

1   The globalization of foreign aid?

CIDA does not 'do' sanitation

It was a bright, sunny morning in February 2001 and I was walking through an informal settlement (*katchiabadi*) on the outskirts of Peshawar, Pakistan. Fresh out of a Master's degree in International Development Studies, I was there as an official of the Canadian International Development Agency (CIDA) – the organization that delivered Canada's foreign aid to countries throughout the world. A colleague and I were toured about by the head of a local community organization running informal schools and undertaking other community development activities in the area. The tour was impressive. The group was doing excellent work on behalf of the community and had received funds for their education programmes from a larger CIDA project in the area. At the most basic level, this was what successful development was supposed to look like.

We asked the group leader about the community and what else CIDA could do to help them in the area. His one word answer: 'Sanitation.' Looking around the community, it was understandable why this was his response. The gutters in the makeshift streets were host to standing water that looked as unsanitary as it smelled and surely posed a health risk to children and others in the community. It was with a pit in my stomach that I nervously splurted out something like: 'I'm sorry sir, CIDA does not *do* sanitation in Pakistan anymore. Our new country priorities for Pakistan are education, governance, and gender equality.' He looked about as crestfallen as I felt. Having to decline to help what appeared to be a rather successful community-based organization with its sanitation concerns because CIDA's aid priorities for Pakistan had been focused in other directions was a tough lesson for an idealistic new development officer.

The problem was, that beyond CIDA not *doing* sanitation in Pakistan at that time, I knew other donors were also leaning away from programming in that area. Instead, donors were lining up to support the local governance devolution reforms of the military government at the time. It seemed unfair that a bona fide local need on the outskirts of Peshawar would go un-served simply because CIDA, DFID, USAID, Sida, and others had different priorities. In the end, there was little I could do. But the question was planted in my mind: 'Why do foreign aid donors tend to think and look alike when it comes to their aid priorities?'

After a few years of asking myself questions like this from within CIDA, I left to embark on research on this very topic. This book is the result of more than a decade of my thinking and research on the subject and my efforts to explain why aid donors think and act so similarly despite the fact they exist in very different domestic political, social, and economic contexts. I label this phenomenon of donor similarity the 'globalization of aid policy' – a phrase I will come back to throughout the book.

Globalization is an appropriate framework through which to view this phenomenon, as what emerges in the chapters that follow is a story of the convergence of donor policy and programming priorities around specific issues and norms that have truly global origins and scope. These convergences, I suggest, account for why so many donors look so similar in what they do and prioritize at any given time, and are a topic that has, to this point, received insufficient attention in the study of aid, donors, and how they function.

The globalization of foreign aid

Foreign aid (or development assistance) grew out of reconstruction efforts in Europe in the post-Second World War era to become the responsibility of all wealthy democratic states over the past sixty years. More recently, even non-democracies and middle-income countries are getting into the foreign aid game. Providing aid to poorer countries is now a taken-for-granted function played by all countries that want to be viewed as players on the global stage. In 2015, this assistance amounted to more than 130 billion USD in foreign aid provided to developing countries by the then 28 donor members which comprised the Organization for Economic Cooperation and Development's (OECD) Development Assistance Committee (DAC). This substantial transfer of resources from donor to recipient countries is ostensibly guided by both recipient development objectives and donor policy priorities and has the potential to shape development outcomes in much of the world for better or worse; however, recent calls for aid that acknowledge the diversity of local contexts and experiences have not always been answered with unique solutions. Instead, donor policy discourse in the aid sector has increasingly referred to 'emerging global consensus' around development issues as diverse as water management, poverty reduction, governance, security-sector reform, sustainable development, and others (World Bank Group 2000, 2002; USAID 2002b; UNFPA 1994; UN 2003, 2015; ADB 1997; CIDA 2002). This type of consensus can limit recipient country options to guide their own development and has seldom been examined in the development research literature.

If this topic has received so little attention, then why am I arguing we should be concerned about the globalization of foreign aid policy? Beyond the jarring inspiration of having to refuse a CIDA investment in sanitation in

Peshawar, I believe that the relevance and importance of this topic stems from three interrelated concerns that arise from the globalization of aid:

1. The globalization of aid policy priorities limits the potential range of development interventions deemed acceptable by donors and there-fore limits recipient countries in how they structure their development interventions.
2. The globalization of aid also limits innovation and fresh approaches from the donor perspective – if a donor consensus exists around an issue like gender or security it becomes very difficult to propose alternative approaches to these issues within donor agencies.
3. The rise of donor consensus around policy priorities leads to a reduced need for donors to undertake research and analysis linked to various pri-orities and contributes to a shift of donor focus to process rather than developmental concerns.

Each of these factors reinforces my belief in the importance of gaining a bet-ter understanding of processes of globalization at work within the foreign aid sector globally. Indeed, left unexamined, these processes of globaliza-tion could leave us with an extremely narrow, inflexible, and stagnant range of approaches to development and foreign aid with little room for locally appropriate, innovative, or evidence-based solutions to emerge from outside the emerging global consensus. Indeed, left unchecked, the 'global consensus' may become yet another barrier to development.

Regrettably, few researchers have tackled the question of why donors act alike or have similar policy priorities. And yet, four *plausible* arguments can be derived from some of the most influential past writing on aid, develop-ment and globalization. The first possibility (*the 'Realist' argument*) is that these sets of policies are linked directly to donor political, commercial, and military interests (Morgenthau 1962; Alesina & Dollar 2000). The second possibility (*the 'Humanitarian' argument*) is that these similar policies sim-ply reflect humanitarian interests in promoting development and combating poverty globally (Lumsdaine 1993; Opeskin 1996). A third possibility (*the 'World Systems/Post-Development' argument*) is that donors could simply be enacting unequal discourses of development and reinforcing a capitalist world system intended to dominate the developing world and reinforce the power of the North over the South (Chase-Dunn 1989; Chase-Dunn and Grimes 1995; Escobar 1991; Ferguson 1994; Wallerstein 1979). A final pos-sibility *(the 'World Society' argument)* is that these similar policy models and priorities are evidence of globalizing influence on nation-states to adopt similar institutions and norms devised by the international organizations, experts, and other civil society groups (Boli and Thomas 1999a; Hwang 2006; Lechner and Boli 2005; Meyer, Boli, et al. 1997). It is this final possi-bility – the world society argument – which I explore in this book to unravel the globalization of foreign aid.

The World Society?

Researchers describe the World Society as a collection of organizations, states, and individuals which create and enact models of behaviour which are translated into policy and institutions throughout the world (Meyer, Boli, et al. 1997; Lechner and Boli 2005; Boli and Thomas 1999a). World society theory holds that the similarity of these institutional models explains the similar appearance of states and organizations in the realms of citizenship, human rights, justice, educational systems, and even scientific advancement. World society, in the form of international and intergovernmental organizations, exerts pressure on states, domestic organizations, and individuals to move towards common goals and models of legitimate organization behaviour, leading to a globalization of policy and institutional forms based on a common 'world culture'. Like any theoretical argument, this approach to understanding global politics has strengths and weaknesses.

Strengths: explaining diffusion

Explaining diffusion is a strength of the world society approach. It is effective at examining global spread of models, policies, and institutions. For instance, research from this perspective has explained the spread of diverse policies and institutions ranging from the enfranchisement and political participation of women (Ramirez, Soysal, and Shanahan 1997; Swiss 2009) to the adoption of national environmental policies (Meyer, Frank, et al. 1997) and the ratification of United Nations treaties (Wotipka and Ramirez 2008). Two factors which have been shown to consistently influence successful diffusion include: (1) organizational embeddedness; and (2) policy density.

Embeddedness refers to a country or organization's level of involvement in international and inter-governmental networks and organizations – sometimes also referred to as the penetration of world society into a state (Schofer and Hironaka 2005). This embeddedness takes the form of membership in specific international organizations (Hironaka 2002), but has also been discussed in terms of ties to global networks of intergovernmental or international non-governmental actors (Beckfield 2003, 2008, 2010; Huges et al. 2009; Paxton, Hughes, and Reith, 2015). When considering diffusion, the argument goes that the more embedded a state, the more likely policy models are to diffuse into it.

Density, on the other hand, refers to the existing prevalence of a model or institution in the community of nation-states. One of the ways in which density functions is that a norm or institution becomes so widely held that it becomes costly to the perceived legitimacy of nation-states to *not* adopt or enforce a model (Hafner-Burton and Tsutsui 2005). Density effects also occur at local or regional levels, where institutions/events in nearby countries are argued to shape the outcome of diffusion processes (Ramirez, Soysal, and

Shanahan 1997). Here, the diffusion argument is that the denser the policy or normative model, the more likely other states are to adopt it.

This spread and refinement of policy models is also due to 'recursive processes' at work in the elaboration and change of world society (Meyer, Boli, et al. 1997, 151). The relationship between world society/international actors and the nation-state is not one-way. Recursive processes reflect the change and influence that a range of actors exert on the World Society in response to the adoption and implementation of world society models. The interaction of enactment and recursive processes combine to further diffuse these world cultural models. In short, the answer to why all states look and act so similarly is that they are all trying to do the same things to be legitimate.

Weaknesses: genesis, power, and levels of analysis

At times, the focus on diffusion has neglected to offer detailed explanations of how world-level models develop in the first place. World society models are spread by the various actors – in most cases international associations, organizations, and epistemic communities that operate at the global level. Yet, research has seldom made detailed analysis of how an idea is transformed by these groups from discourse into practice and accepted as a norm, model, or policy script at the global level (Keck and Sikkink 1998). In effect, though we might explain the spread of an environmental regime or educational standard, we often fail to explain the genesis or reshaping of such models.[1]

Another weakness of the world society approach is its limited emphasis on power imbalances between nation-states, between organizations, and between individuals (Finnemore 1996). North/South, East/West, rich/poor, and superpower/micro-state cleavages do not receive sufficient attention within world society writing on globalization and isomorphism in today's world. Despite the fact that international inequalities are evident in the reach of the international organizations and networks that compose world society (Beckfield 2003, 2008. 2010), issues of neo-imperialism, ideological hegemony, conflict, and exploitation are too often overlooked within the world society approach. Further, much of this research fails to problematize core/periphery power imbalances seen as central to the world systems theory approach and in so doing tends to downplay the issue of power more generally.

A preoccupation with explanations at the state level to the neglect of explaining similar phenomena at the organizational or individual levels is the last weakness of the world society approach I will address here. Although the foundational world society article by Meyer and his colleagues (1997) explains that the influence of world society functions at all three levels, most research in this literature has examined only the state level. This leaves gaps in the literature with the exclusion of emphasis on organizations and individuals and their relationships to states and the rationalized others of the World Society. Over-emphasis on the state leaves holes to be filled when it comes to explaining the interactions of international organizations with states and other actors. The international and inter-governmental organization ostensibly plays a crucial role in international norm or model formation, but the relations between these entities and the state, let alone with other organizations and individuals remains a little studied aspect of world society. In this book, I adopt a focus on the relationship between states and international and intergovernmental organizations to ameliorate this shortcoming of the world society approach.

My take on the world society argument

Despite these weaknesses and owing to its strengths, I embrace the world society approach to explain the globalization of foreign aid in this book. Building from its strong track record in explaining diffusion, I use a world society lens to examine the diffusion of increasingly similar foreign aid donor institutions and policies. Still, the issues of model genesis/norm formation, power imbalances, and the interaction of multiple actors involved rather than just states require significant attention. In deciphering the globalization of aid policies, I also need to explain how and from where the norms and ideas that underpin policy emerge. To do this, I take seriously the power politics involved in the institutionalization of these norms and the relationships between different actors involved at the civil society, state, and international organization levels. By adopting an approach that examines the social processes at work in the genesis of world models, I hope to avoid some of the limitations outlined above. In the chapters that follow, I examine both the actions of the international organizations and networks of world society and the donor agency representatives of the foreign aid community to explain their role in creating and spreading policy on both security and gender among wealthy donor countries.

To foreshadow my conclusions, the suitability of this world polity argument as an explanation for the globalization of aid is revealed in subsequent chapters' demonstration of the influence of intergovernmental and international organizations on the spread of both gender and security policy models to bilateral aid agencies. If this influence can account for the similarity of policy perspectives adopted by donors, then understanding the mechanisms and social processes by which this influence is exerted is a crucial component of explaining the formation of policy consensus in development assistance. It is these mechanisms and processes which I aim to reveal in this book.

Processes and mechanisms of globalization

In my search for common processes and mechanisms involved in the globalization of aid, I borrow directly from earlier research on the social mechanisms and processes of contentious politics (Tarrow 2005; McAdam, Tarrow, and Tilly 2001). This research has identified many social mechanisms implicated in contentious politics across national contexts, issue areas, and history.

Mechanisms like these function in different contexts to yield similar outcomes. These mechanisms include pathways such as certification, brokerage, scale-shift, internalization, and modularity – all of which can be employed by contentious actors to achieve their aims. This process or mechanism tracing approach is sometimes criticized for simply describing how contentious episodes unfold rather than offering explanations of why, for being overly general in scope, and for obscuring complex historical contexts (Welskopp 2004; Simeon 2004; Rule 2004; Kjeldstadli 2004). Regardless of these critiques, I still believe this approach offers significant potential to explain the relational aspects of political phenomena like foreign aid. Indeed, my case studies examine separate instances of the globalization of aid policy to discern these similar mechanisms at work. To be sure, these mechanisms are not *only* the tools of civil society and social movement organizations, but instead of all the actors and organizations that compose the world polity – including states. Disentangling the actors and their actions as different mechanisms are employed in promoting or inhibiting consensus formation on aid policy is one of my chief contributions in this book.

Throughout this book, I expand upon the world society approach with a search for common processes of globalization at the micro-level, stating the case for the globalization of foreign aid to be viewed through macro- and micro-level lenses to achieve a fuller picture of why and what donors do and say is so similar despite divergent domestic social and political contexts.

Premises

My story of the globalization of foreign aid is based on four premises about the global aid sector and how it is influenced by world society: (1) donor policy models are world cultural models; (2) national donor agencies are influenced by key international actors; (3) this international influence is mediated by aid agency structure; and (4) individual actors (aid workers or officials) play a direct role in spreading policy models and priorities. Each of these premises is a key support for the foundations of this book's argument.

Donor policy as world cultural models

World polity theory points to a series of universally applicable cultural models of norms and institutions to explain the striking similarity of structure and policy among the world's states and organizations. Development assistance is one example of these common institutional frameworks (Peterson 2014; Swiss 2011, 2012, 2016a, 2016b, 2017; Swiss and Longhofer 2016). As an international organizational field, development assistance now comprises an entire industry of donors, experts, consultants, firms, and NGOs. At the same time, this industry has concentrated its efforts on more and more similar development priorities and objectives. This focusing of development assistance results from the spread of similar policy models and standards for development aid promulgated by the international development community through international organizations, conferences, treaties, guidelines, and the sharing of best practices. This growing homogeneity leads to readily identifiable policy models for donors which adopt and apply common agendas to address specific topics in a relatively uniform manner in diverse developing country contexts. These common models can be seen in donor approaches to issues as divergent as the environment, microfinance, governance, gender, and security. As an example of the models defined by world society through its interaction with nation-state, organizational, and individual actors, the adoption of these models is the overall dependent 'variable' in our story. In the remainder of this book I aim to show how certain policy models come to be enacted, are institutionalized, and are recursively refined by aid donors.

International actors and the influence of world society

Donor agencies do not act only as representatives of their domestic/national interests. To understand aid policy decisions, we must account for the influence of international organizations on states' policies. The influence of international actors is therefore a primary area of investigation in this book. These actors of world society in the development assistance sector include a range of organizations, both intergovernmental and international non-governmental. The spread of development as a concept in the twentieth century was reflected in a growth of organizations in this field which aim to promote and achieve development in poorer societies. This growth included the proliferation of development-oriented INGOs (Chabbott 1999), as well as the creation of several highly influential intergovernmental bodies that explicitly deal with development, like the OECD's Development Assistance Committee (DAC), the World Bank's International Bank for Reconstruction and Development (IBRD) and International Development Association (IDA), the regional development banks, and the United Nations Development Programme (UNDP).

   This array of international actors, in concert with internationally oriented domestic development NGOs in donor states all exert influence on donors to implement specific policy models and to work on specific development priorities. As contributors to the discourse on development assistance, civil society and intergovernmental organizations interface with the nation-state donors to define and refine the standards and norms of development and work to craft the policy models that donors adopt. Research underscores the critical role that international organizations play in shaping the policy directions and actions of the nation-state. Given this important role, the influence of international actors and their relationship with donors is a chief concern of this study. Indeed, I demonstrate throughout, the critical role of international actors in the social processes which mediate donor agency adoption and institutionalization of world polity models for development assistance.

Donor agency structure and the interface with world society

Donors adopt global level models, often at the behest of international actors, but these processes are also mediated by the structure of donor agencies. Evidence suggests that the nature of the domestic institutions mediates the reflection of world society influences in policy (Hironaka 2002; Ramirez, Soysal, and Shanahan 1997). Applying this notion to the development assistance sector suggests that the presence of a donor agency would be the first step to a nation-state expressing development assistance policy models. Taken further, it suggests some role for the structure of the development assistance donor agency in mediating the interface with world society. Different domestic institutional structures alter the amount of world polity influence evident in each state. This consideration has not generated much attention from previous world polity research.

Throughout this book, I conceptualize donor structure: agency autonomy and locus of decision-making. These factors measure the distance of the agency from central government control and the internationalization of the agency. The concept of agency autonomy is intended here to refer to the status of the institution as either a stand-alone agency/body within the government of the country (autonomous), or as a sub-unit of the Ministry of Foreign Affairs (integrated). Previous research suggests donors that are more strongly independent of their respective ministry of foreign affairs are perceived as being more effective (Gulrajani 2010). The second characteristic, locus of decision-making, refers to the location of primary decision-making on issues of disbursement to countries on a bilateral basis within the organization. When decisions are taken primarily at agency headquarters the donor would be identified as a 'centralized' agency, and in contrast, when decisions are primarily taken in the field offices located in recipient countries points to a 'decentralized' donor (Engberg-Pedersen 2014). Agency-wide policy decisions still tend to be centralized even in this second instance. Since the early-1990s, the OECD DAC has promoted donor decentralization of decision-making as a characteristic of more effective and locally appropriate aid (OECD 2002b). Generalizing from this DAC position, it follows that donors already using decentralized decision-making structures indicate a willingness to adopt internationally sanctioned norms and principles for delivering aid, and thus a greater openness to world society influence. Using these factors, we can create a typology of aid agencies which yields four ideal types, shown in Table 1.1 below.

Table 1.1 Donor structure matrix

	Locus of decision-making	
Agency autonomy	Autonomous centralized	Autonomous decentralized
	Integrated centralized	Integrated decentralized

Throughout the chapters that follow, this structure matrix is assessed for its influence on mediating world polity influence on donors. Although the ideal types are shown, the reality of donor structures is that they are fluid and fluctuate over time and according to the situation. The question of how donor structure influences the integration of world polity policy models into donor policy at the national level is just one aspect of the globalization of aid that is teased out in the pages that follow. I argue that the autonomy and the decentralization of an agency makes a difference in its interface with the World Society, and therefore mediates its level of susceptibility to outside influence, with greater autonomy and decentralization leading to the most susceptibility to world polity influence.

Individual agency in the spread of world society models

The world society approach tends to examine the spread of common policies and institutions at the macro, international level, and discusses the impact of relationships between nation-states or between organizations. Some allowance is provided for in the theory for the influence of individuals on these processes, but research on the world polity has not focused strongly on individual experiences in these processes (Finnemore 1996). Within the foreign aid sector these inter-governmental and inter-organizational relationships are managed by individuals acting on behalf of the donor and on behalf of international actors. In this book, I argue that to better understand the globalization of foreign aid, we must look at how individual actors within aid agencies shape the adoption and institutionalization of aid policy priorities. Part II of this book thus draws heavily on data I gathered from individuals and their experiences working in the foreign aid sector, and details the impact of individuals on the international interface of the nation-state and world society.

Developing consensus?

Based on these premises, I ask three central questions about the globalization of foreign aid:

1. How does world society affect nation-state institutions and what are the processes that promote consensus or uniformity of policy and priorities among foreign aid donors?
2. What role does individual agency play in mediating the interface of world society and the nation-state?
3. What role does civil society play in the spread of world polity models of development assistance?

These questions are united by their focus on the processes through which world society influences the state and promotes universal norms and models. This enactment of global policy models by various actors is at the core of the institutionalist perspective of world society/polity theory. Yet, I argue in this study that without understanding the micro-level social processes which encourage and facilitate this enactment, the theoretical purchase of the world polity perspective is diminished. By identifying processes which promote consensus or uniformity of policy, I aim to offer a more effective argument for how world society influences the state. Indeed, my case studies reveal that individual agency and civil society actors should both be expected to play a role in mediating this interface of world society and the nation-state through social processes of globalization that encourage uniformity and consensus in the development assistance sector, effecting the globalization of aid.

These questions are important to advancing the understanding of foreign aid. This critical redistributive function of global politics is intended to play a significant role in improving the lives of billions of people in the developing world, and is expected to continue to grow in magnitude in many countries in coming years. For instance, in wake of the 2005 Group of Eight meetings which saw the leaders of the world's richest nations commit to doubling aid to Africa by 2010, we witnessed a staggering increase in aid dollars. Even in the wake of the persistent global economic crisis from 2008 onwards, many donors have maintained if not expanded aid budgets, with new countries attaining the 0.7% target (the UK, for instance), and many new and emerging donor countries becoming larger donors in their own right (Gulrajani and Swiss 2017). As such, it is of great significance to understand how the growing homogenization of or consensus around development assistance policy and priorities arises because of its direct impact on future increases in aid.

If this phenomenon remains unexamined and unchecked the development options of many developing societies may become even more limited and curtailed to a narrow agenda pushed by the major Western donor agencies and international organizations. Past research on aid has placed little emphasis on how or why donors march in lock-step with uniform policies and priorities. This book's contribution thus reveals important aspects of how this policy isomorphism arises, and as a result, how outside activists and other civil society groups might act to help reshape or diversify the development assistance agenda. Better understanding of why donors are so uniform in their foreign aid policies is critical to shaping aid in the future which is both (1) better adapted to local contexts in developing societies and (2) more responsive to the priorities of the people in those societies rather than an international agenda of rich donor societies.

A research roadmap

In one respect, the aim of this research is to test the fit of the world society approach to our understanding the globalization of aid policy to offer a novel explanation of the apparent consensus or striking similarity of policy models and priorities among foreign aid donors. To this end, I focus my research on exploring the priorities and practices of the very type of governmental organization responsible for providing aid to the developing world: the bilateral donor agency. These agencies have not been a major research focus in the global/transnational and development sociology literatures; although they have been examined more fully in other disciplines and development studies research (Black and Tiessen 2007; Brown 2007, 2012; Brown and Grävingholt 2015; Brown, Black, and den Heyer 2016; Lancaster 2007; Woods 2005).

Between its inception as a research question in a Pakistani slum in 2001 to this quantitative and qualitative exploration of the globalization of aid at the macro and micro levels, I have spent more than fifteen years thinking and writing on this issue. In its final form, the book's explanation of the globalization of foreign aid hinges on mixed-method case studies of two specific policy issues which have been prominent in the development assistance sector in recent years: (1) gender; and (2) security. I selected these vastly different, but sometimes intersecting, development issues as case studies because they have both prompted aid donors to adopt an increasingly common international agenda despite being driven by different underlying motivations and links to donors' national interests.

I use the case studies to tease out the common social processes which underpin similar policy models and priorities despite the diverse donor country contexts in which these aid agencies operate. Part I of the book examines the spread of the gender and development model and the conflict and security model among donors at the global level, drawing on cross-national statistical analysis from the 1960s onward.

Building on this macro-level cross-national analysis, in Part II of the book I analyze the qualitative interview data I collected within three different donor countries from 2006 to 2008 – Canada, Sweden, and the United States – to examine the gender and security cases separately to identify the common micro-level processes of globalization at work in each country's donor agency. Though more than a decade has elapsed since this data was collected, the stories it tells stand the test of time and provide evidence of how globalization works within aid donor organizations.

The three case study countries represent very different points on the donor spectrum when considering characteristics of their foreign aid programmes like generosity, donor structure, and perceived underlying motivations for giving. This variety of contexts allows my comparative analysis to tease out how common positions adopted by donors emerge in very distinct domestic contexts.

The book

To begin unpacking the globalization of foreign aid, in Chapter 2,[2] I show how the world society perspective provides a strong base upon which to build the book's multi-level analysis of the globalization of aid and introduce my analysis of the globalization of aid at the macro level, discussing the results from quantitative cross-national statistical models. Using macro-level quantitative evidence to demonstrate how the spread and adoption of women in development/gender and development policies among the major Western aid donor countries was the result of the global level influence of world society on donors. This influence is strong, and agencies are subject to several channels through which it is exerted, including international conferences, the behaviour of other donors, and ratification of international treaties. These results provide the macro-level base upon which I build my investigation of globalizing mechanisms in Part II of the book. Detailed results of these models are presented in a methodological appendix at the end of the book which I hope will appeal to the statistically savvy reader while not distracting those readers less interested in the statistical details.

Shifting in Part II of the book to examine micro-level explanations through my qualitative case studies, Chapter 3 introduces the individual country context of the aid sector in the United States, Sweden, and Canada in the 2006–2008 time period of the study to explain the context in which the case studies are based. Readers will gain a solid understanding of the complex politics of aid in each of the case study countries at the time, as well as relevant changes that have occurred since the time of the field research with each donor. This chapter shows how different domestic contexts mediate the interface between donors and world society and is a prerequisite for understanding the social processes involved in promoting common policy agendas and institutional forms that follow in the rest of the book.

Subsequently Chapters 4 and 5 reveal the processes at work in promoting the adoption, institutionalization, and refinement of a women/gender and development model (Chapter 4) and a security-sector reform model (Chapter 5)[3] in the aid agencies of the three case study countries. Based on data collected through in-depth interviews with donor agency officials and other development workers from each country, these chapters provide rich qualitative evidence to demonstrate that common social processes at work in each case explain why diverse donor agencies adopt similar if not identical approaches to the issue of gender and development and security sector reform.

In Chapter 4's gender case I identify three common processes which are responsible for the common approaches to gender and development and near consensus on the issue that exists in the aid community internationally: (1) processes of internalization and certification of the gender and development issue as a priority; (2) processes of donor agency embeddedness with civil society; and (3) processes of bureaucratic activism on the gender issue within donor agencies.

Chapter 5 shows how a commonly accepted approach to security issues in the development assistance sector has emerged over the past decade or so, and then identifies two social processes evident in my case study countries that explain this phenomenon: (1) catalytic policy processes which drive donors to adopt positions on new issues to maintain their expected participation in international arenas; and (2) processes of donor autonomy from the rest of government, in particular from ministries of foreign affairs.

Part III of book summarizes my findings by showing how linking both quantitative and qualitative findings reveals a fuller understanding of the globalization of aid. Chapter 6 explores in more detail the five processes identified in Part II of the book. I revisit the different processes in the comparative case opposite to the one where they are first identified in an effort to triangulate their broader validity and then discuss their applicability to the broader understanding of world society influence on the nation-state beyond simply the aid sector.

Finally, in Chapter 7, I elaborate on how my arguments about the aid sector contribute to a deeper understanding of how globalization, in the sense of increasingly similar institutions and policies, functions. By looking for micro-level social processes of globalization I offer a compelling argument for how world society influences the policies and priorities of aid donors. I discuss what an understanding of these processes means for donors, recipients, and for civil society groups interested in influencing the aid agenda. The book closes with a discussion of why understanding globalization in the aid sector is so important to the future of aid delivery and why we need to understand both global (macro) and national (micro) level social processes to adequately explain the so-called 'emerging global consensus' that constitute the globalization of aid.

My goal in this book is to identify common processes of globalization in the aid sector and understand how they unfold in different contexts as a reflection of world society influence on the nation-state. I hope that readers will take away a better understanding of why, in my former life as an aid worker, I had to refuse to support a sanitation project in that Pakistani slum, and why the conflict between local development needs at odds with increasingly uniform donor development priorities arises in the first place.

Notes

1 One exception to this is a detailed exploration of the recursive reshaping of norms around intellectual property of AIDS drugs (Chorev 2012).
2 A modified version of Chapter 2 was published previously as: Swiss, L. (2012). The Adoption of Women and Gender as Development Assistance Priorities: An Event History Analysis of World Polity Effects. *International Sociology, 27(1)*, 96–119.
3 A modified version of Chapter 5 was published previously as: Swiss, L. (2011). Security Sector Reform and Development Assistance: Explaining the Diffusion of Policy Priorities Among Donor Agencies. *Qualitative Sociology, 34*(2), 371–393.

References

ADB, Asian Development Bank. (1997). Microenterprise Development: Not on Credit Alone. Retrieved from www.adb.org/Documents/Books/Microenterprise/default.asp

Alesina, A., & Dollar, D. (2000). Who Gives Foreign Aid to Whom and Why? *Journal of Economic Growth*, 5(1), 33–63.

Beckfield, J. (2003). Inequality in the World Polity: The Structure of International Organization. *American Sociological Review*, 68(3), 401–424.

Beckfield, J. (2008). The Dual World Polity: Fragmentation and Integration in the Network of Intergovernmental Organizations. *Social Problems*, 55(3), 419–442.

Beckfield, J. (2010). The Social Structure of the World Polity. *American Journal of Sociology*, 115(4), 1018–1068.

Black, D. R., & Tiessen, R. (2007). The Canadian International Development Agency: New Policies, Old Problems. *Canadian Journal of Development Studies*, 28(2), 191–202.

Boli, J., & Thomas, G. M. (1999). *Constructing World Culture: International Nongovernmental Organizations Since 1875*. Stanford, CA: Stanford University Press.

Brodhead, T., & Pratt, C. (1994). Paying the Piper: CIDA and Canadian NGOs. In C. Pratt (Ed.), *Canadian International Development Assistance Policies: An Appraisal* (pp. 87–119). Montreal: McGill-Queen's University Press.

Brown, S. (2007). Creating the World's Best Development Agency? Confusion and Contradictions in CIDA's New Development Policy. *Canadian Journal of Development Studies*, 28(2), 203–218.

Brown, S. (2007). Creating the World's Best Development Agency? Confusion and Contradictions in CIDA's New Development Policy. *Canadian Journal of Development Studies*, 28(2), 203–218.

Brown, S. (Ed.) (2012). *Struggling for Effectiveness: CIDA and Canadian Foreign Aid*. Montréal: McGill-Queen's University Press.

Brown, S., Black, D. R., & Den Heyer, M. (Eds.). (2016). *Rethinking Canadian Aid* (2nd Edition). Ottawa: University of Ottawa Press.

Brown, S., & Grävingholt, J. (Eds.). (2016). *The Securitization of Foreign Aid*. Basingstoke: Palgrave Macmillan.

Chabbott, C. (1999). Development INGOs. In J. Boli & G. M. Thomas (Eds.), *Constructing World Culture: International Nongovernmental Organizations Since 1875* (pp. 222–248). Stanford, CA: Stanford University Press.

Chase-Dunn, C., & Grimes, P. (1995). World-Systems Analysis. *Annual Review of Sociology*, 21, 387–417.

Chase-Dunn, C. K. (1989). *Global Formation: Structures of the World-economy*. Cambridge, Mass.: B. Blackwell.

CIDA, Canadian International Development Agency. (2002). Canadian International Development Agency, Departmental Performance Report, 2001–2002. Retrieved from www.tbs-sct.gc.ca/rma/dpr/01-02/CIDA/CIDA0102dpr02_e.asp

Engberg-Pedersen, L. (2014). Bringing Aid Management Closer to Reality: The Experience of Danish Bilateral Development Cooperation. *Development Policy Review*, 32(1), 113–131.

Escobar, A. (1991). Anthropology and the Development Encounter: The Making and Marketing of Development Anthropology. *American Ethnologist*, 18(4), 658–682.

Ferguson, J. (1994). *The Anti-politics Machine: 'Development,' Depoliticization, and Bureaucratic Power in Lesotho*. Minneapolis: University of Minnesota Press.

Finnemore, M. (1996). Norms, Culture, and World Politics: Insights from Sociology's Institutionalism. *International Organization*, 50(2), 325–347.

Gulrajani, N. (2010). New Vistas for Development Management: Examining Radical-reformist Possibilities and Potential. *Public Administration and Development*, 30(2), 136–148.

Gulrajani, N., & Swiss, L. (2017). Why do countries become donors? Assessing the drivers and implications of donor proliferation. Report. London: Overseas Development Institute.

Hafner-Burton, E., & Tsutsui, K. (2005). Human Rights in a Globalizing World: The Paradox of Empty Promises. *American Journal of Sociology*, 110(5), 1373–1411.

Hironaka, A. (2002). The Globalization of Environmental Protection: The Case of Environmental Impact Assessment. *International Journal of Comparative Sociology*, 43(1), 65–78.

Hughes, M. M., Peterson, L., Harrison, J. A., & Paxton, P. (2009). Power and Relation in the World Polity: The INGO Network Country Score, 1978–1998. *Social Forces*, 87(4), 1711–1742.

Hwang, H. (2006). Planning Development: Globalization and the Shifting Locus of Planning. In G. S. Drori, J. W. Meyer, & H. Hwang (Eds.), *Globalization and Organization: World Society and Organizational Change* (pp. 69–89). New York: Oxford University Press.

Keck, M. E., & Sikkink, K. (1998). *Activists Beyond Borders: Advocacy Networks in International Politics*. Ithaca, N.Y.: Cornell University Press.

Kjeldstadli, K. (2004). Mechanisms, Processes, and Contexts. *International Review of Social History*, 49(01), 104–114.

Lancaster, C. (2007). *Foreign Aid: Diplomacy, Development, Domestic Politics*. Chicago: University of Chicago Press.

Lechner, F. J., & Boli, J. (2005). *World Culture: Origins and Consequences*. London: Blackwell.

Lumsdaine, D. H. (1993). *Moral Vision in International Politics: The Foreign Aid Regime, 1949–1989*. Princeton, N.J.: Princeton University Press.

McAdam, D., Tarrow, S. G., & Tilly, C. (2001). *Dynamics of Contention*. Cambridge: Cambridge University Press.

Meyer, J. W., Boli, J., Thomas, G. M., & Ramirez, F. O. (1997). World Society and the Nation-state. *The American Journal of Sociology*, 103(1), 144–181.

Morgenthau, H. (1962). A Political Theory of Foreign Aid. *The American Political Science Review*, 56(2), 301–309.

Morrison, D. R. (1998). *Aid and Ebb Tide: A History of CIDA and Canadian Development Assistance*. Waterloo, ON: Wilfrid Laurier University Press.

Opeskin, B. R. (1996). The Moral Foundations of Foreign Aid. *World Development*, 24(1), 21–44.

Paxton, P., Hughes, M. M., & Reith, N. (2015). Extending the INGO Network Country Score, 1950–2008. *Sociological Science*, 2, 287–307.

Peterson, L. (2014). A Gift You Can't Refuse? Foreign Aid, INGOs and Development in the World Polity. *Studies in Emergent Order*, 7, 81–102.

Ramirez, F. O., Soysal, Y., & Shanahan, S. (1997). The Changing Logic of Political Citizenship: Cross-national Acquisition of Women's Suffrage Rights, 1890 to 1990. *American Sociological Review*, 62(5), 735.

Rawkins, P. (1994). An Institutional Analysis of CIDA. In C. Pratt (Ed.), *Canadian International Development Assistance Policies: An Appraisal* (pp. 156–185). Montreal: McGill-Queen's University Press.

Rule, J. (2004). Review Essay: McTheory. *Sociological Forum*, 19(1), 151–162.

Schofer, E., & Hironaka, A. (2005). The Effects of World Society on Environmental Protection Outcomes. *Social Forces*, 84(1), 25–47.

Simeon, D. (2004). A Unified Field Theory for Contention? *International Review of Social History*, 49(01), 115–121.

Swiss, L. (2009). Decoupling Values from Action: An Event-History Analysis of the Election of Women to Parliament in the Developing World, 1945–90. *International Journal of Comparative Sociology*, 50(1), 69–95.

Swiss, L. (2011). Security Sector Reform and Development Assistance: Explaining the Diffusion of Policy Priorities Among Donor Agencies. *Qualitative Sociology*, 34(2), 371–393.

Swiss, L. (2012). The Adoption of Women and Gender as Development Assistance Priorities: An Event History Analysis of World Polity Effects. *International Sociology*, 27(1), 96–119.

Swiss, L. (2016a). A Sociology of Foreign Aid and the World Society. *Sociology Compass*, 10(1), 65–73.

Swiss, L. (2016b). World Society and the Global Foreign Aid Network. *Sociology of Development*, 2(4), 342–374.

Swiss, L. (2017). Foreign Aid Allocation from a Network Perspective: The Effect of Global Ties. *Social Science Research*, 63, 111–123.

Swiss, L., & Longhofer, W. (2016). Membership has its Privileges: Shared International Organizational Affiliation and Foreign Aid Flows, 1978–2010. *Social Forces*, 94(4), 1769–1793.

Tarrow, S. G. (2005). *The New Transnational Activism*. New York: Cambridge University Press.

Thérien, J.-P. (1994). Canadian Aid: A Comparative Analysis. In C. Pratt (Ed.), *Canadian International Development Assistance Policies: An Appraisal* (pp. 315–333). Montreal: McGill-Queen's University Press.

UN, United Nations (2003). The right to education: Report submitted by the Special Rapporteur, Katarina Tomasevski: E/CN.4/2004/45. Retrieved from www.right-to-education.org/content/unreports/unreport12prt1.html

UN, United Nations (2015). 17 – Partnership for the Goals. Retrieved from www.globalgoals.org/global-goals/partnerships-for-the-goals/

UNFPA, United Nations Population Fund. (1994). Programme of Action of the International Conference on Population and Development. Retrieved from www.unfpa.org/icpd/icpd_poa.htm

USAID, United States Agency for International Development. (2002). Initiative for Southern Africa. Retrieved from www.usaid.gov/pubs/cbj2002/afr/isa/690-012.html

Wallerstein, I. (1979). Dependence in an Interdependent World: The Limited Possibilities of Transformations within the Capitalist World-economy. In I. Wallerstein (Ed.), *The Capitalist World-economy: Essays* (pp. 66–94). Cambridge: Cambridge University Press.

Welskopp, T. (2004). Crossing the Boundaries? Dynamics of Contention Viewed from the Angle of a Comparative Historian. *International Review of Social History*, 49(01), 122–131.

Woods, N. (2005). The Shifting Politics of Foreign Aid. *International Affairs*, 81(2), 393–409.

World Bank Group. (2000). Partners in Transforming Development: New Approaches to Developing Country-Owned Poverty Reduction Strategies. Retrieved from www.imf.org/external/np/prsp/pdf/prspbroc.pdf

World Bank Group. (2002). Improving Water and Sanitation Services for the Poor: An Instrument to Support World Bank Operations. Retrieved from www.worldbank. org/html/fpd/water/bnwp/files/booklet.pdf

Wotipka, C. M., & Ramirez, F. O. (2008). World Society and Human Rights: An Event History Analysis of the Convention on the Elimination of All Forms of Discrimination Against Women. In B. A. Simmons, F. Dobbin, & G. Garrett (Eds.), *The Global Diffusion of Markets and Democracy* (pp. 303–343). Cambridge: Cambridge University Press.

2   Global influences and the diffusion of aid priorities

Why have all major aid agencies adopted some framework or policy for addressing issues of women and gender in their programming? How has this common framework diffused among donors? This chapter tells the story of the spread of women and gender as aid priorities among major Western industrialized countries over the past fifty years by marshalling macro-level data to provide evidence of world society influence at the global level. This is the first step of this book's multi-level analysis of the globalization phenomenon in the aid sector. Drawing on evidence from quantitative analysis of aid institutions, the pages that follow examine the spread of common development assistance policy scripts about women and gender among the major Western donor countries. The story of diffusion at the macro level unfolds such that the spread of a common donor model of women and gender policies among the countries of the Organization for Economic Cooperation and Development's Development Assistance Committee (OECD DAC) closely resembles the diffusion of world polity models and norms seen in other sectors. Results of this analysis at the macro level will then help to shape the micro-level qualitative inquiry in Part II of the book.

By analyzing the timing of the adoption of WID or GAD policies or the creation of a dedicated WID/GAD unit, it is possible to unravel how world polity influence played a role in the spread of development assistance policy and institutions. Indeed, this chapter argues that the bilateral foreign aid sector should be considered a reflection of the enactment of world polity models for development assistance and that donor institutions of the major Western industrialized countries are directly influenced by their interactions with world society.

The diffusion of aid priorities

Between 1961 and 2003, the proliferation of development assistance institutional architecture proceeded with great speed (Chabbott, 1999; Lumsdaine, 1993). Figure 2.1 below illustrates the growth trends in the number of donor agencies and of DAC members in the period from 1960 through 2005. In

1960 – despite aid having been provided for some years by the ministries of foreign affairs of select countries – there was no such thing as a bilateral donor agency; by 2003, there were donor agencies or specialized units dedicated to the provision of development assistance in nearly every major industrialized country across Western Europe, North America, and the Asia-Pacific. At the same time, the growth of the so-called 'Donor's Club' which is the Development Assistance Committee (DAC) of the OECD grew at nearly the same pace – indeed, no major development assistance donor in Western Europe, North America, or the Asia/Pacific region is not a member of the DAC in 2017.

Presently, the DAC acts as a clearinghouse of all things 'development assistance' in the international community. Aside from tracking and accounting for the destination, amounts, and purpose of all Official Development Assistance (ODA) funds globally, the DAC also plays a significant policy role as a forum for discussion and formulation of policy positions and 'best practices' in the development assistance community. The fact that all major donors are also members of the DAC highlights the extent to which this exclusive group plays a significant role in shaping the appearance and function of ODA institutions globally. One way in which this DAC influence occurs is the spread of common policy frameworks through the conduct of conferences and discussions on specific issue areas, the issuing of guidelines for donors to follow in different sectors, and through the policing of standards for donors through a peer review process.

Although the DAC is not the only influence on the adoption of common donor priorities, it is clear in the literature on development assistance that donors have been swayed by distinct trends in the focus of aid throughout the years. Development assistance trends in the past have included focuses on: support for industrialization, basic human needs, structural adjustment, human resource development, good governance, and even budgetary support. This seemingly ever-shifting focus for aid priorities reflects the high degree of uncertainty involved in promoting development through foreign aid. There is no one guaranteed solution to the problem of development, and therefore donors follow the most current aid trends to maintain legitimacy of their aid programmes. Now, despite this uncertainty, early in the twenty-first century, Western donor policy and practices appear to be increasingly similar and reflective of at least a rhetorical 'global' consensus on development objectives and practices. International organizations and donor agencies alike have peppered their development policy documents with mentions of this 'emerging global consensus' on a variety of issues ranging from water management and poverty reduction to governance and security-sector reform (ADB, 1997; CIDA, 2002; UN, 2003; UNFPA, 1994; USAID, 2002; World Bank Group, 2000, 2002).

As Figure 2.1 foreshadows, one example of a common policy framework adopted by nearly all donors is a focus on women or gender inequality in the development process. In 1970, only one Western donor (Sweden) had a

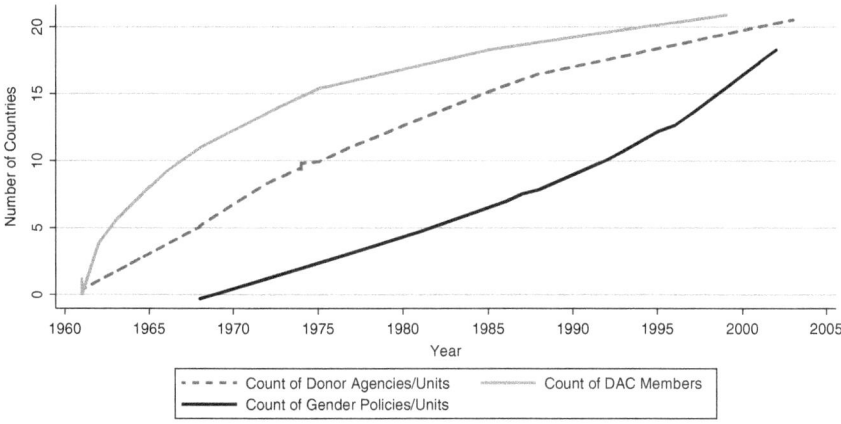

Figure 2.1 Diffusion of development assistance institutions and policies among DAC member countries

Source: Author's coding of OECD and specific donor agency in formation.

dedicated WID unit, but by 2017, nearly all major donors have adopted some form of a WID/GAD policy or have a dedicated unit within their organization to address WID/GAD concerns. This adoption of women and gender as a development priority features frequently in the development literature, tracking the changing nature of donor engagement with these issues over the thirty-five-year period of the study (Moser, 2005; Moser & Moser, 2005; Rathgeber, 1990, 1995; Tiessen 2007; Swiss 2012). Several factors responsible for the internalization of women's rights and gender equality as a development donor concern have been highlighted, and most stem from the creation of a global agenda for states and civil society to support women's rights across society.

World polity research has demonstrated the extent to which women's rights and gender equality developed as a world cultural model during the later twentieth century (Berkovitch, 1999a, 1999b; Lechner & Boli 2005). This growth in support for women's rights across the globe corresponds to the expansion of the women's movement (Berkovitch, 1999a; Paxton, Hughes, & Green, 2006), greater support for gender equality initiatives by international organizations (Berkovitch, 1999b), and increased attention paid to these issues at international conferences like the United Nations World Conferences on Women (Lechner & Boli, 2005). The highlighting of women's issues during the UN Decade for Women (1976–1985) and surrounding the UN conferences also played a strong role in promoting the expansion of the women's movement and the formation of many Women's International Non-Governmental Organizations (WINGOs) (Berkovitch, 1999a). These factors were all instrumental in encouraging nation-states to protect women's rights and promote gender equality across a wide spectrum of issues, including addressing women's health, education, and economic opportunities. International organizations like the UN and the WINGOs of the women's movement collaborated along with governments to establish, refine, and institutionalize a normative model for women's rights and gender equality. World society's influence on the creation of this model was thus strong and wide-ranging.

As these norms encouraging greater protection for women's rights and increased acceptance of the notion of gender equality spread among governments, development NGOs, and international organizations, a concentration on development issues began to emerge as a significant component of this world cultural model. Berkovitch (1999a) argues that this was due to the coinciding of the UN Decade for Women with the Second United Nations Development Decade, leading to the framing of women's issues within the development context and a concurrent focus on both issues in the wider international community. Women's status and development status came to be viewed in the international community as inextricably linked, and gender became a primary concern for development assistance agencies and organizations worldwide (Lechner & Boli, 2005). Donors have subsequently developed specialized units and policies addressing Women in Development or Gender and Development concerns in their work, and the integration of a global model of women's rights into development discourse has become widely accepted in the foreign aid community.

To be sure, the nature of a donor's gender policy and the details of its implementation vary widely amongst the DAC members; however, the fact that they are nearly all engaged with the idea of improving gender equality through development assistance as an objective of their work is indicative of the trends towards conformity or isomorphism within development assistance institutions.[1] Similar evidence can be marshalled to point towards the spread of donor policy models in the areas of environment, human rights, civil society capacity building, governance, and security sector reform among many others.

The emergence and spread of development assistance as a part of the foreign policy machinery of Western industrial democracies is a phenomenon spanning only the last fifty years. Indeed, the process continues still when newly emerging economies and countries transition towards 'developed' status, they are also becoming development assistance donors. Theoretical explanations of this trend in the research literature on development have done little to explore this trend, and therefore research in this area requires alternative approaches to explaining the spread of development assistance and the isomorphism found in policy and institutional frameworks among donor countries. It is worthwhile to briefly touch on the existing literature on the emergence of and motivations for development assistance, and then turn to alternate frameworks which the analysis in this chapter will explore.

Theoretical explanations for development assistance

In the recent literature on development assistance, there have been several explanations of the emergence of and motivations for providing development aid in the post-World War II era. Two main viewpoints identifiable in the literature include: (1) a realist perspective focused on donor national interest: some authors point to the importance of donor country national interest underlying the provision of aid and the insidious domination of the developing world by the power embodied in donor agendas (Alesina & Dollar, 2000; Morgenthau, 1962; Woods, 2005); and (2) a neoinstitutionalist perspective on international humanitarianism: donors are seen to be acting on humanitarian or moral grounds in compassionate partnership with poorer societies of the developing world (Lumsdaine, 1993; Opeskin, 1996; Pratt, 1994). Looked at in historical perspective, development assistance was influenced by *both* national interest and humanitarianism. It is reasonable to assume that no country's aid programme is characterized as wholly uninterested, nor can it be considered fully humanitarian. The complex politics of development assistance build in components of both explanations.

The main shortcoming of both these explanations is their silence on and inability to explain the appearance of nearly identical means of providing development aid in all the major industrialized countries of Western Europe, North America, and the Asia/Pacific. Even if common motivations of either national interest/domination or international humanitarianism underlie the provision of development assistance, these motivations fail to explain why donors have been so conformist in their provision of assistance, following trends of common institutional structures and of common policy priorities or objectives in the face of disparate domestic contexts.

Other research on development assistance and aid agencies also fails to explain the uniformity of policy among aid agencies in a convincing fashion. A Coasian analysis suggesting aid agencies act as facilitators between north and south to cut transaction costs and mediate differing agendas between donor and recipient, explains the existence of these agencies, but does little to examine why they promote such similar policies despite disparate domestic contexts for donors (Martens, 2005). Another perspective suggests that development policy is crafted based on 'prevailing development objectives', 'development theory', and data available to measure performance and test hypotheses at any given point in time (Thorbecke, 2007). This framework again offers little explanation for why the prevailing objectives and theories which lead to similar policy outcomes over time.

Considering the relative silence on the globalization of aid in these perspectives, this part of the book argues that to understand the globalization of foreign aid requires a macro level examination of the influence of world society on aid donors.

World polity / world society explanations of diffusion

World polity research has examined the diffusion of different policies and institutions trans-nationally including the proliferation of environmental policy, the spread of women's political participation, and patterns of treaty ratification (Hironaka, 2002; Ramirez, Soysal, & Shanahan, 1997; Wotipka & Ramirez, 2003, 2008; Swiss, 2009). These quantitative analyses lend support to the relationship between the diffusion of policies and the enactment of world-level cultural models by nation-state actors. The world polity literature suggests that the moving force behind this diffusion is that states enact models to seek legitimacy on the international stage and respond to domestic demands to meet international norms (Meyer, Boli et al., 1997).

Earlier writing on the world polity also demonstrated the institutionalization of national development planning and its evolution as a global definition of development (Hwang, 2006), but has not touched only in a limited way upon the institution of foreign aid (Swiss, 2011; 2012; 2016). These efforts show that development assistance is simply another world polity institutional model intended to be adopted by donor and recipient countries alike in their efforts to display legitimacy as states in the global community. The principles, values, and organizational structures implied in the provision of foreign aid to developing societies are all reflections of world cultural norms of development assistance. Not only have all the major Western democracies created development assistance machineries and a corresponding development assistance sector of experts, NGOs, and aid workers, but developing countries have equally developed means of receiving this aid both at the government and civil society level. This rapid creation and spread of the mechanisms of development assistance in the past half-century is direct evidence of world polity influences of globalization, isomorphism, and growing conformity. Furthermore, this similarity does not end at the simple organizational structure and mandates of development assistance donors, but as this chapter will show, extends to more detailed policy models of development assistance. By adopting policy models that reflect internationally agreed upon best practices of foreign aid, donor countries can demonstrate their legitimacy as international benefactors of the developing world, and at the same time validate the quality of their aid programmes to their domestic constituency and donor peers. It is explicitly for these reasons of legitimacy and validation that donor agencies are likely to be affected by world polity influences in their provision of development assistance. This chapter explores several key factors expected to condition these influences at the macro level:

(1) the 'density' of a policy model: demonstration/contagion effects;
(2) the embeddedness of donors in global civil society networks;
(3) the timing of global conferences and treaties;
(4) the structure of donor agencies; and
(5) levels of donor generosity.

(1) Density, demonstration and contagion: policy isomorphism

Akin to institutional isomorphism is the presence of similar policies shared among diverse institutions/states. Once institutions are similarly modelled after one another, it seems natural that they would share some similarity in policy decisions and priorities. Yet, it may also appear unexpected to some that institutions from different countries operating under different political contexts, and with divergent goals might share the same policy priorities with great frequency. In the development assistance sector, policy isomorphism does appear frequently. Donor agencies share common goals, objectives, and policies that stem from common policy frameworks. Despite different political, societal, and cultural contexts, development assistance is carried out in most instances in a very uniform manner throughout the DAC donor countries. This similarity of policies is argued here to reflect consensus (or consensus-like) agreements that encourage conformity between major donor states at the international level. These agreements yield similar policies in dissimilar contexts, and in turn homogenize approaches to development assistance through the propagation of a limited menu of development assistance models, priorities, and parameters within which to operate.

Development assistance proves a challenge to donor institutions and their related organizational fields, as it is a sector rife with uncertainty regarding both goals and means to achieve them. 'Development' as a goal can mean many different things (Escobar, 1995; Esteva, 1992; Ferguson, 1994; Lumsdaine, 1993; Nederveen Pieterse, 1998; Sen, 1999; Stiglitz, 2002; Woolcock, 1998), and therefore may prove a difficult target to achieve for many states and societies. Assisting in this development proves equally difficult, as there has yet been identified a single guaranteed driver/engine of development behind which donors can martial their resources and energies. Indeed, the story of development assistance over the past sixty-plus years is one of theories offered, tested, and often rejected about how to improve the lives of people and bring about 'development'. This remaining uncertainty about how to achieve the aim of development may therefore lead to a greater propensity of development assistance institutions to emulate what others are also doing as a way of legitimating actions among a group of peers rather than adopting maverick approaches which may appear riskier. In this sense, the uncertainty inherent in development assistance may increase institutional isomorphism and policy isomorphism in ways that appear to increase certainty about means and ends at the same time as they diminish the variety of efforts to promote development (DiMaggio & Powell, 1983). Indeed, earlier world polity research has shown that mimicry and other so-called contagion effects can be shown to bear some responsibility for the spread of common institutions and models among nation-states (Jang, 2003; Ramirez & McEneaney, 1997; Wotipka & Ramirez, 2008).

Part of the tendency to emulate other donors may stem from the nature of the development assistance donors as a 'limited field' (DiMaggio & Powell,

1983). Even with the proliferation of these institutions, we still find only a limited number of donor agencies in the early twenty-first century – only twenty-two major development assistance donors compose the DAC among the 200-plus countries that make up the current international community. As such, these institutions have a very limited group of others from which to model behaviour, form, and policy. A small community of donors may therefore partially explain the high degree of institutional isomorphism in the development sector. As policy models proliferate to more states – sometimes referred to as greater density – states which have already adopted a certain position are liable to influence others to do so. When density of a policy model reaches a certain threshold a 'tipping point' is reached after which comes a 'norm cascade' in which states will adopt a policy or institution to seek greater legitimacy on the world stage (Finnemore & Sikkink, 1998, pp. 901–902). Given these factors, this chapter posits a model of diffusion which assumes: *The greater the number of donors adopting a women in development or gender and development policy, the more likely other donors will adopt such policy, too.*

(2) Embeddedness: the influence of international organizations

One of the chief influences within the world polity is that of international organizations, whether intergovernmental or non-governmental. Evidence from earlier research has emphasized the rapid growth of international non-governmental organizations (INGOs) in the modern age and their role in spreading world cultural models (Boli & Thomas, 1997; Boli & Thomas, 1999b). INGOs are implicated in the spread of institutions and models ranging from environmental protection to population control policies and much more (Barrett & Frank, 1999; Frank, Hironaka, Meyer, Schofer, & Tuma, 1999). Although INGOs are not the central force in the global system, they nonetheless actively influence nation-state actors and 'lead states, individuals, and organizations to incorporate new purposes and goals in their constellations of interests and to abandon older purposes and goals that fall out of favor in world culture' (Boli, 1999, p. 297). As such, the INGO is a key aspect of the world polity can fill the role of 'rationalized other' offered by Meyer and his colleagues (1997) to denote those groups which generate the discourses that are refined to form world cultural models.

The world polity literature also points to the significant role played by inter-governmental organizations (IGOs) as institutions through which the cultural models of the world society propagate (Meyer, Boli et al., 1997; Meyer, Frank, Hironaka, Schofer, & Tuma, 1997; Schofer & McEneaney, 2003; Wotipka & Ramirez, 2003). Chief among these is the United Nations, an organization which with its numerous sub-bodies and affiliates has provided a structure through which nation-states coordinate on issues such as the environment, food, health, development, and others. The UN system also provides a means of legitimating the state on the global level. All member countries of the UN are held to a common set of standards and expectations which essentially define the roles and responsibilities of the state in the modern era (Meyer, Boli et al., 1997). By being a member of many of these intergovernmental organizations, states are held to a standard of membership that indeed defines institutions and policies at the nation-state level and promote isomorphism and conformity. In the case of development assistance, several these organizations exist, most importantly the OECD DAC, World Bank, and the United Nations.

Within specific substantive issue areas, the influence of focused international organizations may be more relevant than the membership in a more broadly based organization like the UN. For instance, in the area of environmental protection, past research indicates that the growth of the international environmental movement and the role of international environmental organizations strongly influenced the adoption of environmental policies and institutions (Hironaka, 2002; Meyer, Frank et al., 1997; Schofer & Hironaka, 2005). Other research reveals that the growth and influence of the international women's movement has affected women's political representation in parliaments throughout the world (Paxton et al., 2006). The theorized influence of the women's movement and the growth of international feminist discourse on issues of women's involvement in society and on gender inequalities can thus be seen to operate at least partially through the influence of international women's organizations. This influence operates through a nation-state's level of integration into these movements and organizations and can be termed its level of embeddedness in the actors that compose world society. In the case of the spread of WID/GAD policy among development donors, the model of diffusion proposed here includes the following proposition regarding embeddedness: *The greater the number of women's international non-governmental organizations in which a country's residents are members, the greater the likelihood of donors to adopt a WID/GAD policy.*

(3) On the global agenda: international conferences and treaties

Aside from actual membership in international organizations like the UN or the OECD DAC, world polity influence is also exerted by attention drawn to issues through the creation of international treaties on the matter or the conduct of high-level international conferences on the subject.

Treaties are perceived as a means of standardizing nation-state approaches to an issue through embracing common definitions, expectations, and objectives. Throughout the lifespan of the United Nations, there have been many treaties that have been responsible for disseminating common concepts and norms throughout international law, particularly around human rights. Notable examples include the Universal Declaration of Human Rights, the Convention on the Rights of the Child, and the Convention on the Elimination of All Forms of Discrimination Against Women (CEDAW). Some world polity research has highlighted how the diffusion of treaty ratification throughout the international community itself can be considered a function of world polity influences (Wotipka & Ramirez, 2008; Cole 2013). At the same time, treaty ratification implies a common framework being applied in multiple nation-state contexts. In the case of the growth of WID/GAD policy in development assistance, the most influential treaty would be the CEDAW and its focus on protecting women's rights and furthering gender equality. Countries ratifying this treaty in the period after 1979 should be more likely to integrate some of its principles into their development assistance framework in the form of a WID/GAD policy.

Earlier research has also highlighted the extent to which UN conferences, for instance, can be considered a form of 'global ritual' through which principles and messages are disseminated and reinforced among nation-state participants (Lechner & Boli, 2005). Indeed, major UN conferences on the topics of environment, human rights, population, and women have had substantial impact on shaping global consensus on these subjects. In the case of the diffusion of WID/GAD policy, the influence of the four major UN conferences on women from 1975 through 1995 are the most salient, with these conferences progressively integrating the notion of women's rights as human rights more fully into development discourse with each meeting (Lechner & Boli, 2005; Moser & Moser, 2005). Due to the heightened attention drawn to women's issues and gender inequalities surrounding these conferences, it can be expected that in the periods following each conference, countries should be more likely to engage with WID or GAD ideas and therefore be more likely to introduce a WID/GAD policy or unit within their donor agency.

Given the focus drawn to women's rights and gender inequality by CEDAW and the four UN conferences on women this chapter examines whether: *The ratification of the CEDAW or the occurrence of the UN World Conferences on Women increases the likelihood of donors to adopt a WID/GAD policy.*

Domestic factors

The common thread running through most research on the world polity remains the testing of international influences such as INGOs, treaties, and contagion effects, however; less often has world polity research focused specifically on domestic factors shaping the nation-state interface with world cultural models. Some research has included a focus on the nature of nation-state structures as intervening factors on how world polity policy and institutional models are translated within the state (Hironaka, 2002; Ramirez et al., 1997). As such, the macro-level model put forward here includes two domestic aspects of the development assistance sector: donor agency structure and donor generosity.

(4) Donor agency structure

Donor structure can be viewed as consisting of two components: agency autonomy and locus of decision-making. Agency autonomy refers to the status of the institution as either a stand-alone agency/body within the government of the country (autonomous), or as a sub-unit of the Ministry of Foreign Affairs (integrated). Locus of decision-making refers to the seat of primary decision-making regarding decisions related to ODA disbursement to countries on a bilateral basis. When these decisions are taken primarily at agency headquarters we identify a 'centralized' decision-making type, and in contrast, when decisions are primarily taken in the field offices located in recipient countries are identified as 'decentralized' donors. Agency-wide policy decisions still tend to be centralized even in this second instance (Engberg-Pedersen, 2014).

The contention that donor structure can be a determining factor of influence of world polity policy models on a donor state merits further investigation. An integrated donor would be more likely to resist externally generated models that were possibly not in keeping with national interests, whereas a more autonomous donor may be more likely to adopt such models. More autonomous donor agencies would be more likely to seek legitimacy from other donor agencies internationally and therefore be more readily influenced by processes of mimetic isomorphism like those identified by Dimaggio and Powell (1983). A donor agency autonomous from the Ministry of Foreign Affairs would face greater uncertainty regarding its policy mandate, as it would be less closely coupled to national foreign policy concerns. Therefore, the autonomous donor agency would seek to legitimate its foreign aid focus by modelling best practices of behavior from other donors, rather than relying on policy direction from within the rest of the government. Unfortunately, this argument has not been previously tested in the literature, and therefore the reasoning applied here is based on an argument that greater distance from policy-makers grounded in national interest would increase uncertainty and open an organization to externally generated policies which are more universal in nature. The donor's decision-making locus may also mediate world polity influence, in that a decentralized donor may have greater exposure to world polity rationalized others, and therefore is more likely to adopt policy scripts than a centralized donor. Indeed, donor decentralization was promoted by the DAC for much of the last decade as a means of diminishing donor country national interests in devising effective development assistance programmes that more appropriately suit local conditions and priorities. To account for these structural factors, this chapter contends that: *The greater the autonomy of a donor agency, the more likely they will adopt externally generated policy scripts related to WID/GAD.*

(5) Donor generosity

Earlier research has shown that levels of donor generosity, aid measured as a proportion of national income, are directly related to domestic political structures such as the magnitude of the welfare state and state commitment to social democratic values (Noël & Thérien, 1995). Implied in the argument that development assistance can be seen to be in the more generous countries simply an externally oriented extension of the welfare state is an underlying motivation of humanitarianism. Given that higher generosity reflects greater humanitarianism, the final piece of the macro-level model laid out here is that greater generosity also reflects more openness to outside ideas, therefore more susceptibility to world polity influence.

Diffusion of WID/GAD policy in the development assistance sector

Examining the world polity influences of density and embeddedness, along with the timing of treaties, the staging of major international conferences, and looking to key domestic factors within the development assistance institutions, this part of the book aims to detail the effects of the world polity on the nation-state – especially as it pertains to the globalization of aid policy. The next section summarizes a quantitative analysis of this model to provide insights into the working of the world polity and its interface with the nation-state in the development assistance sector.[2]

World society and diffusion: macro-level globalization

Each of the factors laid out in the model above can be seen to play a part in the diffusion and adoption of WID or GAD policies or functional units within the major donor countries of the OECD DAC: (1) policy density and contagion; (2) embeddedness in international organizations; (3) influence of the international community through treaties and conferences; and (4 & 5) domestic development assistance sector characteristics. The remainder of this chapter addresses each of these areas.[3]

First, policy density and nation-state embeddedness in international organizations appear to be important determinants of the diffusion of world culture policy models. Quantitative results show support for the idea that, when taken on their own, both policy density and embeddedness appear to be salient factors in the diffusion of gender policy among the community of development assistance donors. Figure 2.2 shows the predicted effects from my statistical models of a one standard deviation increase in both policy density and embeddedness on the likelihood of adopting a gender unit or policy, all else equal.[4] In the case of policy density, relative risk of adoption increases by 101.2% with approximately every four donors already adopting the model. For embeddedness, for every 3.5 additional WINGO memberships a country holds, the likelihood of policy adoption increases by 64.1%.

Measuring density as the count of donors already possessing a gender unit or policy allows us to convey the notion of a critical mass of donors adopting the idea and influencing their peers in doing so. The fact that the latter half of the donors considered in the sample adopted a WID/GAD policy or unit in a ten-year period from 1992 to 2002, suggests that in the early nineties a critical mass of donors sufficient to cause a tipping point or norm cascade that caused the spread of the policy priority to the remaining DAC members (Finnemore & Sikkink, 1998). Furthermore, given that many of the most

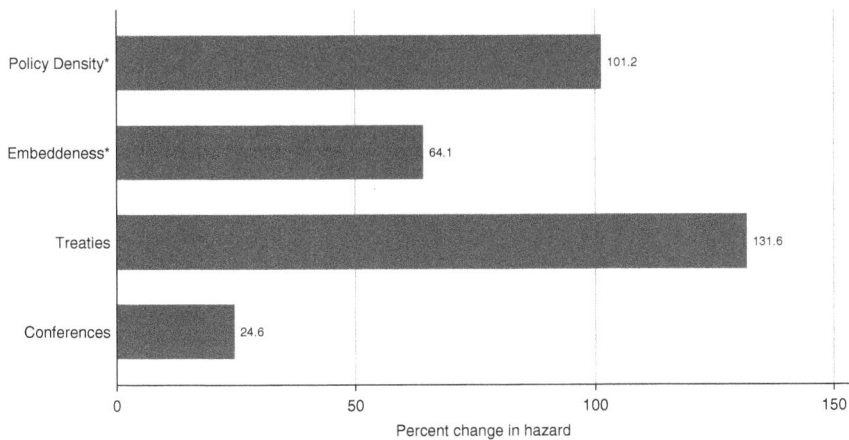

Figure 2.2 Marginal effects of international influences on WID/GAD policy adoption

Note: * Effect of one standard deviation change in policy density (global gender policy adoptions) and embeddedness (WINGO memberships) measure; Effect of Treaties (CEDAW ratification) and Conferences (post-1985 period) are binary. Predicted effects calculated using results from quantitative models 2–5 in Table A.2. in the Methodological Appendix (see page 160).

influential donors (Sweden, United States, United Kingdom, and Canada) had adopted a WID/GAD policy early on may also have influenced later adoption by some of the smaller donors.

The embeddedness of donors in the international women's movement also appears to affect their expression of women's rights and gender equality in their development assistance donor policies. The spread of these values among donor institutions cannot be separated from the spread of similar principles throughout Western democracies in the last few decades. Indeed, these principles are directly linked to the work of the international women's movement (Berkovitch, 1999a, 1999b; Paxton et al., 2006). Other international organizations could equally be considered in playing a role in shaping donor policy. For instance, the rapid growth in the number and type of international development NGOs in the past century can also be expected to demonstrate some effect on donor policy (Chabbott, 1999), however; because of the direct link of donor WID/GAD policy to values and norms championed by the WINGOs of the international women's movement, donor embeddedness in this type of organization is the most relevant for this case.

Second, the influence on donors of the international community through treaties and conferences is another world polity factor that helps to explain the diffusion of common policies among diverse donors. Controlling for donor characteristics, the ratification of CEDAW was powerful enough to shape donor institutions to include a women's rights or gender unit or policy, as the requirements of the convention set out expectations for government institutions in adopting countries to adopt special measures to combat gender inequality and discrimination against women. Figure 2.2 shows that in my statistical models a country ratifying CEDAW increases the predicted relative risk of adopting the gender policy/unit model by more than 130% relative to a country that had not ratified. However, the relationship between donor policy adoption and ratification was not robust through both stages of quantitative analysis.

The fact that ratification is not statistically significant across all stages of the statistical analysis raises some alternative explanations that need to be considered. For instance, the implementation of international treaties following ratification does not always do justice to the spirit of the values and principles outlined within treaties (Wotipka & Ramirez, 2008). Given that all but three of the donors included in the study ratified CEDAW in the 1980s, but more than half of the sample of donors did not develop a donor gender policy until later in the 1990s, the notion of decoupling evident in slow implementation of CEDAW principles needs to be considered. The symbolic support for women's rights evident in CEDAW ratification is not matched immediately by more substantive change in donor policy.

This decoupling and lack of substantive conformity to CEDAW expectations may have been rectified to some extent by the renewed focus on women's rights and gender equality that surrounded the world conferences on women in Nairobi in 1985 and Beijing in 1995, as each country in the sample participated in both conferences. This effect is more modest than the other global influences discussed above, but Figure 2.2 still indicates that countries were 24.6% more likely to adopt a gender policy or unit in the donor agency in the post-Nairobi period than they were earlier. What are some possibilities in how this influence was exerted? One option is that the donor role in supporting the attendance of many developing country NGO participants in parallel meetings to the Beijing conference may have helped to spur a donor focus on gender that was only weak in earlier periods. In addition, donor representatives included in the official government delegations to these conferences may have played a role in returning to the donor agency with greater motivation to adopt policy in the gender and development area. These possibilities also exist at less high-profile international meetings on the gender topic, including the annual meetings of the DAC network on gender. Since 1981, the DAC has had an internal network of donors to discuss and explore women's issues and gender equality. On a smaller scale, these DAC network meetings can work to serve a similar function to donors that the UN conferences play at a national level. As such, the role of both international treaties and conferences or meetings seem to have a role to play in the diffusion of common donor policies, whether at the national level or in terms of individual donor participation in some aspect of an international conference or meeting.

Finally, despite weak quantitative evidence to support the argument that the structure and level of generosity of the development assistance donor influences the readiness of a donor to accept externally generated world polity policy models bears further investigation. The evidence suggests that the assertion that the more generous donor – those associated with greater humanitarian motivations rather than national interest – will more quickly adopt the policy models of the world polity cannot be rejected. This argument, however, would only hold in the case of a world polity model which has underlying humanitarian motivations. In the case of a policy area such as security-sector reform or conflict prevention, this relationship may not hold because of the closer link of that policy model to the national interests of donor countries. In such an instance, we might expect the opposite relationship to hold. Those donors with more motivation linked to national interest – less generous, and possibly more closely linked to their ministry of foreign affairs – would then be more likely to adopt a world polity model derived from national interest values and norms.

The quantitatively measured relationships between variables representing different macro-level aspects of the world polity nation-state interface identified here do only a little to explain social processes at work in the world polity. The detailed interactions of the nation-state and the international community are in fact always person-to-person interactions involving officials, experts, and organization representatives. It is possible that these interactions account for the actual transfer of world cultural models from the world society to the nation-state level, and to other organizations and individuals. Using the example of the creation of gender policies and units in development assistance donors has simply been a means of illustrating this process at the highest level. Indeed, this chapter highlights the complexity of modelling a social process quantitatively at the macro international level, and arguably points towards the need for other research methods to flesh out in richer detail the processes at work in this situation. As Part II of this book will show, by drilling down into the actual micro-level interactions and human agency involved in taking policy decisions, we can more fully comprehend the process of globalization in the foreign aid sector. By combining the findings from this macro-level analysis with Part II's qualitative cases, it is possible to illustrate in greater detail how world polity influences in the development assistance sector have led to greater consensus and conformity of policy among donors in recent years.

Notes

1 Indeed, the diversity of implementation of these policies and units shows that despite similar form (isomorphism) within the world polity, there is striking differences between states when it comes to application of these common models. This leads to the phenomenon of decoupling within the world polity.

2 For a more detailed explanation of this analysis, please see Swiss, 2012, or refer to the methodological appendix included in this book.

3 The results underpinning the conclusions drawn in this section of the chapter are included in the methodological appendix.
4 See the details of the statistical model in the methodological appendix.

References

ADB, Asian Development Bank. (1997). Microenterprise Development: Not on Credit Alone. Retrieved from www.adb.org/Documents/Books/Microenterprise/default.asp

Alesina, A., & Dollar, D. (2000). Who Gives Foreign Aid to Whom and Why? *Journal of Economic Growth*, 5(1), 33–63.

Barrett, D., & Frank, D. J. (1999). Population Control for National Development: From World Discourse to National Policies. In J. Boli & G. M. Thomas (Eds.), *Constructing World Culture: International Nongovernmental Organizations Since 1875* (pp. 198–221). Stanford, CA: Stanford University Press.

Berkovitch, N. (1999). *From Motherhood to Citizenship: Women's Rights and International Organizations*. Baltimore, MD: Johns Hopkins University Press.

Berkovitch, N. (1999). The Emergence and Transformation of the International Women's Movement. In J. Boli & G. M. Thomas (Eds.), *Constructing World Culture: International Nongovernmental Organizations Since 1875* (pp. 100–126). Stanford, CA: Stanford University Press.

Boli, J. (1999). Conclusions: World Authority Structures and Legitimations. In J. Boli & G. M. Thomas (Eds.), *Constructing World Culture: International Nongovernmental Organizations Since 1875* (pp. 267–300). Stanford, CA: Stanford University Press.

Boli, J., & Thomas, G. M. (1997). World Culture in the World Polity: A Century of International Non-governmental Organization. *American Sociological Review*, 62(2), 171–190.

Boli, J., & Thomas, G. M. (1999). *Constructing World Culture: International Nongovernmental Organizations Since 1875*. Stanford, CA: Stanford University Press.

Boli, J., & Thomas, G. M. (1999). INGOs and the Organization of World Culture. In J. Boli & G. M. Thomas (Eds.), *Constructing World Culture: International Nongovernmental Organizations Since 1875* (pp. 13–49). Stanford, CA: Stanford University Press.

Chabbott, C. (1999). Development INGOs. In J. Boli & G. M. Thomas (Eds.), *Constructing World Culture: International Nongovernmental Organizations Since 1875* (pp. 222–248). Stanford, CA: Stanford University Press.

CIDA, Canadian International Development Agency. (2002). Canadian International Development Agency, Departmental Performance Report, 2001–2002. Retrieved from www.tbs-sct.gc.ca/rma/dpr/01-02/CIDA/CIDA0102dpr02_e.asp

Cole, W. M. (2013). Government Respect for Gendered Rights: The Effect of the Convention on the Elimination of Discrimination against Women on Women's Rights Outcomes, 1981–2004. *International Studies Quarterly*, 57(2), 233–249.

DiMaggio, P., & Powell, W. W. (1983). The Iron Cage Revisited: Institutional Isomorphism and Collective Rationality in Organizational Fields. *American Sociological Review*, 48(2), 147–160.

Engberg-Pedersen, L. (2014). Bringing Aid Management Closer to Reality: The Experience of Danish Bilateral Development Cooperation. *Development Policy Review*, 32(1), 113–131. doi:10.1111/dpr.12046

Escobar, A. (1995). *Encountering Development: The Making and Unmaking of the Third World*. Princeton, N.J.: Princeton University Press.

Esteva, G. (1992). Development. In W. Sachs (Ed.), *The Development Dictionary: A Guide to Knowledge as Power* (pp. 6–25). London: Zed.

Ferguson, J. (1994). *The Anti-politics Machine: 'Development,' Depoliticization, and Bureaucratic Power in Lesotho*. Minneapolis: University of Minnesota Press.

Finnemore, M., & Sikkink, K. (1998). International Norm Dynamics and Political Change. *International Organization*, 52(4), International Organization at Fifty: Exploration and Contestation in the Study of World Politics), 887–917.

Frank, D. J., Hironaka, A., Meyer, J. W., Schofer, E., & Tuma, N. B. (1999). The Rationalization and Organization of Nature in World Culture. In J. Boli & G. M. Thomas (Eds.), *Constructing World Culture: International Nongovernmental Organizations Since 1875* (pp. 81–99). Stanford, CA: Stanford University Press.

Frank, D. J., Longhofer, W., & Schofer, E. (2007). World Society, NGOs and Environmental Policy Reform in Asia. *International Journal of Comparative Sociology*, 48(4), 275–295. doi:10.1177/0020715207079530

Hironaka, A. (2002). The Globalization of Environmental Protection: The Case of Environmental Impact Assessment. *International Journal of Comparative Sociology*, 43(1), 65–78.

Hwang, H. (2006). Planning Development: Globalization and the Shifting Locus of Planning. In G. S. Drori, J. W. Meyer, & H. Hwang (Eds.), *Globalization and Organization: World Society and Organizational Change* (pp. 69–89). New York: Oxford University Press.

Jang, Y. S. (2003). The Global Diffusion of Ministries of Science and Technology. In G. S. Drori, J. W. Meyer, F. O. Ramirez, & E. Schofer (Eds.), *Science in the Modern World Polity: Institutionalization and Globalization* (pp. 120–135). Stanford, Calif.: Stanford University Press.

Lechner, F. J., & Boli, J. (2005). *World Culture: Origins and Consequences*. London: Blackwell.

Lumsdaine, D. H. (1993). *Moral Vision in International Politics: The Foreign Aid Regime, 1949–1989*. Princeton, N.J.: Princeton University Press.

Martens, B. (2005). Why Do Aid Agencies Exist? *Development Policy Review*, 23(6), 643–663.

Meyer, J. W. (2007). Globalization: Theory and Trends. *International Journal of Comparative Sociology*, 48(4), 261–273. doi:10.1177/0020715207079529

Meyer, J. W., Boli, J., Thomas, G. M., & Ramirez, F. O. (1997). World Society and the Nation-state. *The American Journal of Sociology*, 103(1), 144–181.

Meyer, J. W., Frank, D. J., Hironaka, A., Schofer, E., & Tuma, N. B. (1997). The Structuring of a World Environmental Regime, 1870–1990. *International Organization*, 51(4), 623.

Morgenthau, H. (1962). A Political Theory of Foreign Aid. *The American Political Science Review*, 56(2), 301–309.

Moser, C. (2005). Has Gender Mainstreaming Failed? *International Feminist Journal of Politics*, 7(4), 576–590.

Moser, C., & Moser, A. (2005). Gender Mainstreaming Since Beijing: A Review of Success and Limitations in International Institutions. *Gender and Development*, 13(2), 11–22.

Nederveen Pieterse, J. (1998). My Paradigm or Yours? Alternative Development, Post-Development, Reflexive Development. *Development and Change*, 29(2), 343–373(331).

Noël, A., & Thérien, J.-P. (1995). From Domestic to International Justice: The Welfare State and Foreign Aid. *International Organization*, 49(3), 523–553.

Opeskin, B. R. (1996). The Moral Foundations of Foreign Aid. *World Development*, 24(1), 21–44.

Paxton, P., Hughes, M. M., & Green, J. L. (2006). The International Women's Movement and Women's Political Representation, 1893–2003. *American Sociological Review*, 71, 898–920.

Pratt, C. (1994). Humane Internationalism and Canadian Development Assistance Policies. In C. Pratt (Ed.), *Canadian International Development Assistance Policies: An Appraisal* (pp. 334–370). Montreal: McGill-Queen's University Press.

Ramirez, F. O., & McEneaney, E. H. (1997). From Women's Suffrage to Reproduction Rights? Cross-national Considerations. *International Journal of Comparative Sociology*, 38(1–2), 6.

Ramirez, F. O., Soysal, Y., & Shanahan, S. (1997). The Changing Logic of Political Citizenship: Cross-national Acquisition of Women's Suffrage Rights, 1890 to 1990. *American Sociological Review*, 62(5), 735.

Rathgeber, E. (1990). WID, WAD, GAD: Trends in Research and Practice. *The Journal of Developing Areas*, 24, 489–502.

Rathgeber, E. (1995). Gender and Development in Action. In Marianne H. Marchand & J. L. Parpart (Eds.), *Feminism/Postmodernism/Development* (pp. 204–220). London: Routledge.

Schofer, E., & Hironaka, A. (2005). The Effects of World Society on Environmental Protection Outcomes. *Social Forces*, 84(1), 25–47.

Schofer, E., & McEneaney, E. H. (2003). Methodological Strategies and Tools for the Study of Globalization. In G. S. Drori, J. W. Meyer, F. O. Ramirez, & E. Schofer (Eds.), *Science in the Modern World Polity: Institutionalization and Globalization* (pp. 43–74). Stanford, Calif.: Stanford University Press.

Sen, A. K. (1999). *Development as Freedom* (1st Edition). New York: Knopf.

Stiglitz, J. E. (2002). *Globalization and its Discontents* (1st Edition). New York: W.W. Norton.

Swiss, L. (2011). Security Sector Reform and Development Assistance: Explaining the Diffusion of Policy Priorities Among Donor Agencies. *Qualitative Sociology*, 34(2), 371–393.

Swiss, L. (2012). The Adoption of Women and Gender as Development Assistance Priorities: An Event History Analysis of World Polity Effects. *International Sociology*, 27(1), 96–119.

Swiss, L. (2016). A Sociology of Foreign Aid and the World Society. *Sociology Compass*, 10(1), 65–73.

Thorbecke, E. (2007). The Evolution of the Development Doctrine, 1950–2005. In G. Mavrotas & A. Shorrocks (Eds.), *Advancing Development: Core Themes in Global Economics* (pp. 3–36). Basingstoke: Palgrave Macmillan.

Tiessen, R. (2007). *Everywhere/Nowhere: Gender Mainstreaming in Development Agencies*. Bloomfield, CT: Kumarian Press.

UN, United Nations. (2003). The Right to Education: Report submitted by the Special Rapporteur, Katarina Tomasevski: E/CN.4/2004/45. Retrieved from www.right-to-education.org/content/unreports/unreport12prt1.html

UNFPA, United Nations Population Fund. (1994). Programme of Action of the International Conference on Population and Development. Retrieved from www.unfpa.org/icpd/icpd_poa.htm

USAID, United States Agency for International Development. (2002). Initiative For Southern Africa. Retrieved from www.usaid.gov/pubs/cbj2002/afr/isa/690-012.html

Woods, N. (2005). The Shifting Politics of Foreign Aid. *International Affairs*, 81(2), 393–409.

Woolcock, M. (1998). Social Capital and Economic Development: Toward a Theoretical Synthesis and Policy Framework. *Theory and Society*, 27(2), 151–208.

World Bank Group. (2000). Partners in Transforming Development: New Approaches to Developing Country-Owned Poverty Reduction Strategies. Retrieved from www.imf.org/external/np/prsp/pdf/prspbroc.pdf

World Bank Group. (2002). Improving Water and Sanitation Services for the Poor: An instrument to support World Bank Operations. Retrieved from www.worldbank.org/html/fpd/water/bnwp/files/booklet.pdf

Wotipka, C. M., & Ramirez, F. O. (2003). Women in Science: For Development, for Human Rights, for Themselves. In G. S. Drori, J. W. Meyer, F. O. Ramirez, & E. Schofer (Eds.), *Science in the Modern World Polity: Institutionalization and Globalization* (pp. 174–195). Stanford, Calif.: Stanford University Press.

Wotipka, C. M., & Ramirez, F. O. (2008). World Society and Human Rights: An Event History Analysis of the Convention on the Elimination of All Forms of Discrimination Against Women. In B. A. Simmons, F. Dobbin, & G. Garrett (Eds.), *The Global Diffusion of Markets and Democracy* (pp. 303–343). Cambridge: Cambridge University Press.

Part II

Donors think alike?

3 The donors

Canada, Sweden, and the United States

Since 1945 almost all major industrialized countries have developed an institutional framework and series of relationships for providing foreign aid to poorer countries. Striking similarity in the policies, practices, and institutions of foreign aid have emerged over that time between the major donors. In recent years, the increasing conformity of policy priorities among development assistance donors has emerged as a concern to recipient countries and civil society groups alike. Indeed, development assistance plays a large role in shaping the nature of development in many countries of the developing world and the impact of donor consensus on development priorities or conformity among donors about specific development objectives runs the risk of homogenizing development assistance in a manner deleterious to concepts of locally appropriate and contextualized development.

As I discussed in earlier chapters, similar trends towards conformity and similarity of institutions and practices have been explored in earlier research on the international expansion and diffusion of similar models and common practices in areas like science, education, environmentalism, feminism, and even politics. This body of research highlights the influence of 'scripts' or 'models' created by international organizations and networks of experts of the world polity on the institutional isomorphism in each of these sectors. Still, little past research actively investigates the social processes and mechanisms through which this world polity influence is exerted (Swiss 2011, 2012). In this light, the isomorphism of aid institutions and policies can also be viewed as a reflection of world polity influences on the nation-state; however, the processes through which this influence occurs requires further investigation.

The processes through which foreign aid policy scripts influence nation-state actors are expected to lead to similar outcomes in disparate contexts. Given this, the purpose of this chapter is to differentiate the three donor contexts that come under scrutiny in my qualitative analysis in the following chapters. To distinguish the variation across the case study countries requires the examination of the major components which comprise the 'Development Assistance Sector' in each donor state. This chapter briefly outlines the salient components of this sector in the book's three country cases as of 2006–2008 period in which the case studies were conducted.

Four main components of the development assistance sectors in Canada, Sweden, and the United States are considered, along with the underlying motivations for the provision of development assistance in each society: (1) the level of public support for development assistance; (2) the structure of the primary aid agency in terms of both decision-making and independence from the rest of government; (3) the degree of involvement of civil society in the development assistance endeavour; and (4) recent legislative frameworks which work to shape the delivery of development assistance in each country. At the end of the chapter, I address the major changes that have occurred in each country's development assistance sector since the case study was conducted in 2006–2008, arguing that despite these changes my findings still help explain the globalization of aid seen in each case.

By exploring these four components of the development assistance sector in each country, the chapter establishes the diversity among the case study countries. These countries, though similar in many ways, address foreign aid in very different ways and with different motives: Canada is revealed as a picture of inconsistency when it comes to its aid; Sweden appears as humanitarian-inspired aid superpower; while, the United States occupies the paradoxical position of being the most generous aid donor by volume, but one of the least generous relative to its own wealth. Understanding these diverse contexts is the first step to understanding and identifying the common social processes and mechanisms that promote conformity and consensus on development assistance at the global level, despite such donor differences.

Canada

Canadian development assistance: persistent inconsistency

Canadian development assistance is based on contradictory motivations of helping assist worse-off countries and peoples and maintaining Canadian national interests (Noël, Thérien, and Dallaire 2004; Otter 2003; Pratt 1994c; Rawkins 1994; Morrison 1998; Black 2014; Swiss 2014). As Canada has no geographic proximity to the developing world, and no foreign colonial history, its direct ties to most countries of the developing world are limited. Aid provided by Canada originally began under the Colombo plan of the British Commonwealth, targeting post-war reconstruction and development in former British colonies of South and Southeast Asia, partially to stem the spread of communism in the region. In 1960, the External Aid Office (EAO) was formed as a branch of the Department of External Affairs to consolidate Canadian aid efforts. In the same year, Canada joined the Development Assistance Committee (DAC) of the Organisation for Economic Co-operation and Development (OECD). Then, in 1968, the Canadian International

Development Agency was formed as a separate government agency tasked with managing Canada's official development assistance (Morrison 1998).

In 1961, before the formation of CIDA, Canada's bilateral aid was focused on thirty-three countries and amounted to 0.16% of GNP.[1] This expanded sharply several years after the formation of CIDA to eighty-four countries and 0.5% of GNP in 1976, and to an even greater number of countries in the 1990s and early 2000s (Pratt 1994b). In terms of ODA as a percentage of GNP, the commonly held measure of donor generosity among DAC donors, Canada has never exceeded the 0.5% reached in 1976 and again in 1988, and indeed Canadian aid levels have been consistently in flux since the 1970s. As such, by 2008 Canada had never reached the 0.7% of GNP ODA target established by the UN, despite rhetoric outlining its desire to do so. Fluctuations in aid levels were not drastic in the 1970s and 1980s, but by the mid-1990s, drastic cutbacks in aid levels were underway to parallel austerity measures imposed on all Canadian governments by conservative spending policies in reaction to economic crisis and high public debt (Otter 2003). These cutbacks led to the lowest level of aid spending by Canada in more than thirty years when in 2001 ODA was only 0.22% of GNP (UNICEF 2007). From 2002 to 2008, the trend was towards slightly more aid, with the aid-to-GNI ratio averaging 0.29% of GNI between 2002 and 2008 (OECD 2017). At these levels, Canada's development assistance levels fell below the DAC average, and research criticized levels of generosity of the Canadian aid programme as costing Canada any claim it had to being a leader in development assistance (Noël, Thérien, and Dallaire 2004).

The motivations behind Canada's aid have also been in flux over the nearly sixty years of its operations. In the early years of aid, before the formation of CIDA, Canada's aid was more closely linked to commercial objectives, trade relationships, and foreign policy objectives – all tied to issues of national interest. After 1968 and the formation of CIDA, some research has pointed towards a departure from this national interest position and an attempt by CIDA to make Canadian aid truly benefit poor countries supported by lobbying from civil society (Lumsdaine 1993). However, after 1977, the interlinking of Canadian aid to its foreign policy and other national interests has for the most part characterized Canada's aid programme (Pratt 1994a; Morrison 1994). In this respect, Canada's development assistance is underpinned both by altruistic humanitarian concerns and by promotion of Canadian interests (Black 2014; Swiss 2014). One example of this is the proliferation of the aid programme to more than 100 recipient countries in the 2000s, but at the same time the high level of tied aid in contrast to many other donors emphasizes the concern with national interests.[2] For instance, in 2000, the OECD DAC reported that Canadian aid was 75% tied (OECD 2002a). In 2005, still 40% of Canadian aid was considered tied, nearly 15% more than the next closest DAC donor reporting these figures (OECD 2006b). Tied aid ensures that development assistance contracts and procurement end up tied to the donor economy and society. Canada's resistance to untying its aid in this period protected those in the Canadian economy who benefit directly from the ODA programme. In contrast, countries like the United Kingdom or Ireland (100% untied), and the Nordic countries (all greater than 95% untied) had entirely or almost entirely untied their aid by 2008, allowing more opportunity for aid funds to end up in recipient country economies. Thus, though Canada disbursed its aid to many less-developed countries, some of this aid came with ties back to Canada that supported Canadian interests. Efforts following the 2005 Paris Declaration on Aid Effectiveness to narrow the number of countries to which Canada provided aid also furthered the national interest motivations, given that many prioritized countries were those with foreign policy (Afghanistan, Iraq), economic (China), or diasporic (Philippines, Ukraine) ties to Canada rather than the poorest of poor countries. Previous analysis of trends in the destination of Canadian aid confirmed the importance of self-interest as a motive (Macdonald and Hoddinott 2004; Swiss 2014).

Canada was, and by all accounts continues to be, a very inconsistent donor, both in terms of aid levels and in terms of motivations underlying its development assistance. This inconsistency is seen in later chapters to reflect itself elsewhere in the Canadian aid programme, particularly in terms of the adoption and application of development assistance policy scripts derived from world polity sources.

Canadian public support for development assistance

The Canadian public's support for development assistance in the period of my study was relatively consistent in public opinion surveys but demonstrated a clear lack of awareness and understanding about the aid programme (Noël, Thérien, and Dallaire 2004). Indeed, in a 2004 opinion poll conducted for CIDA, 78% of Canadians claimed to support Canada's aid programme, consistent with previous studies that found 83% support in 2003, and 75% support in 1998 (Environics Research Group 2004). In 2002, 83% of the Canadian public supported development assistance or the general principle of helping poor countries, however this ranked Canada only thirteenth in level of public support among the then twenty-two Western donors of the OECD DAC (Fransman and Solignac Lecomte 2004). The Canadian public was thus relatively consistent in its support of aid; with approximately four in five Canadians supporting the principle of aid, however, this level of support was demonstrably lower than support shown by many European publics.

Furthermore, this support was marked by a general lack of understanding about the aid programme, in particular about levels of Canada's generosity and correspondingly confusion about public support for changes to Canadian aid. In particular, the Canadian public seemed to have little understanding about the amount of aid Canada provided each year, with many in the public believing Canada to be more generous than it really was (Noël, Thérien, and Dallaire 2004). In 2004 for instance, polling evidence showed that Canadians believed on average that 5 cents of every dollar spent by the government went towards foreign aid. In 2002 this level was perceived at 10.5 cents, and in 1998 at 7 cents on every dollar (Environics Research Group 2004). The fact that Canadian aid spending at the time was approximately only 2% of government expenditure highlights the fact that most Canadians are not aware of Canada's aid programme commitments.

This lack of awareness about actual aid expenditures was perceived by some to contribute to lower levels of support for increasing Canada's aid because the public believed Canada is more generous than it really is (Environics Research Group 2004; Noël, Thérien, and Dallaire 2004; Smillie 1998). Indeed, even after being informed of the actual levels of aid spending, only 43% of Canadians polled in 2004 supported an increase in aid, with another 43% favouring the status quo (Environics Research Group 2004). Furthermore, the Canadian public was more accustomed to hearing about the negative outcomes and failings of development assistance programmes than their successes, as most media attention in Canada in the early 2000s focused only on the problems with Canadian aid (Noël, Thérien, and Dallaire 2004). As such, Canadian public views on aid tended to be perceived as consistent in principle, weak in understanding, and not very supportive of increased generosity – a trend that has persisted to the present day. This is in keeping with the assessment that in many donor countries publics are not strongly motivated to support and fight for more or better aid programmes, suggesting that public support can be considered 'a mile wide and an inch deep' (Smillie 1998, 23).

Given that Canadian aid reached what were historic low levels in the 1990s and early 2000s, the low levels of support for increasing aid in the Canadian public, and the lack of awareness about actual spending levels did little to push Canadian politicians and governments to turn around the decline in Canadian aid. Domestic concerns remained consistently a greater priority to the public than foreign aid generosity (Noël, Thérien, and Dallaire 2004). This low level of support for aid increases led to a corresponding lack of political will among Canadian political parties and governments to make any dramatic increases in the level of Canadian aid spending. Despite evidence from the 2000 Canadian Election Study that showed 20% of Liberal party supporters favoured increases in aid spending, the Liberals in fact presided over the biggest decline in Canadian aid levels ever from 0.44% of GNP in 1991/1992 to only 0.22% of GNP in 2001/2002 (Noël, Thérien, and Dallaire 2004; UNICEF 2007). Even among supporters of Canada's most left-leaning major political party, the New Democratic Party, only approximately 40% supported an increase in aid. The fact that successive Liberal governments cut Canadian ODA in half in terms of a percentage of GNI over the period of a decade, but public opinion levels stayed relatively consistent, highlights the disconnect between public support and political will on aid (Otter 2003).

Even though Canadian aid spending increased significantly from its low in 2001/2002, by 2008 there was still no strong public or political commitment to making the drastic steps needed to achieve the 0.7% goal for aid spending. The disconnect between public support and the reality of Canada's development assistance levels underscored the general lack of concern or involvement of the public in the official development assistance offered by Canada.

CIDA structure

The Canadian International Development Agency was the primary conduit of Canadian ODA, until it was merged with the Department of Foreign Affairs and International Trade in 2013. During the period of my case study, CIDA was responsible for the expenditure of almost 80% of Canada's international assistance envelope (CIDA 2007). This amounted to just over 3.1 billion CAD in the federal government fiscal year 2005–2006 (CIDA 2006a). Although CIDA's structure appeared to be in constant flux, the bulk of the funding was spent through three main programming arms at CIDA in this period: (1) geographic programmes; (2) multilateral programmes; and (3) partnership programmes. The geographic programme branches were responsible for managing Canada's bilateral aid relationships with developing countries worldwide. In 2007, there were four geographically defined bilateral branches within CIDA including Africa Branch, Americas Branch, Asia Branch, and Europe, Middle East, and Maghreb Branch. Additionally, in early 2007 a special Afghanistan Task Force was hived off from Asia Branch to accommodate the high level of effort dedicated to Canadian aid to Afghanistan. These branches were responsible for managing Canada's foreign aid programmes in the countries under their respective regional purview. The Multilateral Programmes Branch was responsible for managing Canadian assistance channelled through multilateral agencies such as the United Nations bodies, the regional development banks, and other multilateral international institutions – though core contributions to these institutions were managed by the Canadian Department of Finance. Finally, the partnership programmes were focused on funding development activities primarily through the work of Canadian civil society groups and institutions.

CIDA was an agency of the Canadian government, and reported to the Minister of International Cooperation. Accountability for CIDA decision-making and spending rested with this Minister, and most major policy and programming decisions needed ministerial approval before being implemented. In 2008, the Minister for International Cooperation was, according to Canadian legislation, a Minister under the Department of Foreign Affairs and International Trade and it is in fact the Minister of Foreign Affairs who was designated as controlling and managing CIDA (Canada 1985). This relationship to Foreign Affairs had, in the early-2000s been somewhat arm's-length, although earlier in the 1970s and 1980s CIDA was more beholden to the direction imposed on it by the then department of External Affairs (Rawkins 1994). Indeed, in the 1970s, many CIDA managers were former External Affairs employees and their circulation into the agency ensured close ties between the two. The appointment of a former External Affairs manager as President of CIDA in 1977 was, indeed, noted as a major reason for altering CIDA's underlying motivations for aid to include Canadian economic benefit from that point forward (Pratt 1994c). By 2008, the relationship to Foreign Affairs was mostly consultative at the programme level, with the aid programmes regularly in contact with the country and regional desks within Foreign Affairs when it came to bilateral aid. At the corporate policy level and in terms of strategic direction for Canada's development assistance, CIDA played a strong role in negotiating its place among Canada's foreign policy in this period – something demonstrated in its contribution to the 2005 foreign policy statement issued by the Government of Canada (Canada 2005). This relative independence from Foreign Affairs despite the official relationships prescribed in legislation made CIDA primarily an autonomous agency in the classification of agency autonomy outlined earlier.

In 2005–2006, CIDA employed approximately 1,600 people, of which 114 were in Canadian Embassies and High Commissions in recipient countries (CIDA 2006a). With only 7% of staff located in recipient countries, CIDA's decision-making structures were primarily centralized. In effect, most major policy directions and programming decisions for CIDA's aid took place at its headquarters in Canada's capital region. Despite rhetoric in the early-2000s about increasing CIDA's field presence and making the field staff more central to policy and planning processes, the ultimate locus of decision-making remained in Canada. This centralized structure was in part reflective of CIDA's decision-making and accountability requirements as an agency of the Canadian government and the necessity of having all major decisions and programmes approved by the Minister for International Cooperation. As such, it was difficult for even relatively small spending decisions at CIDA to be concluded in the field without the assent of the Minister. This need for accountability forced CIDA into adopting a centralized decision-making scheme when considering the locus of decision-making as a characteristic of CIDA structure. Later chapters of this book argue that, despite CIDA's relative autonomy, CIDA's centralization made it more resistant to adopting certain world polity scripts that did not meet with the prevailing directions of Canadian government foreign policy.

Canadian civil society involvement in development assistance

Canada has a history of a high level of support for Canadian civil society involvement in development assistance both in terms of official development assistance and private giving to development-related civil society groups (Brodhead and Pratt 1994). Beginning with the creation of an NGO division in 1968 which provided aid to NGOs at a 3:1 matching ratio, by the late 1980s, Canada was one of the top three DAC donors in terms of both volume of and percentage of aid provided to NGOs (Thérien 1994; Brodhead and Pratt 1994). In 2008, this support came in two forms: (1) core support for NGOs; and (2) targeted support of specific NGO projects and programmes. By 2004–2005 this amounted to more than 600 million CAD committed to the

Canadian voluntary sector by CIDA throughout its different programming branches, approximately 6.9% of Canadian ODA (CIDA 2006b). By 2008, however, Canadian development assistance provided through Canadian civil society organizations had declined, particularly in terms of the core support offered to NGOs. Civil society groups were more frequently being required to tailor their programmes to meet with CIDA priorities in developing countries, or were being sidelined altogether by shifts at that time towards a greater emphasis on sector-wide approaches (SWAPs) or direct budgetary support in keeping with aid effectiveness norms. Indeed, Canadian Partnership Branch support to the voluntary sector declined between 2000 and 2006 (CIDA 2006b). This decline was due both to changing aid modalities at CIDA mirroring international trends towards more government-to-government aid, as well as problems perceived with aid effectiveness and accountability.

Part of the problem encountered with CIDA's relationship to Canadian civil society involved in development assistance was its broad dispersion – with more than 750 organizations funded on an annual basis, creating what a DAC peer review described as a substantial administrative burden for CIDA as an organization (OECD 2002a). These organizations include the entire spectrum of non-governmental agencies, including faith-based groups, Canadian arms of international NGO networks, academic institutions, think-tanks, and even professional associations. Overseeing and managing such a high number of organizations and their relations with all arms of CIDA created a complex web of relationships and requirements for civil society groups to adapt to and maintain, as well as a distinct problem for CIDA to monitor and evaluate performance of all its NGO partners. This dispersion also posed problems for some Civil Society Organizations (CSOs) in that they were at times made to compete for limited funds from CIDA, forcing all competitors to conform to CIDA's requirements and priorities and perhaps stifling unique and innovative approaches that did not meet with CIDA's bureaucratic needs.

Indeed, the influence of Canadian civil society on policy direction at CIDA and with the whole of the Canadian development assistance envelope had been limited by the dilution of civil society voices into such a large number of CIDA partners. Apart from the most sizeable Canadian development NGOs[3] and the national umbrella organization for development civil society, the Canadian Council for International Cooperation (CCIC), it was difficult during the period of my study to see how Canadian NGOs attempted to influence the directions taken by Canada's aid. Some civil society groups were involved in campaigns to lobby politicians and government to set and meet new aid commitments, as was seen in 2005's widely publicized 'Make Poverty History' campaign; however, most of the large number of voluntary sector groups involved in delivering Canadian development assistance held little sway with the policies and directions taken at CIDA. Earlier in its history, some civil society influence was exerted on the organization through the personal ties of CIDA officers and managers to civil society. Indeed, for a period that accompanied the expansion of CIDA in the 1970s, personnel recruitment relied heavily on individuals with civil society or NGO experience (Pratt 1994c). By the 2000s, however, these personnel links to civil society had become less common, and the flow of personnel was more frequently from within CIDA outwards to civil society groups following retirement or career shifts for many senior CIDA officers.

Canada had been generous in its support of Canadian civil society involvement in development assistance for many years; however the degree of embeddedness of CIDA within Canadian civil society was lessened to some degree by the diffuseness of the relationships it maintained with such a large number of organizations and the relative lack of influence that Canadian civil society had on policy or programming outcomes at CIDA.

Legislative mandate: Bill C-293

Apart from legislation already discussed mandating the Minister of Foreign affairs control over the management of CIDA, Canada's aid programme had operated in a relative legislative vacuum for decades. Indeed, from its creation in the 1950s no act of parliament existed to outline either the objectives or the nature of Canada's aid programme (Morrison 1998). In 2007, however, a private member's bill was put before the Canadian parliament with multi-partisan support and a high degree of support from development-oriented Canadian CSOs. Bill C-293 – the Official Development Assistance Accountability Act or the 'Better Aid Bill' as it was called by some civil society groups – outlined three requirements for Canada's ODA: (1) that it contribute to poverty reduction; (2) that it take into account the perspectives of the poor; and (3) that it is consistent with international human rights standards (Canada 2007). In addition, the Bill also outlined reporting and accountability requirements for the Minister of International Cooperation. Bill-293 passed into law in mid-2008, but at the time of my case study it remained to be seen what impact it was to have on Canadian development assistance. The Act's passing into law was one of the few examples of civil society in Canada successfully exerting their influence on the directions taken by Canada's development assistance programme in the 2000s. The fact that it could only happen through political channels outside of government (i.e. a private member's bill sponsored by a Liberal MP) suggests the limited scope for use of this sort of influence in the future.

The fact that for more than five decades Canada's development assistance was conducted without a legislated mandate is a sign of both the low priority that governments have placed on aid and the degree of relative independence the aid programme has had from the rest of the Canadian government.

Key characteristics of the Canadian development assistance sector

Based on this overview, four key factors characterized the Canadian development assistance sector and its level of engagement with world polity scripts and norms about development assistance during my case study research:

(1) CIDA's low level of embeddedness in Canadian civil society, heavily influencing Canadian CSOs but not being influenced strongly in return; (2) the inconsistency of public support for development assistance and a corresponding low level of political will from government to make major changes or advances in development assistance; (3) CIDA's centralized but autonomous agency structure; and (4) the primacy of national-self-interest motivations over humanitarian altruism as motivations for Canadian aid. In Chapters 4 and 5, these factors are used to explain Canada's approach to integrating international influences on development assistance policy consensus into its own policies and to differentiate this approach from the American and Swedish cases.

Sweden

Swedish development assistance: a humanitarian superpower[4]

Development assistance in Sweden emerged from campaigns for international solidarity in the late 1950s with oppressed populations in South Africa and later in French-Indochina. These campaigns were distinctly anti-colonial in nature and found broad support in Swedish student and academic groups who championed solidarity with these oppressed groups and contributed to efforts to improve the situation of the oppressed. As Sweden had little to no colonial past in the developing world, this solidarity with certain parts of Africa and Asia was based mostly on values of justice and equality. In contrast to many donor countries with former colonies, it was instead this motivation of solidarity that came to inspire Sweden's first efforts in development assistance in the early-1960s.

In 1962, the Swedish government began to provide development assistance funds for technical assistance by creating its first aid agency, and provided financial assistance through the Ministry of Finance. This approach continued until the formation of the Swedish International Development Agency (SIDA) in 1965, consolidating technical and financial assistance under one organization. SIDA became the dedicated development agency in Sweden, and took responsibility for the delivery of Swedish foreign aid to a limited number of countries mostly in Anglophone southern Africa. The destination of Swedish aid paralleled many of the efforts of the international solidarity movements within Sweden at the time, and soon came to include parts of Indochina and eventually to a broader spectrum of West and East Africa, supporting liberation struggles there. By 1995 Swedish aid was provided to 114 countries in every region of the world (Danielson and Wohglemuth 2005). From 1989 to 1999, the amount of Swedish aid as a percentage of Swedish Gross National Product (GNP) exceeded the internationally agreed target for all donors of 0.7% in every year, and exceeded 1% in 1992 (OECD 2005a). Although initially focused primarily on economic development and the provision of technical assistance in areas of strength within the Swedish economy, in the 1970s Swedish aid started to integrate a focus on social development concerns such as health, education, and gender.

By the mid-1970s, Sweden was established as a generous donor focusing largely on social issues, but also supporting trends in development assistance such as structural adjustment. Questions began to emerge domestically about the efficacy and value of Sweden's generous aid programme, particularly from the Swedish research community (Danielson and Wohglemuth 2005). As the result of this questioning, Sweden's government undertook to reform the delivery of Swedish aid by creating additional aid agencies specializing in different sectors/types of aid provision. First, the Swedish Agency for Research Co-operation (SAREC) was created to focus on support to research on development both within Sweden and in developing countries. Subsequently, SWEDFUND was formed as an agency responsible for industrial cooperation, BITS was formed and given responsibility for delivery of Swedish technical assistance programmes, and then in 1991 the Swedish International Enterprise Development Corporation (SWEDCORP) was created and was responsible for private sector-related assistance. By 1992, including SIDA there were at least five agencies of the Swedish government established specifically for delivering development assistance, in addition to that provided through the Ministry of Foreign Affairs and others.

This disaggregated approach to aid delivery continued until 1995 with another government commission recommending the consolidation of aid efforts in the creation of a new agency combining SIDA, BITS, SWEDFUND, and SWEDCORP into the Swedish Agency for International Development Cooperation, known commonly as Sida – the use of lower case letters denoting its distinction from the earlier SIDA. Sida then became again the main delivery arm for Swedish aid, responsible for almost all of Swedish bilateral aid (country-to-country), while the Ministry of Foreign Affairs retained control over most multilateral assistance to UN agencies and the various development banks. Between 1995 and 2005, Sida delivered increasing amounts of aid by volume, but fluctuating as a percentage of GNI. In 2006 Sida exceeded the 1% of GNI ODA target again in 2006 for the first time since the mid-1980s, rebounding from a low of 0.78% in 2004 (OECD 2006b) and leading the DAC as the most generous donor in terms of aid-to-GNI ratio. With its humanitarian motives and high levels of aid as a proportion of national income, Sweden could rightly be considered a development assistance superpower.

Swedish public support for development assistance

Support for development assistance within Swedish society has always been strong compared to many countries in the rest of Europe and in North America. For instance, in 2002, 91.9% of the Swedish public polled supported the Swedish aid programme and the principle of helping poor countries (Fransman and Solignac Lecomte 2004). This strong support of development assistance stems from the heavy involvement of international solidarity movements in urging Sweden to offer aid to developing countries early on during the history of Swedish aid; additionally, Sweden is renowned as possessing one of the most liberal social-democratic welfare states in the industrialized world, and public support for ODA can be viewed as an externally oriented outgrowth of Swedish support for the welfare state. Support of the welfare state is a significant factor in explaining ODA levels of industrialized countries (Noël and Thérien 1995). This interplay of domestic and foreign welfare has made the Swedish public consistently one of the most supportive societies in the world when it comes to their backing of a generous aid programme founded on principles of humanitarian concern. For instance, in 2005, 96% of Swedes polled felt it was either important or very important to help people in poor countries develop (the highest level of support in the entire EU), and 74% favoured an increase in aid spending (Eurobarometer 2005).

A corollary of the high level of support from the Swedish public is a relatively high degree of political will demonstrated by both government and opposition parties in Sweden. This was evident in the 2006 parliamentary election campaign in Sweden where all but one major political party publicly committed to the level of 1% of GNP as their ODA target; the one dissenting party was only willing to commit to the internationally agreed standard of 0.7%. Political will measured as a degree of political party support for aid, therefore, was and continues to be high in Sweden. Successive Swedish governments have maintained high levels of aid, and even increased aid as a percentage of GNP to levels unmatched among the other DAC donors (reaching 1.4% of GNI in 2015). Swedish governments have made sure to echo the support for development assistance evident in the Swedish public. High levels of public support for development assistance suggest a public that is more aware of foreign aid levels than we saw in the Canadian case. Political will to support development assistance thus combines with public support to provide a strong base of public and political wherewithal to prioritize aid as a major component of Swedish foreign policy and an outgrowth of the already firmly entrenched Swedish welfare state. As the analysis in subsequent chapters unfolds, it is worthwhile to consider the critical role this public support of and political will has played in establishing the institution of development assistance in Sweden, and in opening Sweden to the possibilities of development assistance policy innovation through the adoption of world policy scripts and norms.

Sida structure

The Swedish Agency for International Development Cooperation or Sida is the primary agency of the Swedish government responsible for bilateral development assistance. Sida is a government agency reporting to the Ministry of Foreign Affairs (MFA). As a government agency, Sida can work mostly independently of the MFA, but must operate under a framework of terms, conditions, and budgets set out by the government (Sweden 2007b). In contrast to the

Canadian case, although the Swedish Minister for International Cooperation is a part of the MFA, Sida does not report directly to the Minister. Instead, Sida's Director General is responsible for carrying out the directives of parliament with advisory support from the Board of Sida. In 2007, the Board consisted of ten members plus the Director General and included members of parliament from several of the major parties as well as representatives from civil society, academia, and the private sector (Sida 2007b).

In 2006–2007, when this research was conducted, Sida consisted of thirteen departments reporting to the Director General, and one evaluation and audit department that reports directly to the Board. The thirteen departments were split into three categories: (1) regional departments covering the four main regions where Sida provides aid (Asia, Middle East, and North Africa; Africa; Europe; and Latin America); (2) sector departments covering various thematic issues such as democracy, social development, the environment, or humanitarian assistance; and (3) support departments focused on corporate needs such as human resources, finances, and policy development. Each department had a head who reported to the Director General (Sida 2007b). Together the thirteen department heads and the Director General comprised the management group within Sida. As of 2006 the agency consisted of approximately 900 individuals, with 190 of those working overseas in field offices and embassies while the remainder were located at Sida headquarters in Stockholm (Sida 2007a). With more than 20% of their workforce located in recipient countries, Sida was a relatively decentralized organization. However, ultimate decision-making responsibilities for country programmes remained at headquarters in Stockholm. As such, Sida was only partially decentralized in terms of the donor agency decision-making classification outlined earlier in this chapter.

In 2007 Sida's relationship with the Ministry of Foreign Affairs was arm's length, but the MFA played a role the policy direction provided to Sida – particularly as it related to the terms and conditions under which Sida operated. The MFA also played a role in the Swedish government's overall policy for relations with the developing world, with other development agencies, and international organizations, including Sweden's relationship to the DAC. Furthermore, the MFA also contained departments for development policy and methods which were responsible for crafting some aspects of Swedish development assistance policy. An example of this included the August 2007 announcement by the Swedish Minister of International Cooperation of a new policy for country focus within development assistance which outlined and limits which countries Sweden would provide aid to and under which conditions (Sweden 2007a). This new direction involved limiting Swedish bilateral assistance to thirty primary countries in an effort improve the 'quality' and 'effectiveness' of Swedish aid. Such policy decisions taken by MFA directly impacted the nature and location of the work undertaken by Sida, but the main decision-making power over such direction rests with MFA. Sida did have its own policy development functions, but they tended to be more thematic and sectoral, rather than about strategic direction. Sida's relationship to the MFA thus can be considered only tacitly arm's-length, as many of the fundamental decisions about development assistance in Sweden rested outside of the agency with the MFA. In this respect, Sida could be considered an only partially integrated organization in terms of the agency autonomy classification illustrated above.

In terms of the donor agency ideal-types outlined earlier, Sida was most closely aligned with the integrated-decentralized type. The ramifications of this structure and their impact on Sweden's adherence to and adoption of world polity scripts of development assistance policy are further explored below.

Swedish civil society involvement in development assistance

Sweden's development assistance included very active involvement of Swedish civil society organizations – both organizations oriented specifically around overseas development issues and those with broader domestic mandates. Indeed, in the mid-2000s Sida had a special relationship with a group of fourteen Swedish CSOs called the Frame Organizations (referred to as the SEKA funding mechanism in Swedish) (Sida 2007b; Danielson and Wohglemuth 2005). These groups were all umbrella organizations which included smaller Swedish CSOs as members, and provided them the opportunity to access Sida funding to conduct development programmes in the Global South and Eastern Europe. These frame organizations were constituted of labour-based groups with members including unions and trade groups, secular development networks with many development NGOs as members, politically affiliated groups tied to mainstream Swedish political parties, and finally religious-based organizations with direct ties to various Swedish churches. In keeping with the importance that Sida and the Swedish government placed on delivering development assistance through civil society these framework groups received nearly one-tenth of the bilateral aid budget that Sweden channelled through Sida. In 2006 this amounted to 1.187 billion SEK, of a total 15.7 billion SEK disbursed by Sida – over 13% of all Swedish ODA (Sida 2007b). Swedish civil society, and particularly the framework organizations, thus played a significant part in delivering development assistance overseas.

Development assistance delivered by Swedish civil society groups was present in nearly every region of the developing world in 2007. Though there are few pre-existing relationships because of a colonial past, the spirit of humanitarian solidarity that underlines Sida's development assistance is magnified even further in the work of civil society. Some groups were geared specifically at demonstrating solidarity with certain regions or countries, whereas others took a more broad-based approach geographically and in terms of sector involvement to undertake comprehensive development programming. Aside from Sida funding, several of the major development assistance CSOs in Sweden also mobilized funds and other support from individual and group memberships. Examples of this could be seen in both labour and faith-based

CSOs. The bulk of the development assistance delivered by these groups – funded by government or otherwise – was aimed at collaborating with local civil societies in developing partner countries. It was rare for Swedish CSOs to collaborate directly with recipient country government partners. Swedish development-related civil society therefore represented a significant actor in carrying out the development assistance process and linking Sweden to development assistance recipients throughout the world.

Domestically, Swedish civil society played a strong role in influencing the government of Sweden when it came to policy and decisions related to development assistance and international relations with the Global South. Indeed, several framework organizations undertook explicit campaigns to lobby the government and other competing political parties regarding key development assistance issues and priorities. Examples included: campaigns to change the way Sweden voted at the World Bank, campaigns to ensure that Sweden maintained the 1% of GNP ODA target, and campaigns to limit spending of Swedish ODA on security/military related programmes. Of the four framework organizations included in my study, three were very actively involved in lobbying the government and other politicians/parties to influence Swedish development policy. Interestingly, however, little of this lobbying was directed at government officials within the bureaucracy. This is not to say there was not contact between officials and CSOs, but simply that officials tended not to be the target of lobbying efforts. Instead, campaigns were oriented towards politicians and the political process, as well as at mobilizing public support towards these ends.

Despite not being the target of CSO lobbying efforts, one interesting feature of the Swedish government's development assistance machinery was the close personal ties of its officials to members of civil society. In fact, during my research, it became clear that many officials within Sida had experience working previously in civil society.[5] At the time my field work was conducted in Sweden, the Minister for international cooperation within the GOS was the former head of the Olaf Palme International Center, a prominent Swedish development CSO. This exchange of personnel between civil society and government played an important role in the Swedish official development assistance sector, and arguably led to a much closer relationship between government and civil society than seen in either of the Canadian or American cases. This embeddedness within civil society needs to be considered a defining characteristic of the Swedish model of development assistance.

Legislative framework: Policy for Global Development 2003

One manifestation of the effective lobbying of Swedish civil society and the embeddedness of the donor agency was the Policy for Global Development of 2003. This piece of legislation outlined an updated set of terms and conditions for Swedish development assistance and situates development within a broader whole-of-government approach to poverty alleviation. The PGD not only confirmed Sweden's prior humanitarian solidarity motivations for development assistance, but actually made it official government policy. The whole-of-government approach extended these motivations in the name of policy coherence to ensure that other policy areas such as foreign relations, immigration, investment, trade and so on cohesively worked to promote poverty reduction in the developing world. This policy coherence approach reflected the international trend towards greater coherence promoted by several international NGOs and other prominent donors. The PGD was the outcome of a Swedish government commission called GLOBKOM established in 2001 to examine Swedish government policy and its overall interaction with the issues of globalization and poverty (Danielson and Wohglemuth 2005).

One interesting outcome of the PGD was the ability for both Sida and Swedish civil society to refer to a strong legislative mandate for development cooperation. Sida now had the ability to point towards legislation to justify its endeavours and make policy priority decisions based on the terms outlined in the PGD. At the same time, Swedish development CSOs were able to refer to the PGD to assert claims to the legitimacy of their objectives, and to police Sida's work by ensuring that its efforts were aligned with the spirit of development cooperation outlined in the PGD. Indeed, by 2006, some civil society organizations had already begun referring to the PGD to discourage Sida from expanding its support to security-related development cooperation that CSOs felt contravened the humanitarian solidarity underpinning Swedish aid.

Key characteristics of the Swedish development assistance sector

In the chapters that follow, four key factors are shown to characterize the Swedish aid sector and its openness to world polity scripts and norms about development assistance: (1) the degree of Sida's embeddedness in Swedish civil society and the amount of personnel exchange between governmental and non-governmental bodies; (2) a high level of public support for development assistance met with a correspondingly high level of political will from government and opposition parties alike; (3) the structure of Sida as a mostly decentralized and only partially autonomous agency; and (4) the importance of the underlying development assistance motivations of solidarity as a form of humanitarian altruism. These factors illustrate Sweden's approach to integrating international influences on development assistance policy consensus into its own policies and differentiate this approach from the Canadian and American cases.

United States

American development assistance: the generosity paradox[6]

American development assistance began in the years following World War II with the Marshall Plan, focused on emergent European reconstruction. In the years following the conclusion of the Marshall Plan in 1951, Congress created several agencies under various pieces of legislation to unify American military, economic, and technical assistance aid under a common approach. By 1960, with a lack of public support and declining support in Congress for the ongoing approach to foreign aid, reforming American foreign aid became an issue in the 1960 Presidential election. Thus, in 1961, the Kennedy administration launched the process of reforming American foreign assistance, which ultimately yielded the Foreign Assistance Act of 1961 which was responsible for refocusing American aid on the developing world, and for the creation of the United States Agency for International Development (USAID). One of the major changes implemented under the act was a new approach to long-term country-by-country planning for development (USAID 2005b).

Over time, American assistance faced success and challenges. One of these challenges was the distinct motivations underlying assistance, including the different motivations between US official development assistance and US Security-Supporting assistance (Lumsdaine 1993). American aid in the period from 1961 through 1990 was frequently held to champion Cold War strategic aims of national interest rather than humanitarian support of impoverished countries. However, as Lumsdaine (1993) illustrates, if ODA is disaggregated from security-related assistance, these motivations are more distinguished, with an average of at least 41% of American ODA being linked provided to the world's poorest countries. These competing motivations for aid continued into the 1980s and 1990s when a greater emphasis on national economic interest was put in place by the Reagan administration. In the 2000s, strategic interests increasingly dominated the destination of American ODA following the advent of the Global War on Terror under the second Bush administration (Moss, Roodman, and Standley 2005). From 2001, an increasing amount of ODA was focused on countries linked to American military intervention overseas, or to countries with a perceived important role in combating terrorism. Indeed, the amount of American ODA delivered by USAID declined from 50.2% in 2002 to only 38.8% in 2005, whereas that provided by the Department of Defense increased to 21.7% from only 5.6% in 2002 (OECD 2006c). Arguably, the primary underlying motivation of American development assistance in the mid-2000s was a focus on protecting national interests and furthering foreign policy aims. This became even more evident with the release of the USAID/State Department Strategic plan for the 2007–2012 period, where the first aim for both organizations was the promotion of peace and security, rather than poverty reduction (USAID and State Department 2007).

With national interest as the primary underlying motivation for aid, American development assistance is an interesting phenomenon when contrasted with other DAC donors to compare contributions. Despite relatively high levels of contribution in the 1950s and 1960s which exceeded the DAC median, American aid levels as a percentage of GNP have declined and remained relatively low since the 1970s. Over the course of the 1980s,

American assistance ranked near the bottom of DAC donors in terms of the aid-to-GNP ratio. In that period, the US provided on average only 0.22% of GNP as ODA (Lumsdaine 1993). From the late 1990s to the mid-2000s, American ODA fluctuated widely, reaching lows of only 0.1% of GNI in 1998–2000 and a high level of 0.22% of GNI in 2005 (OECD 2006b, 2006c). This low level of giving in terms of percentage of GNI is misleading in terms of overall volume, as in 2005, the United States provided more than 25 billion USD in ODA, the most of any donor. This is the paradox of generosity, where the United States is both the most generous and least generous of donors: providing more aid by volume than any other country, but less as a percentage of its overall economic wherewithal. As later chapters demonstrate, this generosity paradox has implications for the amount and type of influence that American development assistance policies and directions have on the international development assistance community globally.

American public support for development assistance

American public support for development assistance has traditionally been much lower than many of the other DAC donor countries. In the early 1980s, only 50% of the American public favoured their country providing foreign aid (Lumsdaine 1993). By other accounts this support had risen to 54% in 1986, but then declined to only 47% in 1995 (Otter 2003). Research shows that, in contrast to Australia, Canada, Denmark, and Japan, the United States public had the lowest level of support by nearly 30% (Otter 2003). In the early 2000s, however, evidence pointed to increased public support for aid, with 79% of Americans polled in 2002 supportive of development assistance, and with 65% of those polled in 2005 supportive of the US striving to attain the 0.7% aid-to-GNP goal established by the international community (PIPA 2005; Fransman and Solignac Lecomte 2004). Disaggregated by major political party support, supporters of the Democratic Party were more likely to support attainment of the 0.7% goal (PIPA 2005). These widely varying results call into question both the American public's awareness and understanding of its aid programmes, and also the methodology behind opinion polling on the subject (Otter 2003).

What can be gleaned from the relatively low level of support shown in earlier surveys, and the fluctuation in levels of support from different surveys, is that the American public did not appear to have a strongly vested interest in American development assistance. Indeed, like the Canadian case, polls show that the American public believed that their government was much more generous when it comes to foreign aid than it was (Otter 2003). The fact that levels of support for aid were apparently increasing in the late 1990s at the same time as the American Congress was making substantial cuts to official development assistance, reaching its lowest ever levels in 1997 at only 0.09% of GNP, suggests a disconnect between public support of aid and the political will of the American government.

Isolationism in American foreign policy can explain the reduction in aid spending during this time, as can crisis in the international economy, but the levels of public support for aid in that period were increasing at the same time as aid levels shrank significantly. Not only does this highlight the disconnect between government and public, but it can also be taken as a sign of the power that the American Congress can wield from year to year on the American development assistance programme due to its role in approving annual appropriations for aid (Otter 2003). A 2006 DAC peer review of American assistance highlighted the need to promote a better understanding and awareness of US development assistance to the public so that the true aims and outcomes of American assistance could be publicized rather than a focus on failures, shortcomings, and general cynicism about aid programmes (OECD 2006c).

USAID structure

USAID is the government agency which manages the largest portion of the American ODA envelope (OECD 2006c). USAID reports to a presidentially appointed Administrator who as of in January 2006 also held a position in the State department as the Director of Foreign Assistance, the equivalent of a Deputy Secretary of State (State Department 2007). As such, USAID and the State Department have had a very close working relationship, and indeed USAID receives a high degree of foreign policy guidance from the State Department (OECD 2006c). Indeed, in 2007, USAID and the State Department revealed a joint strategic plan for a five-year period, uniting under a common framework of goals and objectives (USAID and State Department 2007). Given this joint approach, USAID's autonomy was limited, and therefore falls into the category of an integrated donor agency, even though it does ostensibly exist as a separate government agency. The close ties to the State Department limited the independence of USAID as an organization.

In the mid-2000s, USAID functioned as a relatively decentralized development donor. Much of the decision-making authority on country programmes rested in the field. This was reflected in the fact that approximately one-third of USAID's almost 2,400 directly hired staff were located in the field offices in recipient countries (OECD 2006c). This decentralization of decision-making on country programmes was reflective of 'aid effectiveness' trends in the international donor community in the mid-2000s, but was a feature of USAID before the Paris Declaration came about.

USAID faced several challenges as a donor agency in the mid-2000s: the shrinking portion of American ODA actually managed by USAID, the formation of additional development assistance delivery arms like the Millennium Challenge Corporation (MCC), and the growing role of the Department of Defense in American ODA delivery, all pointed to a diminishing significance for USAID as a donor. With its close relationship to the State Department and its decentralized decision-making at the country level, USAID proved to be an integrated but decentralized donor – something that I argue limited its receptiveness to the adoption of world polity policy consensus.

American civil society involvement in development assistance

American civil society involvement in development assistance in the mid-2000s was significant, both as implementers of American ODA and as participants in development assistance through private giving (OECD 2006c). USAID worked closely with many large, well-funded development NGOs or Private Voluntary Organizations (PVOs) as they were known at USAID. USAID's partnership with NGOs aimed at supporting the entire spectrum of American non-governmental organizations including faith-based, educational, health, and cooperative groups. In 2005, USAID channelled approximately 2.4 billion USD to NGOs in both contracts and grants, whereas the same group received approximately 18.6 billion USD from private sources (USAID 2007). This highlights an important feature of American civil society involvement in development assistance: the great reliance on private sources for funding. In particular, the existence of many large private foundations with significant endowments serve to provide a sizeable share of these private funds. Foundations like the Gates, Ford, Soros and others were and remain heavy contributors to private development assistance. The role of private funding does not diminish the role that USAID plays in partnering with American civil society groups, but it does put it in stark contrast with the amount of private funding available to some groups to implement development activities outside of official channels. As such, USAID's influence over these groups, and in turn, their influence over USAID must be considered within the shadow of the large pool of funding available to NGOs elsewhere. This lack of reliance on USAID for organizational survival in many cases diminished the overall amount of embeddedness within civil society for USAID. However, on certain issues, the relationship with civil society is closer, and therefore degrees of embeddedness varied.

Legislative framework

Apart from annual appropriations approved by the Congress and Senate, in the mid-2000s there was no notable recent legislative mandate for the American development assistance programme managed by USAID. Instead, the one interesting legislative development in this period regarding American ODA was the creation of the MCC through the *Millennium Challenge Act of 2003* (MCC 2007). This parallel US government corporation was established ostensibly to create a 'new compact on global development' between developing and developed countries, but had not, by 2006 been clearly integrated into the broader programme of American development assistance in a concrete manner (OECD 2006c). A 2006 OECD DAC peer review of American ODA raised the possibility of the MCC creating a problematic duplication of requirements on recipient countries and working against the effectiveness of aid. The overall impact of the MCC on American aid programmes was still unclear during the period of my case study research, but in the first three years of its operation, it began to provide ODA funds to a limited number of countries that met strict MCC criteria. The assistance provided by MCC, did, however, aim to support initiatives and development priorities set locally in these countries, which was commended by some other DAC donors (OECD 2006c).

Key characteristics of the American development assistance sector

As we examine the American development assistance sector's engagement with and openness to world polity scripts of development assistance, it is important to bear in mind the following key characteristics of American aid in this period: (1) USAID's varying level of embeddedness in civil society with a limited ability to influence American CSOs who fail to strongly influence USAID in return; (2) the inconsistency of public support for development assistance and a corresponding low level of political will from government to make major changes or advances in development assistance; (3) USAID's decentralized but integrated agency structure tying it closely to the State Department and broader American foreign policy and security objectives; and (4) the primacy of national-self-interest – and most recently national security motivations over humanitarian altruism as motivations for American aid. These factors will all be shown to influence the US approach to integrating international influences on development assistance policy consensus into its own policies and differentiate this approach from the Canadian and Swedish cases.

Donors and domestic context

Clearly, the snapshots provided of the development assistance sector in Canada, Sweden, and the United States suggest that the donors have much in common, while they also have many differences. At the root of the development assistance endeavour in each state is the function of delivering foreign aid to poorer countries throughout the world. To do so, these three states have evolved a complex system of development assistance institutions and relationships within society. In each country there is a certain amount of public support for development assistance. Each country has created and sustained for many years a government agency dedicated to the delivery of foreign aid abroad. In each case there is some degree of civil society involvement in development assistance. Finally, in each case, there is some form of legislation aimed at shaping the outcomes of development assistance for the country. These similarities point towards a high degree of institutional, and in some cases, policy isomorphism. As only three of the twenty-two major donor countries of the OECD DAC in this period, these cases are reflective

Table 3.1 Summary of development assistance sector characteristics

Characteristic	Case study countries		
	Canada	Sweden	United States
Public support/ awareness	Low	High	Low
Generosity	Low	High	Low
Motivations	National interest	Humanitarian	National interest
Civil society embeddedness	Low	High	Low
Donor structure	Autonomous & Centralized	Integrated & Decentralized	Integrated & Decentralized

of the great extent of conformity among donors when it comes to providing development assistance.

At the same time, examining the common components of the development assistance sector highlights the differences and discrepancies that exist between these donors. Beneath the veneer of common institutions and practices lies a measure of dissimilarity that derives from the extent to which certain practices, policies, and institutions are embodied or implemented. Table 3.1 displays some of these differences. Public support for and awareness of development assistance is far higher in Sweden than in Canada or the United States. In terms of generosity, Sweden is much more generous than either Canada or the United States. In terms of state involvement with civil society in the development assistance process, Sweden and Canada have a much closer relationship to civil society than does the United States. As far as underlying motivations for providing aid, Canada and the United States are much more driven by securing national interests than is Sweden. Finally, CIDA stood out as a more autonomous but centralized donor agency in contrast to the integrated-decentralized forms seen in Sida and USAID. These differences demonstrate that even with a broadly similar mandate and function in each country, the development assistance sector of each operated in distinct ways. This heterogeneity within institutions with ostensibly homogenous objectives is revealed in the chapters that follow to influence to a great degree the mechanisms and social processes at play in each case when it comes to the adoption and expression of similar world polity policy scripts for development assistance.

Ten years later: differences remain

The picture of donor contexts outlined above reflects the state-of-the-art of aid in the three countries at the time this book's qualitative analysis was conducted between 2006 and 2008. In the nearly ten years that have elapsed since, there have been major global and domestic political and economic events that have influenced the place of aid in each of the case study countries. For instance, the global economic downturn beginning in 2008, the election of the Obama and then Trump administrations in the United States, and the longer-term impact of Conservative governments in Canada and Sweden are all factors shaping the evolution of the aid sectors in Canada, Sweden, and the US, and at the same time contributing to the persistence of difference between the countries.

In Canada, the decade or so that has elapsed since these case studies were conducted has seen the coming and going of a new governing party – first as a Conservative minority government and then as a majority, and then a return to Liberal rule in 2015. The effects of these political changes, as well as the global economic crisis that gripped much of the world over this period had only minimal implications for the various features of the aid sector addressed above. Aid levels increased slightly from under 4 billion USD in 2006 to over 5.2 billion in 2010 for an increase in aid as a percentage of GNI from 0.29 to 0.34 in 2010 (OECD 2011). These increases did not continue; however, as the Canadian government cut aid spending in the 2012 budget and as such, the amount of aid as a percentage of GNI dropped as low as 0.24% in 2014 and rebounded only to 0.26% in 2016 under the Liberals' Trudeau government. Public opinion seems to have followed this trend as in the wake of the 2008 economic crisis globally, polling showed that Canadians are less likely to report feeling that Canada is giving too little aid (24% in 2010) than they had been in previous years, while most Canadians polled felt Canada's aid levels were the 'right amount' (54%) (Environics Institute 2010). Following the dissolution of the Afghanistan-Pakistan Task Force and significant discussions in the policy community about alternate structures where CIDA could be granted even further autonomy (Gulrajani 2010; Carin and Smith 2010) or folded into DFAIT (Senate Standing Committee on Foreign Affairs and International Trade 2007), the biggest change for Canadian aid in this period was the folding of CIDA into the former Department of Foreign Affairs and International Trade by the Harper government in 2013. The new merged department – now dubbed Global Affairs Canada by the Trudeau government – maintains the former CIDA's past ODA mandate, but now integrates the development arm of foreign policy alongside the diplomatic and trade functions. In mid-2017, the Trudeau government announced a new Feminist International Assistance Policy for Canadian aid (Brown and Swiss, Forthcoming), the impact of which remains to be seen at the time of writing.

CIDA's relationship with civil society during the Harper years (2006–2015) became more tumultuous than it was in the past with a series of funding rejections to longstanding CIDA partners, some of which have been deemed politically motivated retribution for advocacy viewed to contradict Harper government priorities (Berthiaume 2010). Longstanding CIDA partners such as Kairos, MATCH International, the North-South Institute, and the Canadian Coalition for International Cooperation saw their funding proposals rejected in this period as a result, placing a severe chill on the government–CSO relationship. Initial impressions suggest this chill has lifted somewhat under the Trudeau government. Finally, the effects of the ODA Accountability Act which came into force in 2008 have been deemed to have a limited effect on shaping Canadian aid outcomes. A report by the Canadian Council for International Cooperation, for instance, suggested that CIDA and the Canadian government's reporting on the act 'falls short in meeting the spirit and intention of the Act' (CCIC 2011: 2). Arguably, much has changed in the Canadian aid sector, yet, I would argue that some of the key features that shape the processes I explore in Chapters 4 and 5 remain salient even in today's Global Affairs Canada.

Like Canada, Sweden's aid sector has seen minimal change in the years that have elapsed since the case study was conducted there in 2006. Shortly after the collection of data in Sweden in 2006 a conservative government coalition was elected to govern the country. The effects of this change in governing party had seemingly little impact on levels of aid spending by Sweden. Between 2006 and 2010 aid consistently exceeded 4 billion USD, and aid as a percentage of GNI ranged from a low of 0.93% in 2007 to a high of 1.12% in 2009 (OECD 2011). Public support in Sweden for sustained commitment to aid remained strong, even in the wake of the global economic crisis. In 2009, for instance, 93% of Swedish respondents still felt that it was either very important or important for their country to help people in developing countries, although the number responding 'very important' had declined from 73% to 57% since 2004 (Eurobarometer 2009). This decline in the strongest level of support may be linked to the economic downturn that gripped global markets in the intervening years, and also might be due to the fact that Sweden had been either approaching or exceeding their 1% of GNI aid target in those years. Sida structure and its relationship to the Ministry of Foreign Affairs remained consistent, but there have been a series of internal reorganizational changes within Sida in recent years. These have not affected the nature of the relationship of Swedish aid to civil society, and in 2017 there are now seventeen Swedish 'framework organizations' through which most of Sida's support to civil society is channelled in close partnership. The legislative framework for Swedish aid in the context of the Policy for Global Development of 2003 remains in place still in 2017, and support for this framework has continued despite several changes in government in the intervening years. Beyond this overarching framework the Swedish Government has also released policy statements on the issues of both gender and peace/security as it relates to Swedish aid (Sweden 2010; 2011). These new policy statements worked within the PGD framework and indeed demonstrate the Swedish commitment to the policy priorities that are the subject of investigation in the chapters that follow.

Hard hit by the financial crisis of 2008 and with significant policy changes linked to the arrival of the Obama administration, in the American case, these political and economic changes in the years since the case study data was collected have not translated into significant change for the American aid sector. Indeed, until the arrival of the Trump administration in early 2017, the context of its aid sector remained relatively consistent with the snapshot above. Levels of aid in the US increased slightly in the initial years of the Obama administration, with aid volumes jumping from 23.5 billion USD in 2006 to over 30.3 USD billion in 2010, representing a change in ODA as a percentage of GNI from 0.18% to 0.21% (OECD 2011). Although these figures show a significant increase in volume, the total increase as a percentage of national income is minimal. Furthermore, from 2012 onwards, American ODA as a percentage of GNI fell to around 0.18% and remained at about that level. The fact, however, that ODA levels increased in the context of a major economic meltdown in the US was indicative of sustained support for aid under the Obama administration. Unfortunately, the aid budget has been an early target for the Trump administration, with rumoured cuts of between 30 and 40% a possibility, though the final impact of these cuts is not yet clear. If the Trump administration does cut USAID's budget to this extent, the generosity paradox will be exacerbated further, with the US providing much less aid relative to its national income but still likely the largest overall amount of all donors.

Public opinion figures reflecting American views on aid from 2010 suggested that Americans continued to vastly overestimate the amount of aid provided by their government and therefore support a reduction in aid levels (World Public Opinion 2010). In this poll respondents were asked what percentage of government expenditure they believed was dedicated to foreign aid, and what percentage they believed *should* be dedicated to aid. In response to the first question the median amount was 25% and the median amount of desired aid spending was 10%. The fact that US government aid expenditure hovered around only 1% of total expenditure underlines the significant and persistent disconnect between what is spent and what the American public perceives. Given this gap between reality and perception, it is not surprising that American aid levels have not made any major shifts in the years since my case study was conducted, proposed Trump administration cuts aside. The relationship between USAID and the State Department remained a close one during the Obama administration, and the State Department under the leadership of Hillary Clinton appeared to take a greater interest in the aid function than had been demonstrated in the previous administration. Indeed, the connection between the two departments can be seen in their continued adherence to a joint strategic plan in place until the end of the 2017 fiscal year. Civil society's place in the American aid context is relatively unchanged for now. Several larger American voluntary organization continue to receive significant amounts of funding from USAID,[7] while the role of private philanthropic foundations continues to sustain many civil society groups involved in the aid process. The legislative terrain for USAID and American aid has remained more or less consistent with the context discussed above. The Obama administration's continued support for the MCC and the organization has been institutionalized as another arm of American foreign assistance. As of mid 2017, it appears that the MCC will survive the initial round of the Trump cuts to aid.

In the years which have elapsed between the conduct of the case studies presented in the next two chapters and the publication of this book, there has been only a minimal degree of change in the aid sectors of the three countries, when viewed through the context of the features examined above – the merging of CIDA and DFAIT in Canada aside. In this respect, the time that has passed since the case study data was collected was less a period of momentous change and more correctly should be considered a continuation of the differences demonstrated between the various donor contexts. This persistent difference in the aid sectors of the three countries makes the identification of common processes of globalization that follow in the subsequent chapters all the more compelling given their ability to explain policy convergence in such distinct and shifting political and economic contexts.

Case study approach

In the context of the diverse domestic characteristics of my three-country sample, the case studies that follow adopt a comparative approach which offers great explanatory value in describing social processes at the international level (Moore 1967; Kohli 2004; Huntington 1991; Goodwin 2001; Seidman 1994; Wood 2000; Skocpol 1979; Rueschemeyer, Huber, and Stephens 1992; Evans and Stephens 1988). The comparative lens is focused on two types of comparisons: (1) between the two issue areas of security and gender; and (2) between national contexts of the three country cases. The analysis employs a 'method of agreement' comparisons between countries of both cases where the outcomes were similar (Van Evera 1997). Comparing similar outcomes allows us to look for shared causal processes at work in each case. These comparisons illustrate the commonality and uniqueness of the approach to both security and gender issues in each national context, with the aim of answering the question of what social processes account for increased consensus on development assistance. The cases selected will examine the factors both promoting and inhibiting adoption of these concerns as donor consensus.

The two cases of consensus formation examined in Chapters 4 and 5 include the rise of the women and gender as development priorities and the securitization of aid through a focus on security as a key concern for development assistance. Both policy concerns saw widespread acceptance and adoption by bilateral and multilateral donor agencies. These cases were selected because, despite addressing disparate issues of gender equality and security, policy in both these areas has arisen in a manner that shows a common agenda among donors, the influence of international actors on donor agencies, and yet different underlying political motivations and links to national interest. As such, the two policy cases are comparable, but have distinct features which enable generalization to other development assistance policy areas with which they share similarities. The gender case provides findings which can help to better explain how common approaches to issues that are inspired by humanitarian motivations can arise, whereas the security case illustrates why common policy models more closely linked to donor national self-interest come about. The consensus on these two issue areas is indicative of that found in other policy areas like aid effectiveness, governance, the environment, or education. Analysis of the social processes and mechanisms which help these policy models to evolve is thus likely to reveal similar processes at work on other development assistance policy agendas.

Notes

1 This chapter refers to aid as a percentage of either Gross National Product (GNP) or Gross National Income (GNI). These are closely related measures, but are not the same. In earlier data, the OECD DAC collected this data as a measure of aid as a percentage of GNP. More recently, they have moved towards measuring aid as a percentage of GNI. Thus, the discrepancy in the use of the two measures reflects the timing of when the data was collected.

2 Tied aid refers to ODA funds which require spending on contracts, services, and products originating in the donor country. It is a means of supporting the development sector in donor economies, and tying project outcomes in the developing world to Northern suppliers of expertise and goods. Tied aid has been heavily criticized by recipient countries and more recently by a larger group of OECD donors. Many donors have been moving towards the untying of aid in recent years.

3 Most of which tend to be Canadian satellites of larger international NGO networks. Examples include Oxfam, World Vision, CARE, Medecins sans Frontieres, and the Aga Khan Foundation.

4 The brief history that follows is derived primarily from: Anders Danielson, and Lennart Wohglemuth. 2005. 'Swedish Development Cooperation in Perspective.' Pp. 518–545 in *Perspectives on European Development Co-operation: Policy and Performance of Individual Donor Countries and the EU*, edited by O. Stokke and P. Hoebink. London: Routledge.

5 During the process of data collection in Sweden two Sida officials were interviewed who had this experience personally, but also heard mention of this exchange occurring in a rather commonplace manner.

6 This brief history is primarily drawn from: USAID. (2005). 'USAID: USAID History.' Retrieved September 14, 2007, from www.usaid.gov/about_usaid/usaidhist.html.

7 For instance, Save the Children was slated to receive more than 128 million USD from USAID in the 2011 fiscal year, while organizations like World Vision were anticipated to receive more than 50 million USD in aid funding in the same period.

References

Berg, B. L. (2004). *Qualitative Research Methods for the Social Sciences* (5th Edition). Boston; London: Pearson/Allyn and Bacon.

Berkovitch, N. (1999). *From Motherhood to Citizenship: Women's Rights and International Organizations*. Baltimore, MD: Johns Hopkins University Press.

Black, D. R. (2014). Humane Internationalism and the Malaise of Canadian Aid Policy. In S. Brown, D. R. Black, & M. Den Heyer (Eds.), *Rethinking Canadian Aid* (pp. 17). Ottawa: University of Ottawa Press.

Brodhead, T., & Pratt, C. (1994). Paying the Piper: CIDA and Canadian NGOs. In C. Pratt (Ed.), *Canadian International Development Assistance Policies: An Appraisal* (pp. 87–119). Montreal: McGill-Queen's University Press.

Brown, S., & Swiss, L. (Forthcoming). Canada's Feminist International Assistance Policy: Game-Changer or Fig Leaf? In K. A. Graham (Ed.), *How Ottawa Spends, 2017–2018*. Ottawa: School of Public Policy and Administration, Carleton University.

Department of Foreign Affairs and International Trade Act, R.S., 1985, c. E-22, s. 1; 1995, c. 5, s. 2. (1985).

Canada. (2005). Canada's International Policy Statement: A Role of Pride and Influence in the World: Development.

Canada. (2007). Bill C-293: Official Development Assistance Accountability Act. Retrieved from www2.parl.gc.ca/content/hoc/Bills/391/Private/C-293/C-293_3/C-293_3.PDF.

CIDA. (2006). Canadian International Development Agency: Departmental Performance Report For the Period Ending March 31, 2006. Retrieved from http://publications.gc.ca/site/eng/302621/publication.html

CIDA. (2006). Statistical Report on Official Development Assistance, Fiscal Year 2004–2005. Retrieved from http://publications.gc.ca/collections/Collection/CD4-39-2006E.pdf

CIDA. (2007). CIDA in Brief. Retrieved from www.acdi-cida.gc.ca/CIDAWEB/acdi-cida.nsf/En/JUD-829101441-JQC

Danielson, A., & Wohglemuth, L. (2005). Swedish Development Cooperation in Perspective. In O. Stokke & P. Hoebink (Eds.), *Perspectives on European Development Co-operation: Policy and Performance of Individual Donor Countries and the EU* (pp. 518–545). London: Routledge.

Drori, G. S., Meyer, J. W., Ramirez, F. O., & Schofer, E. (2003). Loose Coupling in National Science: Policy versus Practice. In G. S. Drori, J. W. Meyer, F. O. Ramirez, & E. Schofer (Eds.), *Science in the Modern World Polity: Institutionalization and Globalization* (pp. 155–173). Stanford, Calif.: Stanford University Press.

Environics Research Group. (2004). Canadian Attitudes Towards Development Assistance: Focus Canada Omnibus. A report by Environics Research Group, prepared for the Canadian International Development Agency, Gatineau, January 2004. Report # PN5407.

Eurobarometer, S. (2005). Attitudes towards Development Aid. Retrieved from Brussels: http://ec.europa.eu/commfrontoffice/publicopinion/archives/ebs/ebs_222_en.pdf

Evans, P., & Stephens, J. D. (1988). Studying Development since the Sixties: The Emergence of a New Comparative Political Economy. *Theory and Society*, 17(5), 713–745.

Frank, D. J., Hironaka, A., Meyer, J. W., Schofer, E., & Tuma, N. B. (1999). The Rationalization and Organization of Nature in World Culture. In J. Boli & G. M. Thomas (Eds.), *Constructing World Culture: International Nongovernmental Organizations since 1875* (pp. 81–99). Stanford, CA: Stanford University Press.

Frank, D. J., Hironaka, A., & Schofer, E. (2000). The Nation-state and the Natural Environment over the Twentieth Century. *American Sociological Review*, 65(1), 96.

Fransman, J., & Solignac Lecomte, H.-B. (2004). Mobilising Public Opinion Against Global Poverty (2). Retrieved from Paris: www.oecd-ilibrary.org/development/mobilising-public-opinion-against-global-poverty_023738715074

Goodwin, J. (2001). *No Other Way Out: States and Revolutionary Movements, 1945–1991*. Cambridge; New York: Cambridge University Press.

Gorden, R. L. (1998). *Basic Interviewing Skills*. Prospect Heights, Ill.: Waveland Press.

Hironaka, A. (2002). The Globalization of Environmental Protection: The Case of Environmental Impact Assessment. *International Journal of Comparative Sociology*, 43(1), 65–78.

Huntington, S. P. (1991). *The Third Wave: Democratization in the Late Twentieth Century*. Norman: University of Oklahoma Press.

Jang, Y. S. (2003). The Global Diffusion of Ministries of Science and Technology. In G. S. Drori, J. W. Meyer, F. O. Ramirez, & E. Schofer (Eds.), *Science in the Modern World Polity: Institutionalization and Globalization* (pp. 120–135). Stanford, Calif.: Stanford University Press.

Kohli, A. (2004). *State-directed Development: Political Power and Industrialization in the Global Periphery*. Cambridge, UK; New York: Cambridge University Press.

Lumsdaine, D. H. (1993). *Moral Vision in International Politics: The Foreign Aid Regime, 1949–1989*. Princeton, N.J.: Princeton University Press.

Macdonald, R., & Hoddinott, J. (2004). Determinants of Canadian Bilateral Aid Allocations: Humanitarian, Commercial or Political? *Canadian Journal of Economics*, 37(2), 294–312.

MCC. (2007). About MCC. Retrieved from www.mcc.gov/about/index.php

Meyer, J. W., Boli, J., Thomas, G. M., & Ramirez, F. O. (1997). World Society and the Nation-state. *The American Journal of Sociology*, 103(1), 144–181.

Meyer, J. W., Frank, D. J., Hironaka, A., Schofer, E., & Tuma, N. B. (1997). The Structuring of a World Environmental Regime, 1870–1990. *International Organization*, 51(4), 623.

Moore, B. (1967). *Social Origins of Dictatorship and Democracy: Lord and Peasant in the Making of the Modern World*. Boston: Beacon Press.

Morrison, D. R. (1994). The Choice of Bilateral Aid Recipients. In C. Pratt (Ed.), *Canadian International Development Assistance Policies: An Appraisal* (pp. 123–155). Montreal: McGill-Queen's University Press.

Morrison, D. R. (1998). *Aid and Ebb Tide: A History of CIDA and Canadian Development Assistance*. Waterloo, ON: Wilfrid Laurier University Press.

Moss, T., Roodman, D., & Standley, S. (2005). The Global War on Terror and US Development Assistance: USAID Allocation by Country, 1998–2005. Retrieved from: www.cgdev.org/publication/global-war-terror-and-us-development-assistance-usaid-allocation-country-1998-2005

Noël, A., & Thérien, J.-P. (1995). From Domestic to International Justice: The Welfare State and Foreign Aid. *International Organization*, 49(3), 523–553.

Noël, A., Thérien, J.-P., & Dallaire, S. (2004). Divided over Internationalism: The Canadian Public and Development Assistance. *Canadian Public Policy/Analyse de Politiques*, 30(1), 29–46.

OECD. (2002). Development Cooperation Review: Canada. Retrieved from Paris: www.oecd.org/dac/peer-reviews/2409572.pdf

OECD. (2005). DAC Peer Review: Sweden. Retrieved from Paris: www.oecd.org/dac/peer-reviews/35268515.pdf

OECD. (2006). Development Co-operation – 2006 Report – Efforts and Policies of the Members of the Development Assistance Committee. *OECD Journal on Development*, 8(1), 1–238.

OECD. (2006). Aid at a Glance Chart: Canada. Retrieved from www.oecd.org/dataoecd/42/21/1860310.gif

OECD. (2017). Net ODA. Retrieved from https://data.oecd.org/oda/net-oda.htm

OECD. (2006). The United States: Development Assistance Committee Peer Review. Retrieved from Paris: www.oecd-ilibrary.org/development/part-ii-dac-peer-review-of-the-united-states_journal_dev-v7-art41-en

Otter, M. (2003). Domestic Public Support for Foreign Aid: Does it Matter? *Third World Quarterly*, 24(1), 115–125.

PIPA. (2005). Americans on Addressing World Poverty. Retrieved from: www.pipa.org/OnlineReports/ForeignAid/WorldPoverty_Jun05/WorldPoverty_Jun05_rpt.pdf

Pratt, C. (1994). *Canadian International Development Assistance Policies: An Appraisal.* Montreal: McGill-Queen's University Press.

Pratt, C. (1994). Canadian Development Assistance: A Profile. In C. Pratt (Ed.), *Canadian International Development Assistance Policies: An Appraisal* (pp. 3–24). Montreal: McGill-Queen's University Press.

Pratt, C. (1994). Humane Internationalism and Canadian Development Assistance Policies. In C. Pratt (Ed.), *Canadian International Development Assistance Policies: An Appraisal* (pp. 334–370). Montreal: McGill-Queen's University Press.

Ramirez, F. O., & McEneaney, E. H. (1997). From Women's Suffrage to Reproduction Rights? Cross-national Considerations. *International Journal of Comparative Sociology*, 38(1–2), 6.

Ramirez, F. O., Soysal, Y., & Shanahan, S. (1997). The Changing Logic of Political Citizenship: Cross-national Acquisition of Women's Suffrage Rights, 1890 to 1990. *American Sociological Review*, 62(5), 735.

Rawkins, P. (1994). An Institutional Analysis of CIDA. In C. Pratt (Ed.), *Canadian International Development Assistance Policies: An Appraisal* (pp. 156–185). Montreal: McGill-Queen's University Press.

Rueschemeyer, D., Huber, E., & Stephens, J. D. (1992). *Capitalist Development and Democracy*. Chicago: University of Chicago Press.

Schofer, E., & Hironaka, A. (2005). The Effects of World Society on Environmental Protection Outcomes. *Social Forces*, 84(1), 25–47.

Seidman, G. (1994). *Manufacturing Militance: Workers' Movements in Brazil and South Africa, 1970–1985*. Berkeley: University of California Press.

Sida. (2007). Providing Support through Swedish NGOs. Retrieved from www.sida.se/sida/jsp/sida.jsp?d=263&language=en_US

Sida. (2007). About Sida. Retrieved from www.sida.se/sida/jsp/sida.jsp?d=115&language=en_US

Skocpol, T. (1979). *States and Social Revolutions: A Comparative Analysis of France, Russia, and China*. Cambridge; New York: Cambridge University Press.

Smillie, I. (1998). Optical and Other Illusions: Trends and Issues in Public Thinking About Development Co-Operation. In I. Smillie & H. Helmich (Eds.), *Public Attitudes and International Development Co-Operation* (pp. 21–40). Paris: OECD.

State Department. (2007). Senior Officials. Retrieved from www.state.gov/misc/19232.htm

Sweden. (2007). Ministry of Foreign Affairs: Government Agencies. Retrieved from www.sweden.gov.se/sb/d/2059/a/32231;jsessionid=aRUi3ZvKMk34

Sweden. (2007). Focused Bilateral Development Cooperation. Retrieved from www.sweden.gov.se/content/1/c6/08/65/95/c70b05d5.pdf

Swiss, L. (2014). Mimicry and Motives: Canadian Aid Allocation in Longitudinal Perspective. In S. Brown, D. R. Black, & M. den Heyer (Eds.), *Rethinking Canadian Aid* (pp. 101–124). Ottawa: University of Ottawa Press.

Thérien, J.-P. (1994). Canadian Aid: A Comparative Analysis. In C. Pratt (Ed.), *Canadian International Development Assistance Policies: An Appraisal* (pp. 315–333). Montreal: McGill-Queen's University Press.

UNICEF. (2007). 0.7% Background. Retrieved from www.unicef.ca/portal/Secure/Community/502/WCM/HELP/take_action/G8/Point7_EN2.pdf

USAID. (2005). USAID: USAID History. Retrieved from www.usaid.gov/about_usaid/usaidhist.html

USAID. (2007). 2007 VOLAG: Report of Voluntary Agencies. Retrieved from Washington D.C.: http://pdf.usaid.gov/pdf_docs/Pnadi999.pdf

USAID, & State Department. (2007). Strategic Plan Fiscal Years 2007–2012: Transformational Diplomacy.

Van Evera, S. (1997). *Guide to Methods for Students of Political Science*. Ithaca: Cornell University Press.

Wood, E. J. (2000). *Forging Democracy from Below: Insurgent Transitions in South Africa and El Salvador*. Cambridge, UK; New York, NY: Cambridge University Press.

4 Women and gender
World society and bureaucrat agency

Women and gender as aid priorities

As earlier chapters have shown, existing research has not questioned why donors act alike or have similar policy priorities, but several possible explanations can be derived from relevant literature on development and globalization. One area where growing uniformity of donor policy is evident is in approaches to women and gender in development assistance (Moser and Moser 2005). Chapter 2 showed how foreign aid donors paid increasing attention to women and/or gender and development policies from the 1970s onwards.[1] Common approaches to women and gender diffused throughout the major donors of the development assistance community over that time achieving widespread acceptance (Swiss 2012). A large majority of Western donor agencies now has some sort of policy or unit to address these issues in their work. Prevalence of this gender model highlights the relative homogeneity of the donor community when it comes to policy and priorities. Arguably, these similarities reflect the globalization of development assistance policy, with donor agencies appearing increasingly uniform and acting in lockstep on a range of development priorities. The influence of world society on the nation-state and the adoption of world cultural models of gender and development assistance by donors has not been widely examined. Chapter 2 confirms world society influence on the adoption of women and gender models by aid donors through macro level cross-national statistical methods, but concludes that more detailed investigation of how this influence operates is needed (Swiss 2012). Building on that macro-level analysis, I turn in this chapter to the micro-level processes of globalization through which donors arrive at, institutionalize, and refine these models of women, gender, and development.

This chapter employs a qualitative micro-level case study with an analysis of interviews conducted with individuals working in the aid sector in Canada, Sweden, and the United States. These donors share commonalities in their approaches to various aid priorities, including gender and security. At the same time, they have very diverse domestic contexts. In this chapter, several common processes and mechanisms of globalization evident in all three country cases are identified despite the apparent differences between donors. The commonalities that emerge – the globalization of foreign aid policy – are a result of social processes and mechanisms dedicated to mediating the interface of nation-state institutions with the World Society and directly influence the degree of uptake of world cultural models like donor approaches to gender.

Gender equality and women's rights as a world society model

World society research demonstrates the extent to which women's rights and gender equality have grown as a world cultural model over the course of the later twentieth century (Berkovitch 1999b, 1999a; Lechner and Boli 2005). Growth in support for women's rights across the globe corresponds to the expansion of the women's movement (Berkovitch 1999a; Paxton, Hughes, and Green 2006), greater support for gender equality initiatives by international organizations (Berkovitch 1999b), and increased attention paid to these issues at international conferences like the United Nations World Conferences on Women (Lechner and Boli 2005). Focus on women's issues during the UN Decade for Women (1976–1985) and surrounding the UN conferences also played a strong role in promoting the expansion of the women's movement and the formation of many Women's International Non-Governmental Organizations (WINGOs) (Berkovitch 1999a). These factors were all instrumental in encouraging nation-states to protect women's rights and promote gender equality across a wide spectrum of issues, including addressing women's health, education, and economic opportunities. International organizations like the UN and the WINGOs of the women's movement collaborated with governments to establish, refine, and institutionalize a normative model for women's rights and gender equality. World society's influence on the creation of this model was strong and wide-ranging.

As norms encouraging greater protection for women's rights and increased acceptance of gender equality spread among governments, development NGOs, and international organizations, a concentration on development issues began to emerge as a significant component of the world cultural model. Berkovitch (1999a) argues that this was due to the coinciding of the UN Decade for Women with the Second United Nations Development Decade, leading to the framing of women's issues within a development context and a concurrent focus on both issues in the wider international community. Women's status and development status came to be viewed in the international community as inextricably linked, and gender became a growing concern for development assistance organizations worldwide (Lechner and Boli 2005).

Gender as a development concern

The combination of a women's rights model with development themes first appears in the early 1970s. Research by Boserup (1970) identified the need to examine discrimination against women in development processes and spurred the emergence of the Women in Development or WID approach to foreign aid. WID focused on securing women's increased participation in development processes and greater access to the benefits of modernization (Benería and Sen 1981; Jaquette 1982; Rathgeber 1990; Goetz 1997). In the 1970s, many donor agencies, international organizations, and development NGOs began to adopt WID to redress discrimination against women in their projects and activities. These efforts involved the creation of WID units or bureaus, WID policies, and the addition of separate WID initiatives to many development assistance programmes (Goetz 1997).

Eventually WID was critiqued for failing to promote greater social and political empowerment for women. Critics called for more focus on unequal power relations between men and women that prevent women from participating as equals in all facets of life. From these critiques emerged the Gender and Development (GAD) approach (Goetz 1997; Misra 2000; Rai 2002; Rathgeber 1990, 1995).[2] This approach favours solutions which are state or civil society focused and target fundamental changes to socially constructed gender relations. These solutions were less easily adopted by development agencies (Rathgeber 1990, 1995; Parpart 1995).

At present, most development agencies have a formal policy or organizational unit to address issues of women and gender in development (Winship 2004; Moser and Moser 2005; Swiss 2012). A common feature of these policies is the concept of 'mainstreaming' the issue of gender across an organization's development initiatives (del Rosario 1997; Goetz 1997; Jackson 1997; Tiessen 2007). Mainstreaming refers to the integration of gender as a concern for all programmes and staff, rather than simply relying on targeted initiatives or the work of gender specialists or experts.

With the evolution of discourse on gender and development and the advent of gender mainstreaming, gender and development was institutionalized as a de facto component of the global development assistance community. Common approaches to women and gender in foreign aid are representative of the world cultural models highlighted in the world society literature. The nesting of gender and development policy models in the global institutional framework of foreign aid promulgated by world society and a cadre of well-off donor nation-states exemplifies the phenomenon of policy isomorphism in world society. Application of the model – though widespread in acceptance – is varied in implementation. The next section examines the chief characteristics of the gender and development model and its application within the three donor country cases examined later in the chapter.

Donor approaches to gender in development assistance

To demonstrate how the gender and development model is a nested component of a world society framework for aid institutions, it is necessary to outline the chief characteristics of such a model. Arguably, three features indicate the presence of this model in donor institutions: (1) focus on gender through a corporate level strategy/policy; and/or separate organizational unit or personnel dedicated to women/gender; (2) efforts to mainstream gender throughout agency programming; and (3) shifting focus on gender away from a solely Women in Development (WID) approach to incorporate a Gender and Development (GAD) perspective – possibly including a focus on men/masculinities. These characteristics reflect the DAC's *Guidelines for Gender Equality and Women's Empowerment in Development Cooperation* (OECD 1999) and form a basis for identifying a common model of gender and development among donors. These features allow us to observe the adoption, institutionalization, and refinement of the gender and development model within the donor agencies of the three countries I studied.

First, all three countries have either a corporate level gender policy or a dedicated unit within their donor agency tasked with addressing women's or gender issues. Sweden and Canada have had such policies in place since 1968 and 1976 respectively (ILO 2006; CIDA 1999). USAID's Office of Women in Development was created in 1974 following a 1973 congressional amendment of the Foreign Assistance Act (USAID 2006).

Second, each of the countries demonstrates visible efforts to mainstream gender in their aid programming. Canada and Sweden both advocate integration or mainstreaming of gender into all programming in their respective gender policies. For instance, in its 1999 policy, the former CIDA outlined its views on gender equality as an integral part of all its programming, and reinforces the need to undertake gender analysis in all CIDA planning and evaluation. Although not specified in a corporate policy, because USAID is a decentralized agency with much of the decision-making being taken at missions in recipient countries, it is reasonable to expect decisions on gender programmes and policy to be taken in the same manner (Elson and McGee 1995). This decentralized approach should be interpreted as a very high level of gender mainstreaming because the responsibility of promoting gender equality and women's empowerment has been devolved to such an extent.

Finally, with the shift from a WID to a GAD approach present in both of their donor agencies, Sweden and Canada share in demonstrating the third feature of the gender model. As an exception here, until recently, USAID has primarily displayed programming which appears linked to WID principles rather than current GAD approaches.[3] Still, within USAID there are pockets of activity that more closely resemble GAD doctrine. An example can be seen in USAID's Population Reference Bureau's Interagency Gender Working Group (IGWG) – a formal network of USAID officials and American civil society groups. This group acts as an interface between USAID and American development NGOs working on in the population, health, and nutrition areas and features more than sixty groups working with USAID to develop new approaches and best practices on gender to be applied within the agency (IGWG 2007).

Policy isomorphism in gender and development

The similarities in how three separate donors address gender in their development assistance programmes are striking. Despite the diverse domestic contexts of the countries and their development assistance sectors, similar gender and development approaches emerged over time. What explains the homogeneity of the gender and development model as it has been applied in the three cases? How has world society influence on the adoption, institutionalization, and refinement of these gender approaches operated? Earlier macro-level cross-national statistical research on the diffusion of world society gender models in the aid sector identified several determinants of this relationship including: the timing of international conferences; the actions of other donors; and donor engagement with international organizations and civil society (Swiss 2012). Still, the common social processes and mechanisms which underline these relationships at the micro level and mediate the nation-state interface with world society need further exploration.

My central argument is that by identifying mechanisms at work in each case, we can provide a better explanation of how world society influence on the nation-state and the recursive processes of global model refinement occur. In contrast to earlier work, I argue that these mechanisms and social processes can be used to explain not only contentious politics, but also the politics of consensus building and isomorphism within the world polity and the underlying differences that emerge between states. It is within a framework of identifying these common mechanisms and processes of globalization that we now turn to the interview data from the three country cases.

External influences and internal dynamics

Respondents related their experiences about two main categories of influence on how the issue of gender equality was addressed, had been adopted or institutionalized, and was evolving within the donor agency in their country: external influences and internal dynamics. This section provides evidence drawn from interviews to illustrate these two categories of influence and outline the processes and mechanisms that account for policy isomorphism on the gender issue.

World society influence on the nation-state comes in several forms, and involves a range of actors. External influence was conceptualized in the interviews as stemming from agencies and actors outside of the nation-state government, including both international and domestic external influences. Of these influences, there are four main types of influences that were included in the interviews: international organizations, international conferences and treaties, other donor nation-states, and domestic civil society. Respondents were asked about each external factor, and to consider the extent and nature of influence each had on gender equality policy and programming in the donor agency in their country. Internal factors influencing the administration of gender policies and programmes were also discussed with respondents by asking them about the challenges, successes, and nature of the origins and implementation of gender policies within their country's donor institutions.

From this discussion of external and internal influences, three identifiable social processes mediating the interface of donors with world society and directly contributing to the institutionalization and refinement of a gender model in their aid policy and programming were discernible in the data. The first, a process of *internalization and certification* of the gender and development model was caused by mechanisms common to all three donors by which internationally generated agendas became internalized within donor agencies. The second, the donor agency's level of *embeddedness within civil society,* directly influenced the extent to which the gender model implemented by the donor met with international expectations. Finally, the third, a process of *bureaucratic activism* works to counter management resistance within agencies to the gender and development model within agencies. Each of these processes is shown to have direct implications for explaining the similarities and differences found among CIDA, Sida, and USAID in the gender and development case and can be viewed as key factors in shaping the diffusion and institutionalization of other world society institutional models globally.

Internalization and certification

The first social process evident in the interviews and which accounts for the influence of international actors on donor agencies is the process of *internalization and certification*. This is a process by which new norms/policy models are internalized within an agency by looking outwards to certify its legitimacy. This process combines several mechanisms described by respondents during the interview process, including: setting and policing of standards by international actors; appealing to outside authorities to certify the validity of a model; and mimicking other donors and their approaches to gender. All three of these mechanisms combine in a process of model internalization and certification, leading donors to adopt world society models to varying extents. These mechanisms were present in each of the donor countries considered in this case study.

Standards setting/policing and the appeal to outside authority

Two interrelated mechanisms of the internalization and certification process emerging from the interviews were standards setting/policing and the 'appeal to outside authority'.

Standards setting is a mechanism by which an international body comprised of a group of national actors agree to a set of norms or standards as a *de jure* approach to a situation expected to hold for all similar actors. The standards are upheld and monitored by the same body or group through a mechanism of standards policing. The setting of standards can be highly formalized – such as those established under the auspices of the International

Organization for Standardization – or can be informally undertaken by the acknowledged clearinghouse/summit body for a sector.

In the case of the foreign aid sector, bilateral donors come together in three venues which could arguably serve a standard-setting role: The Development Assistance Committee (DAC) of the OECD; the United Nations (UN); and the World Bank. The DAC is open to membership by donors only, whereas the UN and the World Bank Group includes both donors and recipients. Arguably, the case of the aid sector suggests that the broader the membership of the standards-setting body, the less focused, concrete, and enforceable the standards set. As such, standards policing can be less fruitful for standards agreed upon in a more diverse setting, which may appeal to either ideologically motivated goals/objectives or to the lowest-common-denominator of policies. In contrast, those standards set and upheld by a smaller group may have more 'teeth' in the sense that nation-state adherents to a specific standard face more serious repercussions or reprimand among peers. Standards policing is the primary mechanism at the root of the process of the DAC Peer Review. In this respect, the small group of Western donors (twenty-two countries in 2006–2007) might be seen to have greater ability to police standards than say the entire global membership of the UN General Assembly.

Complementary to standards setting and policing is the 'appeal to outside authority'. This mechanism sees appeals to outside authorities to provide greater legitimacy to impending policy shifts or changes. Aid officials follow this path when they are attempting to establish the case for a policy change or generate more support for changes within the agency at the management level. By highlighting the experiences of or support for a policy model by a respected outside agency or individual, aid officials borrow legitimacy from the perceived authority of that outsider.

This outside authority provides greater legitimacy in two ways: (1) by appealing to the aid agency's preference for 'best practices' (i.e. if another donor is already using an approach already deemed a success, then the model gains greater credibility as a new approach to adopt); and (2) by appealing to the donor agency's views on its deficiencies of expertise (i.e. in cases where an agency does not have in-house experience or expertise on an issue, it is easier to accomplish related policy change if outside expertise/experience can be emulated/mimicked in an effort to leapfrog perceived deficiencies). The appeal to outside authority can be especially useful to more junior officials tasked with making change within the agency, as it allows them to package credibility from outside to bolster their claims/advice to senior management who might otherwise adopt a more circumspect approach to the advocated policy model shift. The outside authority can be another bilateral donor agency, an international organization, the outcomes of an international conference, or an individual/consultant/researcher. It is not necessary for the outside authority to actually be engaged in any way with the development agency, and indeed much appeal to outside authority is based on freely available policy documents and statements.

Respondents interviewed for this study were asked about the influence of international organizations active in the aid sector and of relevant international conferences and treaties on their work on gender and development. Targeted questions were asked regarding the influence of the OECD DAC and the UN. Given that the DAC and UN set many international standards for foreign aid on the global stage, it stands to reason they would have direct influence on donors and on donor gender policy. The DAC GenderNet's work to produce a standardized set of guidelines for donors on gender equality, to standardize gender equality reporting of ODA funds, and to ensure that gender is incorporated in other DAC activities and priority areas is a relevant example of this. The UN has also shown the potential to be influential with its inclusion of gender equality in the Millennium Development Goals, squarely placing gender on the global aid agenda.

Respondents provided only mixed support for the idea that international organizations had much influence on donor gender policy or day-to-day approaches to gender programming. Not surprisingly, individuals interacting directly with international organizations claimed a greater amount of influence than those for whom the DAC or the UN seem more distant entities. For instance, a Swedish respondent who participates actively in the DAC's GenderNet suggested that the DAC guidelines and gender network were '...in a way quite influential'. Continuing, the respondent highlighted the inspirational aspect of the DAC's work on gender:

> [T]hose guidelines were also a part of the post-Beijing 1995 push and it affected everyone. [T]he DAC [...] provided a really good forum for people to talk about this. It inspired (well that is what it is supposed to do, it is supposed to inspire!) the members and even the observers and gender has really grown. Just like a lot of the other working parties and networks. To inspire them, you know, to do their own work, to look over their own policies and things like that.
>
> [September 12, 2006a]

This inspiration provided by the DAC network and guidelines has a recursive component, as the DAC consists of donor members and their active contribution. The work of the DAC 'inspires' the network members in their work for their home country's donor agency.

Influence of the DAC guidelines alongside other international factors was echoed by a Canadian donor official as a key factor in shaping CIDA's corporate policy on gender equality:

> Certainly, the work of the DAC, the donors together, and the UN have influenced the policy. We drew on the DAC guidelines on gender equality and the commitments from the Commission on the Status of Women, Beijing and the whole Beijing process.
>
> [October 4, 2006]

Referring to the creation of the 1999 gender policy, this respondent high-lights the work of the DAC, its guidelines, as well the Beijing conference and the UN's Commission on the Status of Women as international influences on CIDA.

Another CIDA respondent suggested the DAC plays a role in setting standards through the collaborative work of its networks and the creation of sets of guidelines:

> GenderNet is a group of donors who get together once a year and dis-cuss pertinent issues to gender equality, but we also have a programme of work [...] We all contribute to that work within the DAC. [...] The OECD DAC peer review mechanism reviews us as donors, so Canada's currently right now in the process of having a peer review of which gender equality is part [...].
>
> [February 13, 2007]

This respondent also highlights the role for DAC standards policing. Referring to the DAC peer review process in which several donor members review the overall development assistance programme of another donor to assess how it matches with DAC guidelines and expectations, she underlines that the DAC can influence its members through its peer review oversight. She continues:

> In terms of our individual donor policies, I'm just going back to last year [...] when all the donors were asked to fill out a questionnaire on, you know, sort of what level of resources (this is for the evaluation part of the DAC) do we commit to gender equality? Do we have a policy? How many advisors do we have? (gender equality advisors in the field, gender equality specialists in the headquarters, etc. etc.) And so, in that way, the DAC collates information on what we're doing individually as donors and puts it together.
>
> [February 13, 2007]

Here, the respondent discusses the DAC's role as a clearinghouse for devel-opment assistance information, data, and best practices by providing the example of how the DAC had surveyed donors in 2006 regarding the overall implementation of their gender policies. This peer review and data collection function demonstrates the standards policing role of the DAC.

In contrast to most official donor respondents, civil society respondents showed little indication of the influence of the DAC on their work on gender, and perceived only marginal influence of the DAC on donor approaches to gender in their respective countries. This is not to say that civil society rep-resentatives were not aware of the DAC, as many echoed concerns about the recent DAC agenda on aid effectiveness which appears to limit the role for civil society in some forms of development assistance. The DAC's perceived influence can be seen to vary depending on how closely an individual is to working directly with the organization. Civil society respondents were less connected to the DAC and thus less likely to report its influence on the donor agency in their country.

UN influence was deemed significant as far as the Millennium Development Goals (MDGs) were concerned, but only because of the focus on gender derived from reframing gender equality as a specific goal in the MDGs. Respondents' discussion of UN influence repeatedly centred on factors like international conferences, treaties, and the MDGs.

Aside from the earlier example where a Canadian official mentions how the Beijing conference and the process of preparing for and responding to it, helped shape CIDA's corporate level gender policy, other respondents also highlighted the influence of UN conferences. An American respondent suggested that the outcomes of the International Conference on Population and Development (ICPD) in Cairo in 1994 and the Platform for Action from Beijing, along with the MDGs, have been a strong influence on gender mainstreaming at USAID:

> Sure, having [gender] be, you know, integrated into the Millennium Goals was really valuable. I think that the work – the gender integration for USAID – only moved forward because of ICPD and Beijing. That was a huge impetus for USAID to work more formally on this.
> [November 12, 2007]

When asked if this influence was due to the issue being given focus on the international agenda by these conferences or because of the actual commitments made by countries at the conference, she responded: 'Both.'

Similar views were echoed by another Canadian respondent suggesting a two-fold means by which international conferences or declarations influence donor nation-states: first, by drawing attention to an issue on the international stage; and second, by policing a nation-state's adherence to commitments made at one of these conferences or when ratifying an international treaty. In this respect, the international conferences and their subsequent statements or treaties can be seen as influencing donors both through standards setting/policing and as an external referent through which they can derive justification for policies within their agencies.

At the same time, dependent on the individual context of the respondent, the influence of these events can also have perceived detrimental effects on a donor's gender policies and programmes. For instance, one Swedish civil society representative suggested that the Beijing Platform for Action had been very influential on donors, but had also led them astray from the overall aims of promoting women's rights and empowerment:

> I would say that the Sida position is totally gender mainstreaming – and that goes for all donors. That is the position of [our organization] as well. But you have to gender mainstream all activities, all programmes, all

projects. Ah, what we are trying to do is […] is going back to Beijing '95. The policy was not gender mainstreaming period. It was gender mainstreaming and continued support to women's organizations and the fight for women's rights. So it was not actually forced out of the agenda, but the big bilaterals like Canadian CIDA or Swedish Sida opted for just understanding the Platform for Action as a gender mainstreaming agenda.

[September 12, 2007b]

From this respondent's perspective, the donors have been overly influenced by the Beijing platform, to the extent that they have lost touch with the original aims of protecting women's rights. In this regard, the powerful influence that the outcomes of the Beijing conference had on donors seems striking. Both Canadian and Swedish donor agencies are accused here of appealing to the outside authority provided by the Beijing Platform for Action to such an extent that their gender programmes became bogged down in gender mainstreaming requirements.

Whether through conference outcome documents or the process of preparing for and taking part in conferences, these events can shape donor enactment of gender policy. The fact that the MDGs refer to gender equality as a goal allows donors to appeal to outside authority and refer to the MDGs as a legitimating factor to justify their gender programming. External referents like DAC guidelines or the MDGs are therefore perceived as valuable by those working on gender within donor agencies, as they provide an impetus for making internal progress towards gender equality.

Mimicry

Mimicry is closely related to the appeal to outside authority. By mimicking policy/approaches of other donors or organizations, aid agencies adopt a policy priority in a rapid manner without having to invest as significantly in the genesis of a new approach or idea as they would for a *sui generis* priority/model (DiMaggio and Powell 1983). Agencies mimic other donors they feel demonstrate success, expertise, or 'best practices' for a given development concern. Employing mimicry as a policy development mechanism, donors look to what their peers are doing for solutions to common problems, rather than taking unique positions or approaches themselves. Indeed, DiMaggio and Powell (1983) argue that this mimicry allows organizations to become more certain of the outcomes of their efforts and in the process, promotes isomorphism within an organizational field or sector. Mimicry does not require complete adoption of model created elsewhere, but sometimes occurs in degrees if a model is adapted and then implemented in modified form. Donors that are mimicked are perceived as 'cutting edge' in terms of policy innovations. Mimicry allows trailing donors to achieve similar results without the need to innovate. Indeed, because of the small community of aid donors, mimicry appears to frequently explain diffusion of policy models and the promotion of consensus. In a policy environment that recently has lauded donor cooperation and collaboration in the context of aid effectiveness, the likelihood of donor mimicry seems to be increased.

The responses of those interviewed for this study suggest mimicry plays a substantial role in the gender and development models adopted and implemented by their agencies. Respondents were asked how other donors and which donors had influenced the approach to gender within their country's aid agency. Not *all* respondents felt that other donors were very influential, but many discussed this influence at length. Within these responses, two main themes emerged: (1) certain donors are viewed as 'leaders' in the gender field and should be emulated; (2) the influence of other donors can be quite indirect, except through the DAC venue or through multi-donor collaboration.

These themes can be seen in the following response from a Canadian aid official who, when asked about the influence of other donors, stated:

> … if you mean specific bilateral donors, yes, we've shared tools. For example, the work that was done by Swedish Sida on the sort of tip sheet approach to prompting people about gender equality aspects across the host of different themes and sectors – we borrowed from them and adapted and did some of our own and we're still doing this kind of work. Likewise, you know, other donors may borrow from us in terms of modeling of some of our programming approaches. DFID [The United Kingdom's Department for International Development] adopted almost an identical sort of gender fund mechanism based on the work we had done. In Pakistan, we've been doing some work trying to do some collaborative work with the ADB [Asian Development Bank] on gender equality and trying to influence them as an institution, but also then, for example, doing a joint country assessment on general equality for Indonesia together…
>
> [October 4, 2006]

Here, she refers to the leadership of Sida on gender issues and mentioned Canada's emulation of Sweden's successful 'gender tip-sheet' approach to assist CIDA in more effective gender mainstreaming. She also refers to CIDA as a leader in the field because one CIDA approach to programming in Asia was being emulated by Britain's Department for International Development (DFID). When probed to further elaborate on other donor influence on CIDA policy, she continued:

> Hmm, influenced by other donors on a gender equality policy. When I saw this question,[4] I did put down the DAC and the UN, like, as a group. But in terms of specific bilateral donors, I think less so. At a country level, we might see a different picture, but, I can give you some examples where, yes, we have been the lead of a donor round table suggesting that we bring

together the donors on gender equality or that there's analysis lacking in the PRSP and how we can address that as a group. On our work with the ADB, it's multiple donors with DANIDA and Norway. It's not just CIDA leading the charge, but I don't think we can take credit for always being the leader. So at a policy level, perhaps it's the broad, you know, like the UN and the DAC. When it comes to programming and tools and practices, then yeah, it's a sharing back and forth, but I can't point to one specific donor that I think has been particularly influential across the board [...] a specific donor doesn't come to mind. At a country level, that might be a different picture, depending on the country.

[October 4, 2006]

Influence at the macro-policy level is not perceived as strong, but when it comes to collaborating on gender work, the influence of others can be felt. Ties built by working together with other donors can therefore be a significant influence.

This idea of collaborating with others and the importance of discussion with other donors as a channel for mimicking behaviour was also raised by an American respondent:

There was a meeting that was funded by Gates, in Washington, that brought together different funders to talk about this important agenda [constructive engagement of men] and kind of think strategically about how to move forward. USAID was a participant, we presented on a panel with other donors. So there has been discussion with other donors, on this area of work and progress so far and how we can promote it further. [...] The organizations that I remember were there were the World Bank, Swedish Sida, Canadian CIDA, and I think DFID might have been there as well.

[November 12, 2007]

USAID collaboration with several other donors including the World Bank, Sida, CIDA, and DFID had moved ahead USAID's engagement on the issue of men in gender programming. Collaboration on a specific issue – the engagement of men in gender programming – brought together multiple donors to strategize over how to move ahead in that area. Sharing experiences between agencies is a significant influence on other donors' gender policy.

Donor mimicry and collaboration may be considered more of a dialogue than a unidirectional mechanism. Indeed, in situations where a donor agency is perceived as a leader, or the leader, in an area like gender – the perception of other donor influence may flow towards other donors rather than inwards. One Swedish official noted when asked about whether other donors had much influence on Sida's gender policy that Sida had, in fact, been influencing others' policies instead, providing the example of New Zealand's aid agency copying parts of Sida's recent gender policy [Interview

September 12, 2006c]. Instead of Sida being influenced by others, the 'progressive' policy they possessed was seen to influence other donors who attempt to emulate it. Donors who are newly developing gender policies looked to Sida as a model. In this sense, a donor with a reputation for leadership on the gender issues is influential, but perhaps not influenced as much by other countries.

Mimicry within the community of donors in the gender field is evident in the data. Donors discussed the copying of specific components of other donor approaches: CIDA's adoption of Sida's gender tip-sheets; Sida's adoption of DFID's help-desk approach; DFID's copying of a gender project format in Asia. Each of these provides an example of mimicry where the influence of other donors takes hold to shape gender policy and programming models.

The internalization and certification process identified above is demonstrated in data from all three donor countries. Standards setting and policing was a strong influence on all three donors, as was the adoption of appealing to outside authority to justify new approaches to gender. Mimicry played a role for both CIDA and USAID, while Sida instead reported being mimicked by others. These three mechanisms all interrelate to encourage a process of internalization by which donors take on an external model as their own and a process of certification which validates that model as acceptable, effective, and appropriate to their needs. The influences of the DAC, the UN, international conferences and treaties, and of other donors are strong determinants of the internalization and certification process. In all three donor country cases examined here, an outwards-oriented perspective was used to enable and justify movement towards a common approach to gender and development.

Embeddedness within civil society

Deriving inspiration from Peter Evans' (1995) concept of embedded autonomy, I define donor agency embeddedness within civil society as the extent to which actions and objectives of the donor are linked to or engage with agendas of development-oriented civil society in the donor country. Indicators of embeddedness include: the presence of donor-led networks involving civil society and donor actors, levels of personnel-exchange between donor and NGOs, personal relationships between donor and civil society personnel, consultation of civil society stakeholders by donors during the policy development process, and donor openness to civil society advocacy. Higher degrees of embeddedness reflect a greater connection between the donor agency and its domestic civil society. The less embedded the donor, the less sway its civil society will have on development assistance outcomes for that country.

Respondents were asked to assess the influence of domestic civil society organizations on their aid agency's gender policy. Questions focused on domestic development NGOs in each country, but some respondents independently touched upon international NGOs involved in this area and spoke of their influence. The amount of reported influence of domestic civil society varied widely between respondents and between case study countries. As might be expected, countries with a greater involvement of civil society in the aid sector tended to report more influence, and those without, less. One contradiction of this was the significant involvement of civil society in USAID's Interagency Gender Working Group (IGWG), and as collaborators with the agency's WID office. Here, USAID is working very closely with NGO representatives to collaborate on defining directions for both the donor and civil society to take on gender in the population and health fields. One respondent described this collaboration as exerting influence in both directions:

> We brought partners to the IGWG who were doing innovative work and really could make technical contributions and help us in advocacy. But at the same time, we also are exerting our pressure as a funder on other cooperating agencies.
>
> [November 12, 2007]

Collaborative networking and sharing between donor and civil society had the effect of influencing USAID's direction on gender, but allowed for donor influence on NGO partners.

Civil society influence on Sida also occurred through a donor-NGO network on gender issues. Though less formalized than USAID's IGWG, this network was perceived by a Sida respondent as a space for:

> sharing of information and sharing experiences and getting to know what is up, what is new, what is happening. [...] Also to discuss our policy [from] last year for example – to get feedback from them.
>
> [September 12, 2006c]

Utilizing a network for consultation of NGO partners on Sida's new gender policy is just one example of how civil society embeddedness functions. The informality of this network, consisting of the two Sida gender advisors and approximately twenty NGO representatives was described by another respondent who participates in the network as a 'strategic and undercover alliance between internal Sida staff and the NGO sector' [Interview September 12, 2006b]. Sida engaging, even informally and inconspicuously, with critical voices from civil society is indicative of the influence of NGOs on the gender model adopted in Sweden. This influence, one respondent suggested, might be more potent because one of Sida's two gender advisors was a recent recruit from an NGO where they had been responsible for gender programming. This raises another issue of external influence through close ties to internal channels, something explored in the final section of the chapter.

CIDA also had some experience recently of consulting with civil society on the directions to take on gender, but not in the form of a formal or informal network with civil society. However, the extent of influence might be questioned given the respondent's difficulty in remembering the incident:

> You know, I'm wracking my brain here. We had a roundtable with our previous Minister a year and a half ago [2004] on gender equality and we'd invited a number of civil society representatives, multilateral and bilateral to comment on our strategy paper back then and yeah, I would say, I mean, there are a number of organizations that throughout time, have had some impact.
>
> [February 13, 2006]

In contrast to responses such as these indicating a significant role for civil society influence on gender policy and approaches, some respondents felt there was less direct influence by domestic civil society on CIDA's gender work, and indeed called into question the progress on gender made by NGOs:

> No, they don't contact us about that [gender]. In fact, we are the ones that have to, quite often, force the issue. Civil society on gender is quite weak. At least the ones we're finding. [T]hese are the best ones and they're still weak. They don't have a gender specialist in a lot of cases and if they get one, they're like: 'Well, look, we have a gender specialist!' Well do something! Write a strategy.
>
> [December 21, 2006]

A former Canadian official suggested that some advocacy had occurred, but it was not always consistent, and often CIDA turned around on these agencies, calling their approaches to gender into question:

> I would say that the pressures on the agenda, the advocacy kinds of pressures have come more from the development organizations that have picked up on the issue. In the earlier days that was groups like Oxfam and so on [...] – CUSO⁵ to some extent. But again, some of those groups didn't do so well internally in their own organizations and then CIDA would come back at them through the CIDA gender equality policy: [...] 'If you want our funding then we want to see this.'
>
> [December 13, 2006]

Civil society's influence is conditional on the type of relationship that the donor has with civil society. If a network existed for the discussion and furthering of gender aims, then civil society was more likely to be perceived as influential. If consultations and advocacy were more limited or ad hoc, then the extent of civil society influence on gender policy was also likely to be perceived as such.

Aid agencies with existing formal or informal donor-NGO networks on gender equality were reportedly more likely to report being influenced by civil society. In turn, civil society influence seemed to push donors toward more fully implementing all the components of the gender and development world society model outlined above. Integration of donor–civil society networks on gender equality into donor work on the issue is a clear marker in the Swedish and American cases of a heightened degree of embeddedness in civil society. Development NGOs in both cases influence the outcome of donor work on the gender issue, and the donors appear to seek out and respond to this influence. In contrast, CIDA shows a relative detachment from civil society, and indeed, provides evidence of the donor shaping civil society agendas rather than vice versa. This may help explain why the Canadian implementation of the gender and aid model at times fails to integrate more advanced forms of mainstreaming and disregards more recent approaches to men and masculinities.

Management resistance and bureaucratic activism

The interaction of management and aid officials within donor agencies reflects how human agency shapes both resistance to and implementation of gender models. This agency most frequently takes the form of activism or advocacy on behalf of gender. Respondents were asked to discuss the challenges and successes of gender approaches. The primary challenge raised in response to the question related to significant levels of management resistance within agencies to implementing gender models. At the same time, respondents repeatedly referred to forms of bureaucratic activism to combat management resistance – activism with significant impact on the application of gender models in donor organizations. Four mechanisms of bureaucratic activism emerged from analysis of the data: gender champions; bureaucrat entrepreneurship; bureaucrat guerrilla tactics; and personnel exchange.

Gender champions

Champions are high profile or long-serving executives tasked with shepherding an issue within the organization. Having a champion focus attention upon an issue, move forward a transformative shift in policy, or bend the ear of senior management relies on the determined leadership of that person to complement the efforts of others. The champion can be a very effective means of refocusing attention on a previously moribund issue, or one deemed in need of reinvigoration of effort. Two possible outcomes offered by championing of an issue are: (1) increased organizational inertia and urgency surrounding the issue; and (2) decreased resistance or indifference to the issue from others in senior management.

A gender champion is typically a senior management member who, although possibly not a gender expert, is respected within the agency and internationally, and takes on a sometimes unofficial role of promoting gender issues through both formal and informal channels. One respondent from CIDA emphasized the importance of champions in recent years in bringing additional momentum to gender and development issues on the international agenda:

I think that's given a renewed focus and like I say, it's been, in my view, had a lot to do with championing as well. You know there have been various champions in the multilateral institutions, but also in the donor agencies and you know the fact that we, at CIDA, have a champion, is giving us a whole lot more energy and attention and... Well, if you get the opportunity to speak to Diane, you'll be amazed by I think, by the dedication and motivation she has for making this work.

[Would it be fair to say that the main advantage of the championing is essentially that it puts a voice for gender equality at the most senior management levels?]

Yes. Yes. And also, so you know, there's obviously the corporate level as well as the international profile leadership, if you want to call it that. I mean, it's on a number of levels, but internally, she champions it. The Executive Vice-President champions it from the point of view of increased resources, looking at revamping the training that the agency receives on gender equality, and essentially ensuring that you know, whether it be CDPFs [Country Development Programming Frameworks] or memos that, you know, that gender equality is continuously there.

[February 13, 2007]

Another CIDA respondent commented on the gender equality champion, suggesting that she was responsible for an increased focus on gender within the agency in the past year and was a useful tool to push gender issues in the agency beyond what the corporate policy can do alone:

I think a big change that I've noticed with CIDA is with the Executive Vice-President coming on board and being named the gender equality champion. She takes that role quite seriously, which is a good or a bad thing because she's a doer, she wants to change things but she also wants has very specific ideas and sometimes she is not always – sometimes she's pushing a little too hard I would say. It's an interesting relationship but her presence has actually been valuable and Africa Branch in May of this year, May 2006, we did a gender equality workshop, a pan-Africa one and the VP went to that and that really seemed to spur her on and she had a chance to listen to people in the field especially and that seemed to – she got a lot of ideas from the workshop report and the recommendations coming from the participants that she been trying to move forward and a lot of the stuff she's been pushing on now or you see in the draft strategy that she has developed very much comes from the workshop that we did and the recommendations coming out of that workshop.

[So the impact of having a champion like that, that has perhaps a little more leverage to focus on these issues – you've seen some positive benefits?]

Oh yeah, she can get people to listen ... right ... you need somebody high up that thinks it's important. I mean we have a policy, which is great. But if it's not being implemented or nothing is making sure if it's being implemented it has limited impact.

[December 20, 2006]

Exposing the gender champion to ideas, people, and experiences can help to motivate and shape their action on behalf of gender equality within the agency. Furthermore, she highlights the importance of having a champion who can 'get people to listen' and has clout with senior management and decision makers.

Other examples suggested that the gender champion did not *need* to be an individual with high profile or clout with senior management. In one example provided from experience within USAID, a respondent noted that champions can simply be recognizable and long-serving individuals working actively on gender issues within the organization. The key combination she highlighted was the need for a champion to have resources behind them – financial backing to achieve specific aims.

Champions can circumvent resistance within senior management of an agency to move forward with a more progressive gender agenda. The responses above illustrate the credit given to effective championing of the issue within CIDA and USAID, and the impact this leadership on an issue provides. Whether from a senior manager or a long-serving and respected expert, the championing of gender issues played a significant role in institutionalizing the gender and development approach within donors by playing a figurehead role among other bureaucrat activists and stemming management resistance to gender approaches.

Bureaucratic entrepreneurialism

In some cases, the line between champion and another type of official working within these agencies can blur. Where gender champions tend to be officially acknowledged or appointed to the role, it often occurs that an individual advances the gender agenda by more independent and unofficial means. In these cases, individuals are able to further gender policies or programmes out of sheer effort despite resistance or unawareness in the agency. One Swedish respondent spoke of an instance where a supportive manager and interested official coexist:

[I]t is the so called perfect mix of a head of division or in some cases head of department, who is interested and has some knowledge and who wants to promote this, and a programme officer who has the same inspiration or whatever. So when they meet, that is when things happen.

[September 12, 2006c]

The confluence of these individuals permits the officer or gender advisor to accelerate policy and programming reforms that, though not necessarily resisted or lauded by the agency, are at least tolerated. Another respondent labelled this as bureaucratic entrepreneurialism, with progress arising from the work of one or two individuals in a way that was accepted but perhaps unconventional within the system.

Bureaucratic entrepreneurialism is found when aid officials act independently to advocate for policy reforms that as yet are not institutionalized within the agency. This internal advocacy appropriates outside information, experience, and resources to advance a specific issue – even in the face of resistance from management or political staff. The entrepreneurial aspect of this behaviour is the 'self-starting' nature of the bureaucrat entrepreneur. These entrepreneurs have no downward pressure from management to advocate for these policy changes, but take it upon themselves to work for a perceived greater good. Individual effort exerts unexpected influence on the policy outcomes of the institution. Bureaucrat entrepreneurs gain prestige within organizations if reforms for which they advocate are eventually accepted. In this way, bureaucratic entrepreneurialism requires an enabling environment of resources and opportunity structures within the organization to permit the entrepreneur to operate openly. If these resources and opportunity structures do not exist, then reforms may only take place in a situation of guerrilla bureaucracy.

Individuals who carve out an entrepreneurial niche for themselves *vis-à-vis* gender equality work in the agency become recognized as the resource to consult on the issues. One USAID gender advisor noted:

… both of us have been in the same position in the same office, for a while. I think that it is very important because there is tremendous turnover and movement within USAID. And often an issue is carried forward because of an individual's commitment and connections and so the fact that there has been some stability, I think, has benefited the work of [the Agency].

[November 12, 2007]

Here, the promotion of gender issues in the agency was linked to 'an individual's commitment and connections,' combined with long experience in a position which enable 'stability' to arise around the gender issue. If individual opportunities to promote gender are matched with a long-term dedication to the issue and latitude within the agency to achieve some results, these gender entrepreneurs can become valued assets within the corporate structure for the implementation of gender objectives and policies.

The important role of bureaucratic entrepreneurialism was most evident in the interviews in the discussion of the early stages of WID and GAD work at CIDA, as well as in the work of the IGWG at USAID. Self-starting individuals who act as internal activists to advocate for gender appear to play a significant role in shaping donor outcomes on gender and the widespread adoption of a gender model under the influence of world society.

Guerrilla bureaucrats

When entrepreneurialism crosses into actions or tactics that run counter to the wishes of senior management or politicians, transgressions can take the form of what several respondents labelled 'guerrilla' tactics. Guerrilla bureaucracy can be seen in instances where officials undertake change or advocacy within the organization which is neither authorized nor supported by management. Such actions occur without the knowledge of apex decision-makers with the intent of building momentum for change so that the initiative/reform becomes irresistible or difficult to ignore when revealed. These actions can make a change a *fait accompli* that cannot be resisted tactfully by management. The guerrilla bureaucrat advocates a resisted or unpopular idea which cannot be stomached by mainstream decision-makers in the organization, and tries to bring the idea to the table in ways that subvert the policy process to their own ends. The guerrilla aspect of these activities arises from the fact that they are conducted by small groups or individuals and have an element of surprise or ambush, hence the comparison to guerrilla warfare. Such tactics are used by bureaucrat advocates as a form of internal activism within an organization or among a senior management that is perceived as resistant to change or resistant to adopt a new policy priority/direction. The distinction from normal bureaucratic activism/entrepreneurialism is the concealed nature of the activities.

A retired CIDA official detailed an instance early in her career when, following a talk on discrimination against women in the Canadian public service, a group of women within CIDA took it upon themselves to push for change within the agency:

> It's almost like guerrilla action. That's a word I would have to use. It comes out of the ways in which people like me had to work just to get things onto an agenda. Get it on the agenda. It was like working [...] to get attention by sometimes even embarrassment of leaders in government who were just not paying attention. [...] [O]ne of the things that we did was: Marcel Massé was the new President of CIDA and he said, 'I want to meet with groups of employees.' So the Executive Assistant

of [a CIDA Vice President] said to me [...] 'Hey, I have to set up these groups, so, we could make an all women group and then talk about these issues.' [...] So we organized and we had this whole thing set up so that specific women were at that lunch meeting and he thought he was just going to have a 'little chat with the gals'. We were going to raise specific issues that came out of – you know – which were then on the agenda from the UN report. So, again you're looking at [...] things like the end of Women's Decade reporting stuff from the UN. So, that's what happened. [...] Yes, after the lunch meeting Massé was thunderstruck enough to say, 'Well I guess you could write me something on this.' So we did.

[December 14, 2006]

By seizing on an opportunity in an unexpected manner, this group of women officers ambushed the CIDA President so that he was forced to respond with moving ahead the Women in Development agenda at the time. This unexpected action was successful in circumventing some of the resistance within the agency to make an impact on senior management and provide impetus to further the gender agenda at CIDA. The guerrilla aspect of such an approach can be seen in the unexpected pathway through which this action managed to 'get it on the agenda' despite perceived resistance.

Guerrilla action was also highlighted by a Sida respondent who discussed difficulty faced by programme officers tasked with gender responsibilities over and above their day-to-day tasks in the face of resistant management:

[T]hey have had to struggle towards their leadership in order to be able to be it. Maybe their leadership does not find it so necessary to put time into it.

[September 12, 2006c]

Discussing the need for officers to 'struggle' to incorporate gender into their work suggests the need to work outside accepted parameters or to disrupt expectations of resistant individuals. According to several of my respondents, this individual agency involved battling resistance and indifference within their donor agency is a critical component to making innovative progress on the gender issue.

The most striking example in the data was the push by the group of women CIDA officials to orchestrate a situation where the CIDA President could not help but to opt for sponsoring the creation of a strategy on how to make CIDA a more equal workplace. This ambush in the face of resistance from others within the organization and totally unexpected from the perspective of senior management, but still yielded a positive outcome. Guerrilla bureaucracy like this is the most overt form of bureaucratic activism shaping gender and development approaches in aid agencies.

Personnel exchange

A additional factor related to bureaucratic activism emerged as a significant consideration in the adoption, institutionalization, and refinement of gender models among all three donors: personnel exchange. This refers not to the high level of turnover reported in each case, but to the origins of individuals brought into aid agencies to fill positions tied to gender equality concerns. In all three donors this phenomenon was seen when individuals tasked with women in development or gender responsibilities were brought into the agency from a previous position with a civil society group, an international organization, or another government body. In the case of Sida for instance, one of the two gender advisors had been freshly recruited from a major Swedish civil society group where she had been responsible for gender programming. CIDA also had gender advisors who had been integrated into the agency from previous roles with the Status of Women Canada (a government department dedicated to women's issues and equality), the United Nations, and even from former roles as independent gender consultants. USAID similarly demonstrated the transfer of people into its WID Office from previous work within the United Nations system. This phenomenon reflects the need to hire people with gender equality expertise to undertake gender work and is therefore unsurprising, but is also indicative of the pathways through which the flow of standardized models, ideas, and norms of gender equality from the international organizations, civil society groups, and expert communities of the world polity into nation-state organizations can occur.

Personnel exchange plays a key role in policy reforms in two ways: (1) exchanged persons have the potential to make easier 'targets' for outside advocacy, as they may prove more sympathetic to former colleagues and causes; (2) exchanged persons bring an outsider perspective on internal matters that make them better suited to adopt activist stances and support significant changes within an organization. It must be noted, however, that this may not be uniformly the case. Exchanged persons may also be less open to advocacy, and less willing to express an outsider perspective if they are in an environment that discourages these views. An organization can therefore be more or less encouraging of personnel exchange.

Personnel exchange also plays a role in all three country contexts. Indeed, gender expertise accrued outside a donor agency is an asset which is apparently valued highly by donors who have brought individuals into their systems from civil society, international organizations, or other government departments. Once integrated into the agency these individuals play a key role in advocating for gender approaches which challenge the status quo. In so doing, exchanged individuals play significant part in supporting bureaucratic activism on gender within aid agencies.

Bureaucratic activism is thus a complex process manifested with several different mechanisms. The most commonly reported and experienced forms of bureaucratic activism were the gender champion, bureaucratic entrepreneurship, and personnel exchange. All of these factors were evident in each of the donor country cases examined here. Guerrilla bureaucracy, on the other hand, was most evident in the case of CIDA, with a few mentions by Sida representatives. This less common, but highly interesting, form of bureaucratic activism also played a role in shaping gender and development approaches in those countries. On the whole, bureaucratic activism is the chief process by which management resistance to the adoption, institution-alization, or refinement of a world society gender model is abrogated.

Gender, aid, and micro-level processes of globalization

Chapter 2 shows that world society influence on the adoption of gender policy by donors is a significant macro-level explanation of the diffusion of the gender model in the aid sector. This chapter's comparative case study of gender and development in three countries expands on these macro explana-tions and shows that there are three common micro-level social processes that account for the striking similarities in application of gender and development models in each donor agency. Analysis of the case study interviews of donor officials and civil society workers in each country shows that – regardless of different domestic contexts facing the aid sector in each case – these common processes and related mechanisms underpin the interface of aid agencies with world society and the gender models it promulgates. The processes of inter-nalization and certification, embeddedness within civil society, and bureau-cratic activism account for the influence of world society on donor uptake of gender and development models in the bilateral aid sector.

The processes identified here add to world society explanations of glo-balization and the diffusion of common gender policies and institutional frameworks among nation-states. Additionally, these processes raise ques-tions about the nature of the relationship between world society and the nation-state; a relationship which is not as clearly demarcated as past research might suggest. Delineating between world society and nation-state becomes exceedingly difficult when considering intergovernmental bodies' role in world society. The DAC, given significant attention in this chapter and the next, is a prime example where disentangling what is world soci-ety and what is nation-state agency becomes difficult, and requires further investigation. At the same time, more research into the globalization pro-cesses identified here may yield a deeper understanding of into the spread of gender policy models in other governments and institutions globally. The next chapter expands on the examination of micro-level globalization pro-cesses by examining similar phenomena in the context of donor approaches to security sector reform.

Notes

1 This is not to conflate women in development with gender and development. Donor approaches have clearly evolved from an initial engagement with Women

in Development (WID) to a more recent acceptance of understanding women's position in the development process as a function of gender inequality thus shifting the focus to Gender and Development (GAD).

2 The research literature on gender in development also includes the Women And Development or WAD school of thought which evolved in response to dependency theory. This chapter does not explore this approach in any depth, as it failed to make any large impact on the development assistance sector and tended not to be addressed by donor agencies.

3 Only in 2011 was USAID's Office of Women in Development renamed the Office of Gender Equality and Women's Empowerment.

4 This respondent only agreed to an interview if they were able to see a basic list of questions in advance. This did not prevent me from exploring other topics and probing further on different responses.

5 Canadian University Service Overseas.

References

Benería, L., & Sen, G. (1981). Accumulation, Reproduction, and Women's Role in Economic Development: Boserup Revisited. *Signs*, 7(2), 279–298.

Berkovitch, N. (1999). *From Motherhood to Citizenship: Women's Rights and International Organizations*. Baltimore, MD: Johns Hopkins University Press.

Berkovitch, N. (1999). The Emergence and Transformation of the International Women's Movement. In J. Boli & G. M. Thomas (Eds.), *Constructing World Culture: International Nongovernmental Organizations Since 1875* (pp. 100–126). Stanford, CA: Stanford University Press.

Boli, J., & Thomas, G. M. (1999). *Constructing World Culture: International Nongovernmental Organizations Since 1875*. Stanford, CA: Stanford University Press.

Boserup, E. (1970). *Woman's Role in Economic Development*. London: Allen & Unwin.

Chabbott, C. (1999). Development INGOs. In J. Boli & G. M. Thomas (Eds.), *Constructing World Culture: International Nongovernmental Organizations Since 1875* (pp. 222–248). Stanford, CA: Stanford University Press.

CIDA, Canadian International Development Agency. (1999). CIDA's Policy on Gender Equality. Retrieved from www.acdi-cida.gc.ca/INET/IMAGES.NSF/vLUImages/Policy/$file/GENDER-E.pdf

CIDA, Canadian International Development Agency. (2002). Canadian International Development Agency, Departmental Performance Report, 2001–2002. Retrieved from www.tbs-sct.gc.ca/rma/dpr/01-02/CIDA/CIDA0102dpr02_e.asp

del Rosario, V. O. (1997). Mainstreaming Gender Concerns: Aspects of Compliance, Resistance, and Negotiation. In A. M. Goetz (Ed.), *Getting Institutions Right for Women in Development* (pp. 77–89). London: Zed Books.

DiMaggio, P., & Powell, W. W. (1983). The Iron Cage Revisited: Institutional Isomorphism and Collective Rationality in Organizational Fields. *American Sociological Review*, 48(2), 147–160.

Elson, D., & McGee, R. (1995). Gender Equality, Bilateral Program Assistance and Structural Adjustment: Policy and Procedures. *World Development*, 23(11), 1987–1994.

Evans, P. B. (1995). *Embedded Autonomy: States and Industrial Transformation*. Princeton, N.J.: Princeton University Press.

Goetz, A. M. (1997). Introduction: Getting Institutions Right for Women in Development. In A. M. Goetz (Ed.), *Getting Institutions Right for Women in Development* (pp. 1–28). London: Zed Books.

IGWG, Interagency Gender Working Group. (2007). Interagency Gender Working Group – About. Retrieved from www.igwg.org/about.htm

ILO, International Labour Organization (2006). *A Profile of ILO Multi-Bilateral Donors' Policies on Gender Equality*. Retrieved from Geneva: www.ipu.org/parline-e/parlinesearch.asp

Jackson, C. (1997). Actor Orientation and Gender Relations at a Participatory Project Interface. In A. M. Goetz (Ed.), *Getting Institutions Right for Women in Development* (pp. 161–175). London: Zed Books.

Jaquette, J. S. (1982). Women and Modernization Theory: A Decade of Feminist Criticism. *World Politics: A Quarterly Journal of International Relations*, 34(2), 267–284.

Lechner, F. J., & Boli, J. (2005). *World Culture: Origins and Consequences*. London: Blackwell.

Meyer, J. W., Boli, J., Thomas, G. M., & Ramirez, F. O. (1997). World Society and the Nation-state. *The American Journal of Sociology*, 103(1), 144–181.

Misra, J. (2000). Gender and the World System. In T. D. Hall (Ed.), *A World-Systems Reader: New Perspectives on Gender, Urbanism, Cultures, Indigenous Peoples, and Ecology* (pp. 105–127). Lanham, Md.: Rowman & Littlefield.

Moser, C. (2005). Has Gender Mainstreaming Failed? *International Feminist Journal of Politics*, 7(4), 576–590.

Moser, C., & Moser, A. (2005). Gender Mainstreaming since Beijing: A Review of Success and Limitations in International Institutions. *Gender and Development*, 13(2), 11–22.

OECD. (1999). *DAC Guidelines for Gender Equality and Women's Empowerment in Development Cooperation*. Retrieved from Paris: www1.oecd.org/dac/gender/pdf/GENDGE.PDF

OECD. (2007). *Aid in Support of Gender Equality and Women's Empowerment*. Retrieved from www.oecd.org/dataoecd/7/55/38898309.pdf

Parpart, J. L. (1995). Deconstructing the Development Expert. In Marianne H. Marchand & J. L. Parpart (Eds.), *Feminism/Postmodernism/Development* (pp. 221–243). London: Routledge.

Paxton, P., Hughes, M. M., & Green, J. L. (2006). The International Women's Movement and Women's Political Representation, 1893–2003. *American Sociological Review*, 71, 898–920.

Rai, S. (2002). *Gender and the Political Economy of Development: From Nationalism to Globalization*. Cambridge, UK: Polity.

Rathgeber, E. (1990). WID, WAD, GAD: Trends in Research and Practice. *The Journal of Developing Areas*, 24, 489–502.

Rathgeber, E. (1995). Gender and Development in Action. In Marianne H. Marchand & J. L. Parpart (Eds.), *Feminism/Postmodernism/Development* (pp. 204–220). London: Routledge.

Razavi, S. (1997). Fitting Gender into Development Institutions. *World Development*, 25(7), 1111–1125.

Sida. (2005). *Promoting Gender Equality in Development Cooperation*. Sida.

Swiss, L. (2012). The Adoption of Women and Gender as Development Assistance Priorities: An Event History Analysis of World Polity Effects. *International Sociology*, 27(1), 96–119.

Tiessen, R. (2007). *Everywhere/Nowhere: Gender Mainstreaming in Development Agencies.* Bloomfield, CT: Kumarian Press.

USAID. (2006). *Women, Men, and Development.*

USAID. (2007). USAID Women in Development (WID): Integrating Gender into International Development. Retrieved from www.usaid.gov/our_work/cross-cutting_programs/wid/gender/index.html

USAID, & State Department. (2007). *Strategic Plan Fiscal Years 2007–2012: Transformational Diplomacy.*

Winship, J. D. (2004). *A Summary of Gender Strategies of Multilateral Development Agencies and Selected Bilateral Donors.* Retrieved from http://pdf.usaid.gov/pdf_docs/Pnada972.pdf

5 Security sector reform
Catalytic policy processes and donor autonomy

Security sector reform and foreign aid

Before the 1990s, bilateral foreign aid donors mostly eschewed issues of security and conflict. When countries experienced conflict and insecurity, development assistance programmes were suspended, and the focus of international donors shifted to humanitarian assistance to stem crises. In the wake of the Cold War, the growth in intra-state conflict in much of the developing world required aid donors to re-examine the approach to dealing with societies in conflict. Indeed, an entire approach to addressing issues of security and conflict in development assistance has appeared in international development discourse. Approaches to human security, and later to security-sector reform, have become a distinct priority for donors and other international organizations. Like in the gender case examined in the previous chapter, the similarities among diverse donors on this issue of security and conflict in development are striking. The influence of organizations like the Organisation for Economic Co-operation and Development's Development Assistance Committee (OECD DAC) and the United Nations Development Programme (UNDP) (OECD, 2004a, 2004c; UNDP, 1994) seem particularly strong. Despite these similarities, this security and development model is applied to different degrees by each donor because of the different experiences of social processes and mechanisms at work within each donor context.

Why have different donor domestic and foreign policy contexts led to convergence around approaches to security and development in the bilateral aid sector? What social processes facilitate global influence on the nation-state to shape donor policy? Recent trends point to a convergence of donor consensus around the issue of security sector reform, but a divergence of implementation. What accounts for this variance in implementation of aid and security approaches by donors? This chapter examines these questions from the world polity viewpoint elaborated throughout this book, using the same comparative, three-country case study of bilateral aid agencies. Analysing additional interviews with donor and civil society representatives from Canada, Sweden, and the United States allows for the identification of common micro-level mechanisms and processes at work in mediating the influence of world society on the nation-state. The commonalities and differences emerging from this data are used to compare and contrast the three countries' approaches to integrating an approach to security sector reform into their development assistance programmes. This chapter argues, despite experiencing convergence stemming from common social processes of globalization at work in each case, that the divergence of implementation of security sector reform frameworks results from the interplay of those processes with donor agency structure and each country's specific context.

World society and state security as a global model

The prescriptive norms and expectations of statehood espoused by world society shape what it is to be a state and how the state should be structured and develop (Kim et al., 2002; Meyer, 2007; Meyer et al., 1997). In keeping with Jepperson and co-authors' (1996) earlier research on world society's influence on state security policies, this chapter makes the case that that security policies and institutions of the state including militaries, police, legal-judicial systems, and correctional systems stem in part from common frameworks or scripts of world society. Ineffective implementation of these structures, and therefore the presence of intra-state conflict, has long been an explanation for the existence of weak states throughout the developing world (Holsti, 1996; Jackson and Rosberg, 1982; Migdal, 1988). It is in this context, therefore, that state security and the security of individuals in society (human security) have become another focus of the world polity. World society has addressed security in the broader context of not only war, militaries, and the police, but also legal/judicial and correctional/penal institutions. The discourse on human and national security has evolved over a long period, and in recent years – particularly following the end of the Cold War era – has been absorbed into the broader discourse on international development and development assistance.

Security as a development assistance concern

Until as recently as the 1990s aid was not commonly directed to areas of insecurity or conflict. The sharp increase in intra-state conflict in the developing world in the 1990s was seen as a driving force for the re-evaluation of the relationship between development and conflict or insecurity (Smith, 2001; Woods, 2005; Brown and Grävingholt, 2016; Duffield 2001, 2007). Donors began to consider the potential vulnerabilities that might emerge from increased conflict in the developing world (Nef, 1999), and some research even implicated development assistance as a contributor to the violence and insecurity (Andersen, 2000; Uvin, 1998, 1999). This merging of security and development concerns has been referred to as the 'securitization of aid' (Brown and Grävingholt, 2016).

The emergence of the human security agenda attempted to frame security as an issue that dealt with people and their lives as a broad spectrum of security concerns, rather than focusing on traditional security concerns of states, territories, and militaries (UNDP, 1994). Human security touched upon most aspects of people's lives, making it difficult to specify what interventions donors should pursue. This lack of precision would play a substantial role in the failure of human security to gain wide acceptance in the development assistance sector globally. Critics of the human security concept suggest it was motivated largely by the development community's desire to obtain a part of the substantial political and financial resources traditionally dedicated to the conventional security sector (King and Murray, 2002; Paris, 2001). Despite efforts by several 'middle power' states such as Canada to craft their foreign policies around a human security agenda and to establish a vibrant international community working on human security initiatives, human security failed to become a major contributor to new directions in development programming (King and Murray, 2002).

The next trend in the evolving relationship between development and security has been a focus on Security-Sector Reform (SSR) in the developing world (Smith, 2001). The OECD DAC defines SSR as seeking to 'increase partner countries' ab ility to meet the range of security needs within their societies in a manner consistent with democratic norms and sound principles of governance, transparency and the rule of law' (OECD, 2004b). Typical SSR initiatives might include: working to disarm and demobilize combatants, police training, judicial and legal reforms, professionalization of militaries, reforms of the intelligence sector, improving overall security policy coherence, and strengthening civilian control over police and militaries (OECD, 2004b; Smith, 2001). Though SSR was already underway in parts of the developing world in the 1990s (Jean, 2005), it was not until the United Kingdom's DFID began working on SSR in the late-nineties that the issue was more widely acknowledged as a priority by donors (Ball and Hendrickson, 2005; Brzoska, 2003; Jean, 2005; Smith, 2001).[1] In 2001 the DAC first began to focus on SSR as a priority, culminating in the DAC High Level Meeting of 2004 which yielded a donor statement on SSR and Development Assistance (OECD, 2004a, 2004b, 2004c). This consensus statement on development assistance and SSR was followed by a set of DAC Guidelines on how donors should best address SSR in their programming. Indeed, the aim agreed to by all DAC donors within these guidelines is to 'promote peace and security as fundamental pillars of development and poverty reduction' (OECD, 2005).

Alongside this SSR agenda emerged renewed calls for the development community to examine the impact of violent conflict on development efforts. Motivated by enlightened self-interest and collective security, this entails approaches to 'conflict sensitive development' and the mainstreaming of conflict analysis into aid programming and planning (UNDP, 2005). Approaches to collective security have led donor nations to not only support development in conflict situations, but also to integrate development activities into broader military and diplomatic efforts in states for post-conflict reconstruction and peacebuilding – Provincial Reconstruction Teams (PRTs) in Afghanistan are a prime example of this approach (Maloney, 2005). This whole-of-government approach to security involves not only donor agencies, but also militaries and ministries of foreign affairs, and has been lauded by the donor community's SSR agenda as the most effective way to address security issues in development (OECD, 2004b, 2005).

Security concerns have become an integral component of development assistance discourse in the twenty-first century and reflective of world cultural values shaped by international actors of the world polity – in this case, the UN and the OECD. With this crafting of an identifiable model of security and development in world society comes the diffusion and adoption of such a model by development assistance donors. The spread and institutionalization of security and development approaches among bilateral development assistance donors in recent years has been striking. Brown and Grävingholt's (2016) volume on the securitization of aid highlights this institutionalization process in at least seven of the DAC member countries, but the institutionalization of this model is further evident in the change in Official Development Assistance (ODA) funds dedicated to the security priority. The OECD DAC tracks annual aid flow data and categorizes aid flows to a range of sector codes. Following the 2004 DAC statement on SSR, the OECD aid statistics database began tracking aid flows dedicated to the broad sector code of 'Conflict, Peace, and Security'. The sharp increases in ODA dedicated to this priority are reflected in Figure 5.1 (total volume of security aid) and Figure 5.2 (security aid as percentage of total ODA). Both figures demonstrate that not only

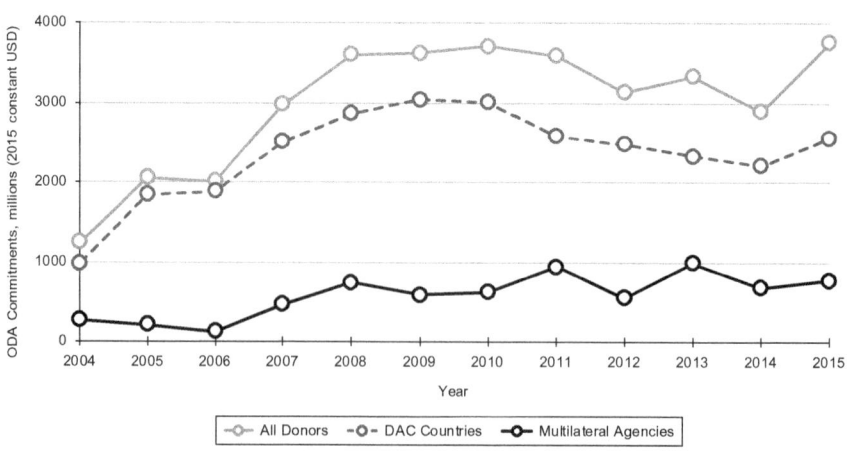

Figure 5.1 Total ODA commitments for 'conflict, peace, and security', 2004–2015
Source: https://stats.oecd.org

the OECD DAC donors, but also Multilateral donors (a category consisting of the World Bank, the IMF, all the regional development banks, and all the major UN agencies) experience a sharp jump in aid spending on the security issue in the years immediately following the DAC agreement. Accounting for inflation, total DAC aid in this sector nearly tripled from 984 million USD to more than 2.9 billion USD in the five-year period between 2004 and 2008, and averaged 2.6 billion USD between 2009 and 2015 (OECD, 2017). The multi-lateral donors experienced a similar increase of nearly 300% from 262 million USD to approximately 740 million USD in the same period between 2004 and 2008 (OECD, 2017). Not only are volumes of aid dedicated to the security priority increasing sharply, so is the overall share of total ODA dedicated to the issue. Figure 5.2 illustrates this increase, with the OECD DAC percentage of aid dedicated to security increasing more than doubling from 1.2% to just over 3% by 2009 and the multilateral donors' percentage of aid dedicated to security more than doubling between 2004 and 2008. In terms of both total volume of aid dedicated to security and the overall share of that aid as percentage of all aid, we see the sharpest increases in the 2004–2008 period, reflecting the institutionalization of the aid model across the donor commu-nity in this period. The consistency of aid flows to this sector in the years since reflect how it has been maintained as an aid priority by both bilateral and multilateral donors following the diffusion of security as an aid priority.

These aid flow figures do not reflect the nature of this institutionalization, but do provide a sense of the scope of the shift in donor priority. Although not all donors have integrated and implemented SSR or whole-of-government approaches as a mainstay of their development assistance programming,

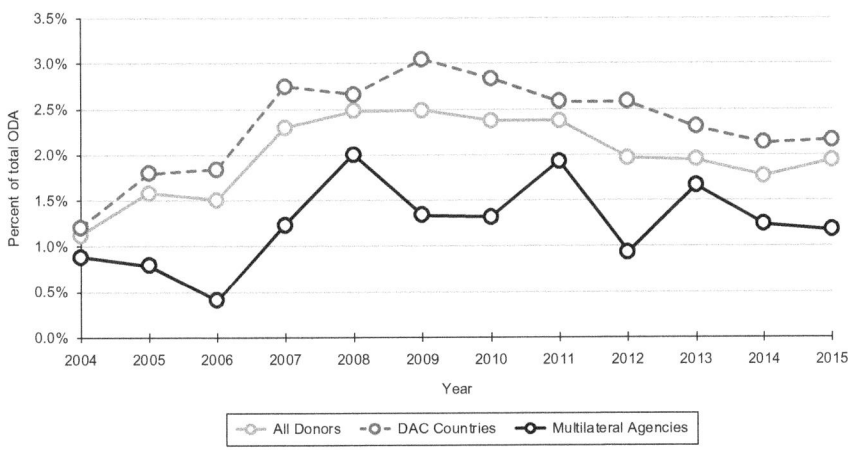

Figure 5.2 'Conflict, peace, and security' aid as percentage of total ODA, 2004–2015
Source: https://stats.oecd.org

different donor countries have adopted some emphasis on security and conflict in their development assistance, with many donor agencies at minimum adopting an agency policy on security/conflict and development (Brown and Grävingholt, 2016). It is this adoption, institutionalization, and refinement of the security and development model by donors that this chapter explains. How has world polity influence on donors functioned to encourage the spread of the security and development model commonly seen? What social processes work to mediate the spread of this model among donors? The next section addresses these questions after briefly examining how donors have institutionalized this model.

Donor approaches to security in development assistance

Bilateral aid agencies have integrated the SSR model into their programming in a number of ways. Three representative characteristics of this model that emerge in donor implementation include: (1) the adoption of an agency-level or corporate policy on security/conflict and development; (2) the creation of a targeted aid mechanism or unit within the donor agency addressing security and development; and (3) either programming in the SSR area, mainstreaming of conflict in development assistance programming, or adoption of whole-of-government approaches to SSR in post-conflict societies. All of these components are reflective of the security and development model outlined above, and are present in the DAC's 2005 guidelines on *Security Sector Reform and Governance* (OECD, 2005). In the case study reported below, these characteristics were employed as the framework for evaluating the institutionalization of the security and development model in each of the donor agencies considered. Before exploring the interview data from each case to examine the social processes at work in the diffusion and implementation of the model, it is necessary to first assess the three characteristics of the SSR model in each country.[2]

The Canadian International Development Agency (CIDA)

CIDA demonstrates two of the features of the SSR model outlined above. First, it had an apparatus for working on security and development initiatives. Second, CIDA has conducted programming in the SSR area and has taken part in whole-of-government approaches to security and development. CIDA does not show full adoption of the model in that it lacks a corporate level policy on security and development issues and it lacks a dedicated agency-level unit to address these issues at the corporate level (Swiss, 2016).

Despite having delivered aid in war-torn and post-conflict countries throughout much of its existence, CIDA did not have a specific policy position or apparatus to address conflict and development until 1996, when the government of Canada's Peacebuilding Initiative was created. Subsequently, CIDA formed its Peacebuilding Fund and corresponding Peacebuilding Unit in 1997 (Thibault, 2003). This fund allocated approximately 10 million CAD annually to fund programmes related to post-conflict peacebuilding – encompassing development programming that was focused on redeveloping areas of conflict and future conflict prevention. In 2006, the Peacebuilding Fund was dissolved and the former Peacebuilding Unit adopted a narrower perspective on peace and security issues that focuses mainly on issues of human rights in conflict situations.

This initiative was part of a broader Canadian government approach to peacebuilding; however, it never translated into a corporate level policy at CIDA. Indeed aside from the Peacebuilding Fund and Unit, the treatment of conflict, security and development at CIDA has been mostly informal. There is no specific unit for peace and security in the agency's policy group. There is no over-arching policy outlining CIDA's approach to security and development, although discussion with CIDA officials suggests that one could be under consideration. The lack of an overall corporate policy to address these issues leads CIDA to address the conflict and security issues primarily in response to recipient country situations which require it. This treatment of issues on a case-by-case basis dependent on country context has seen recent initiatives in Iraq, Afghanistan, Sudan, and Haiti as prominent examples of CIDA's work in conflict zones.

In many of these cases, CIDA's contribution is simply a smaller piece of a whole-of-government approach to failed and fragile states. CIDA's contribution to PRTs in Afghanistan is a primary example of this, where coordination with both the Department of Foreign Affairs and International Trade (DFAIT) and the Department of National Defence underlie CIDA's participation. In 2005, a new initiative with across-government involvement, located at and managed by DFAIT replaced the Canadian government's earlier peacebuilding initiative. The Stabilization and Reconstruction Task Force (START) and its corresponding Global Peace and Security Fund (GPSF) provide Canada's chief interface with the security and development agenda presently. The GPSF funded initiatives which directly support the SSR agenda, and extend even to fund initiatives involving military procurement in some cases (DFAIT, 2007). In this sense, DFAIT is addressing the 'hard' security topics as well as other issues of SSR, while CIDA has been focused on SSR through longer-term developmental and institution-building initiatives addressing the 'soft' side of security on a country-by-country basis.

The Swedish International Development Cooperation Agency (Sida)

Sida's adoption of a security and development approach demonstrates most of the characteristics of the model discussed above: a corporate policy; a security and development unit; and mainstreaming of conflict analysis in development assistance. The extent of the implementation of the mainstreaming initiatives is still undetermined, but Sida programming in conflict countries like Afghanistan and Iraq understandably addresses these issues as a primary concern. All of these features of Sida's approach to security suggest the implementation of a recognizable world polity model for security/conflict and development within the organization.

Sida began examining the nexus of security, conflict, and development in the late 1990s. The first policy to address this area arrived in 1999 as a result of growing awareness of Sida having to increasingly do two things: (1) deliver aid in areas embroiled in conflict or recovering from conflict; and (2) ensure that Swedish aid did not further contribute to conflict in these areas.

This first strategy discussed the importance to Sida of the 'do no harm' perspective on aid which had emerged following the Rwandan genocide in the early 1990s. This approach focuses on fungibility issues and tracking the use of aid funds, but also requires the analysis of conflict in an area to ensure that donor activities do not aggravate tensions or unintentionally align the donor with one party or another in an ongoing conflict. This 1999 effort to integrate a conflict perspective on Swedish aid was neither enthusiastically received nor implemented widely within the agency.

In the context of renewed international interest in security and development post-2001, security emerged as a central theme of promoting development in the 2003 Policy for Global Development (Government of Sweden, 2003). As a result of this greater awareness and engagement with the interaction of conflict and development, Sida formed a separate unit to address the issue in 2005. Instead of the earlier strategy where one officer authored a low-priority policy on conflict, the new Division for Peace and Security in Development Cooperation had five officers and a director working on the topic, and issued a more comprehensive policy on security and development in late 2005. In this policy Sida examines security and development as an issue to be considered in all programming because of the linkages between poverty and insecurity (Sida, 2005). The policy identifies three approaches to development cooperation: (1) risk awareness; (2) conflict sensitivity; and (3) promotion of peace and security. By adopting these three approaches, Sida intends to mainstream conflict analysis in all of its development programming, reflecting the international discourse on the subject crafted by the UN, DAC, and other international actors.

The United States Agency for International Development (USAID)

USAID demonstrates all three features of the SSR model outlined above: corporate policy on security/conflict and development; a unit within the agency addressing security and development; and both programming in the SSR area and adoption of whole-of-government approaches to SSR in conflict and post-conflict situations.

USAID has addressed conflict and development issues since the early 1990s, and some have argued that American aid has always been 'militarized' to achieve geostrategic aims (Spear, 2016). In a significant policy statement from 2002, *Foreign Aid in the National Interest: Promoting Freedom,*

Security, and Opportunity, conflict featured prominently as a main pillar of American development Assistance (USAID, 2002). At present they address security and development issues through several approaches. The primary channel is through their organizational unit and a corporate-level policy on Conflict Management and Mitigation (CMM) which is mainstreamed as a cross-cutting programme in the agency. The main focus of the CMM unit and policy is addressing issues of conflict prevention through assisting relevant country programme field offices to mainstream conflict issues into their pro-gramming (USAID, 2005). The CMM group is also responsible for managing USAID's relationship with the DAC CPDC Network, and plays a sometimes prominent role in the Network's activities.

The CMM policy also broadens USAID's approach to conflict beyond conflict prevention to include post-conflict reconstruction and SSR. The CMM unit and policy are thus very clear representations of the features of the prototypical model for donor approaches to conflict and insecurity in development assistance.

Aside from the CMM group, USAID also has an SSR advisor tasked with assisting USAID field offices and country programmes to develop specific SSR activities, as well as liaising with other government departments in the United States that have an interest and involvement in the SSR agenda. In this respect, USAID's work on conflict and insecurity is closely tied to the broader agenda of the US government. For instance, security features prominently within the Strategic Plan for the US State Department and USAID 2007–2012 (USAID and State Department, 2007). In addition, USAID's role in supporting American foreign policy on security also appears in the 2006 US *National Security Strategy* suggesting it will become more closely linked to the State Department to achieve these aims (United States Government, 2006). USAID's work on conflict is linked very closely to a whole-of-government approach to security and development. This approach was formalized further in 2009 with the issuing of a joint set of SSR guidelines by USAID and the Departments of State and Defense (USAID, 2009).

Policy isomorphism in security and development

The outlines of CIDA, Sida, and USAID above show some striking similari-ties of security/conflict and development approaches among donors: each has had a specific unit responsible for addressing security and conflict issues; each has made some effort to do SSR programming; each has either mainstreamed conflict or participated in whole-of-government approaches to security in recipient societies. Yet, as much as donors acknowledge the importance of the security and conflict issue in development assistance, the extent to which they implement policy and programming on the issue varies, showing diver-gence of implementation. Both Sida and USAID have dedicated policy units tasked with leading the organization on these issues, as well as corporate level policies that accord a priority to security not seen in CIDA and its lack of policy guidance or unit-based leadership on security. How CIDA addresses the security and conflict issue in its programming is shaped by the absence of an agency-wide policy strategy on the issue. Instead, the implementation of a security and conflict approach at CIDA is dominated by ad hoc application in countries where it is required, but a little focus on these issues in other cases. Both Sida and USAID have this same context-based implementation – with a greater effort to address these issues in specific post-conflict societies – but also have a corporate approach to the issue which makes it applicable potentially in all cases, mainstreaming conflict through the agencies' efforts. CIDA lacks this mainstreaming approach on conflict. This chapter contends that the contradiction of the consensus of donors on the priority of security in development assistance and the divergence in the extent to which a common approach to these issues is implemented is reflective of different social processes at work in each country's context.

Part of this difference can be accorded to the close link of the security and conflict issues to national interests in the foreign policy arena. Bilateral aid officials have seen as taboo all things military or defence related, but no longer. In the post-Cold War international security agenda and the recent focus on combating terror, development has been accorded the ability to help stem some aspects of insecurity (Ball and Hendrickson, 2005; Brzoska, 2003; Jean, 2005). At the same time, insecurity is seen as a major barrier to development. Failing or fragile states are therefore seen as a development assistance concern not only for the reasons of promoting human development, but also for stemming insecurity that has the potential to affect not only developing societies, but donor societies also. This notion of enlightened self-interest or collective security cannot be discounted as a key component of the renewed focus on security in the development assistance field. These motives bear consideration as the next section moves to the examination of data collected on this issue from interviews with aid agency officials and civil society representatives in each of the three case study countries.

Micro-level processes: influence on donors

The semi-structured interviews with aid agency officials and civil society representatives working on the security and conflict issues within the development assistance sector in each of the three case-study countries yielded comparable results regarding the factors which influence donors to adopt a conflict and security approach in development assistance.[3] Interviews were recorded, transcribed, and then coded for common themes and emerging similarities across the cases using ATLAS.ti qualitative data analysis software. Particular attention was paid to themes apparent in all three country cases and mentioned by multiple respondents in each country. Common themes and similarities among respondents were examined as markers of underlying social mechanisms and processes which could explain donor adoption of the global model of security and development. These processes and mechanisms, in keeping with the work of McAdam, Tarrow, and Tilly (2001), are those events that work in divergent contexts to change the relations between social actors in similar fashions. In this respect, the processes identified here are those which appear in each case to mediate the interface of donors and the world polity to affect the adoption of a security and development policy approach.

Analysis of the interview data identified two primary social processes at work in shaping the interface of donor agencies with world society and the resulting adoption, institutionalization, and refinement of a security and development model in their policy and programming. First, interview respondents reported common experiences of catalytic policy processes helping to shape a common agenda shared by donors and leading to adoption of common models of security and development. Second, respondents highlighted the important effect that the process of donor agencies asserting autonomy from foreign ministries and the rest of government had in mediating the extent of implementation of a common world polity approach related to security and development. Both of these processes account for the similarities and differences found between CIDA, Sida, and USAID in the security and development case and arguably these micro-level processes are critical factors in shaping the diffusion and institutionalization of other world society institutional models globally.

Catalytic policy processes

The first process identified by respondents can best be described as a catalytic policy process. This process entails an outside discussion or working group activity which drives the internal development of policy within a donor organization to meet a specific deadline or goal. For instance, work towards arriving at consensus on a set of guidelines, directives, or statement on a specific policy issue at an international conference or meeting. This process is considered catalytic when it is the primary mover of internal policy discussion or change. In the absence of such an outside process, the donor organization is unlikely to have a position or policy on a given issue. Because of the expectations that the country/organization will come to the international table with a defined position, the outside policy discussions catalyze internal policy development. This may lead to the organization undertaking work in new, previously untouched areas of policy priority. In such instances, the question of how dedicated or devoted an organization is to initially work in a particular policy area may be called into question, as the main motivation for beginning work on an issue may indeed be simply to have a place at the table amongst its peers, or to not be left behind in an emerging area of concern. This is not to say that afterwards, the result of an outside catalytic policy process cannot be strongly supported policy institutionalized within an organization. Indeed, an argument can be made that many new ideas may follow this trajectory within an organization if the driving forces behind them are mostly external to the organization.

In the aid sector, catalytic policy processes have a number of interna-tional venues from which to originate. Chief among these is the DAC, fol-lowed by both the UN and the World Bank as alternate points of catalysis. One Canadian respondent highlights the DAC's role in initiating policy discussion:

> The process itself is a great accoucheur [midwife]. It really helps the countries to actually make a position. Because the first positive impact is that as you reach a process, you suddenly realize that this is an issue which needs to be dealt with. So it forces you to think about your issue. But this is always done between policy branches. So the weakness of the DAC is that its work is not very visible. It's a highly specialized, close group. So generally, when the DAC takes a position and the min-ister agrees on the creation, it's then sent to the field and sent to the operational branches of the aid agencies and say, 'behold, we have now seen the light and this is the way you shall do it in future'. And this is how those shall do this now. And so because all the agencies suffer from the same problem, they don't, because of time pressures, have the time to actually make their position coming from the field of operations towards the policy branch, towards the DAC, so in that sense, the influ-ence comes afterwards because top-down says, 'this is the way you will be doing it'. So in that sense, the process is important because it gets the policy branches and high management align on a common approach and then it's directed towards the field.
>
> [October 18, 2006]

Describing the DAC process as a midwife when it comes to policy develop-ment is suggestive of how preparation for and participation in DAC discus-sions, meetings, and creation of policy guidelines and directives can in essence deliver a new policy position to an agency where it did not exist previously. In this respect, the DAC deliberations and preparation of standards for donors is viewed as catalytic in generating policy development and positions among donors.

Commenting on the influence of the DAC High Level Meeting declaration on Security Sector Reform from 2004, another Canadian respondent stated:

> I would say it has [influenced CIDA's policy], but I'm not sure it is so much the declaration itself as it is the process of preparing for the decla-ration. That we prepared a position for that, but we were working through these issues anyways. We ended up with the guidelines for CIDA, the best practices, and just generally how to approach these issues in CIDA and preparing for that, I think, benefited CIDA greatly, because we did not have our mind around what that looked like or what that should look like.
>
> [So without the knowledge that CIDA had to prepare for this process, CIDA probably wouldn't have been doing as much on the issue?]

I think we still would have been doing some things, but there wouldn't have been a driver. There wasn't a lever to say that you have to have this done by this time. And without those sort of external levers, it continues festering along for a while and there's no real demand internally to resolve it. So there's been lots of stuff for years on untying, but until they hit the lever of the DAC recommendation they didn't move on it.

[April 11, 2006]

The description of the DAC process as a lever on Canadian policy suggests the external influence of the process of contributing to the DAC declaration on security and development had on CIDA. Describing CIDA's participation in the DAC process as a 'driver' which pushed the agency beyond its lack of internal demand to resolve the issues, illustrates the view of this respondent on the DAC's catalytic role in the security sector question. Without the DAC recommendations in this area, the respondent perceived no 'movement' on the issue within CIDA.

When questioned about the DAC's role in shaping the Canadian approach to security and development, another respondent suggested that despite Canada's past work on peacebuilding from a human security perspective, the DAC could be seen to help push CIDA's focus on security and development from its past focus on peacebuilding to a perspective more akin to the DAC position on SSR:

[Would it be safe to say that there wasn't much movement on developing a Canadian position on these issues before they came before the DAC?]
Yeah. Well, my predecessors ...
[So there had been predecessors in that role at CIDA?]
There have been, had been called different things, had been under different titles, but there had been Canadians who had been working on [security issues] – because the peace building initiative had started earlier. So there had been a policy parallel to the peacebuilding programming and I had had a predecessor who had worked on it and they had worked on the first set of guidelines, but those were peacebuilding guidelines. You know, they were much more, they were focused ... The first set were focused on peace building and post-conflict reconstruction. The second set was looking more at conflict avoidance, and security sector reform and it was broadening the debate and digging down a bit more into lessons learned and more constructive guidelines and ...
[Ok. So there wasn't really any concrete Canadian position on the conflict and development issue? Before 9/11 pushed it to the agenda.]
No. There had been strong support for the guidelines and for peacebuilding and the peacebuilding initiative because Axworthy, while he was there had started the whole ... There was the, you know, the Human Security Fund and the Peacebuilding Fund and part of it was

Foreign Affairs, part of it CIDA and ... So certainly that had been the beginning, but it had been focused on certain types of programming and a certain part of the spectrum from you know, one end of peace to the other.

[So it would be safe to say that the DAC process, to some extent, drove Canada to develop more of a position on these issues?]

Yeah. Yeah.

[January 30, 2007]

This assertion that the DAC process was involved in shaping CIDA policy on the security and development issue lends support to the argument that donor participation in the DAC process of arriving at consensus on the security and development issue actually pushed donors to adopt positions simply so they would have something to bring to the table, and indeed so they could later be able to demonstrate that their new models for addressing security and development were in line with agreed upon international standards defined by the DAC.

An American respondent echoes this view on the DAC's catalytic role. Suggesting there was not an approach to security sector reform in USAID prior to the DAC declaration on the topic in 2004. Instead, the respondent suggests that the DAC guidance on security sector reform allowed for a number of diverse security initiatives throughout the agency to coalesce into a 'more comprehensive programme':

[So, I guess in the time that you've been with the agency – you're in a position which has interestingly enough formed by a reaction to the guidance from the DAC in 2004. In the time that you've been with the organization then, how have you seen the approach to security sector reform change within the agency?]

Well it's hard to say because there wasn't one beforehand. There were a number of different things and those things continue to exist. This programme is really to follow on with what had been a five-year programme, supported through a civil society group called the National Democratic Institute to look at civil military relations. So that was sort of the experience the agency had specifically in a related topic in this area, but obviously we all held a long, deep, history providing rule of law programmes that are related in conflict mitigation programmes which are related and it's important to reintegration part of DDR programme. So there were bits and pieces throughout the agency.

[And subsequent to the DAC guidance that has changed in what way?]

Well, it sort of coalesced into a more comprehensive programme.

[March 27, 2007]

In the view of this respondent, not only did the DAC declaration of April 2004 lead to this coalescing of a SSR programme at USAID, but it also was a direct contribution to the creation of a SSR advisor position within the agency in August of that year. This direct connection between DAC influence and agency reaction through implementing policy and assigning human resources to the issue demonstrates this catalytic role of the international declaration and the process involved in arriving at a consensus position among donors.

The implication here is that the DAC and its guidelines can act as a catalytic external influence because donors know that they will be held to account for their activities in newly emerging priority areas such as Security-Sector Reform. This expectation of being policed on adherence to new DAC standards may explain the reason that donors activate policy development in areas that the DAC deems relevant priorities. One Swedish respondent who had formerly been seconded to the DAC discussed its role in this regard by highlighting the tenuous connection between DAC policy guidelines and the eventual scrutiny being examined by other DAC members in the peer review process:

> Now the link between the policy development and the follow-up, that is peer reviews basically, is not clear. It might look so from the outside, but it's not a clear structure on how you're going to monitor the guidelines and the peer reviews. But you will find, say, in the last eight reviews, that [...] the [DAC] secretariat has tried to cover peace and security issues in a [...] systematic way.
>
> [September 13, 2006]

Despite the absence of a 'clear' link, this respondent does highlight a definite relationship between the DAC's priority setting and the policing of these priorities among donors. Where the peace and security issue quickly emerged in the DAC peer reviews to which the respondent was exposed in his time at the DAC. The catalytic process of DAC participation for donors thus appears to be inspired by a notional expectation that donors will be scrutinized for their follow-up on specific issues of importance to the DAC.

The same Swedish respondent hinted at how some of this catalytic process of participation within the DAC might work, specifically by describing the role of individual experts participating on the behalf of donors in DAC working groups like the Conflict, Peace, and Development Cooperation network:

> It was also interesting to see how, sort of CPDC, has a lot of under groups formed around specific issues such as evaluation or whatever and what the role of the donors are there. That would give you a hint on how you think you actually influence this, because the dilemma in these groups – this is just my own position – is that some people get engaged in this [and] it becomes their own sort of *raison d'être*, and a group can sort of have a life of its own almost, and there is no clear end date, what are you supposed to deliver? There is also sort of, an over, I don't know, sometimes we over-emphasize the impact of results and best practice and so on. So

> I might contradict myself sometimes here, but in a way, you can view the process itself as having the interactions among the donors as really that's where you pursue the agenda.
>
> [September 13, 2006]

Suggesting that individual participants in the DAC groups have an independence and latitude to pursue issues that they take on at their own accord is reflective of the some form of bureaucratic entrepreneurialism. Still, this respondent views the process of the interactions between the donors within the DAC venue as the chief area in which 'you pursue the agenda' or set priorities for the donor community.

This process of networking on the stage within international organizations is a key component of the catalytic policy process. This gathering of donor experts coalescing around security and conflict issues under DAC auspices closely resembles the consensus-building role played by epistemic communities identified in earlier literature on transnational policy formation (Haas, 1992; Kogut and Macpherson, 2008). Indeed, such networks of experts and their joint work towards consensus positions is indicative of the role of what Babb (2001) calls 'expert-isomorphism' within the catalytic policy process. Donor representatives coming together within the DAC context, being forced to formulate legitimate and acceptable positions to share with their expert peers, encourages those experts to reshape their specific agency's policy on conflict and security to resemble the agreed principles developed within the transnational epistemic community of donor experts. Another Swedish respondent highlighted the importance of Sida participation in DAC networks and working groups, suggesting they have a noticeable influence on Sida policy in areas like poverty reduction and security:

> Yes, I would say very influential really. We just had a meeting last week, last Friday with the Minister of Foreign Affairs, with all the people in DAC and various DAC networks and working groups and ah, a lot of people. And in some of these groups Sida in Sweden is very active. Even we chair, for example we are chairing the evaluation network and we will also be a chair of the working party of aid effectiveness from now. So and in some other groups we are very active.
>
> [How has that translated into changes in Sida policy itself? Or has it?]
>
> Yeah, it has been very influential. Like one example I can give is on the poverty. We used to be very active in the poverty network that presented guidelines on poverty reduction. These were very influential when Sida prepared its own strategy or what you call it, prospectus on poverty. That is just one example […]. For example, we had a new policy on Conflict, Peace and Development. I think that is also very influenced by the DAC working group. And many and others [issues] as well.
>
> [September 11, 2006]

Despite North/South inequality in the level of embeddedness of states in the international network of governmental and non-governmental organizations that compose world society (Beckfield, 2003), the influence of these organizations on nation-state actors have been highlighted repeatedly in the literature (Boli and Thomas, 1999; Meyer et al., 1997). The evidence offered by the interview responses in this book's case countries helps to illuminate more deeply how this influence functions. The role of catalytic policy processes initiated within the DAC venue appears to be a powerful driver of policy development and adoption within the three donors examined here. Various mechanisms operate within this catalytic process including bureaucratic entrepreneurialism, networking, and both standards setting and policing. All of these mechanisms concatenate into a process which 'kick-starts' donors to initiate new or revise existing policy positions on the security and development issue to fall in line with international standards regardless of existing domestic wherewithal or priority attached to the issue. This process is a participatory one, in which donors actively shape the international agenda at the same time as they develop domestic responses and implementation plans to meet it. As noted earlier, the initiatives of the United Kingdom's Department for International Development to place the security sector reform issue on the DAC agenda began overall donor engagement with this issue (Ball and Hendrickson, 2005; Brzoska, 2003). The DAC, therefore, is not simply an external force, a *deus ex machina* acting on donors, but instead is an interactive venue where donors indeed establish the external influences which then come to shape their own policy positions on the security and development issue.

Decoupling and autonomy from rest of government

Discussion of the security and development approach of aid agencies with interview respondents, the second process that emerged in the data was the nature of the agency's relationship to the rest of the government, especially the ministry of foreign affairs. Respondents identified issues related to the relative autonomy that the donor agency in their country had from the rest of government. The level of autonomy from rest of government refers to the nature of the relationship between the bilateral donor arm of a state and the government apparatus. Part of this is owing to a question of donor agency structure: Is the donor a sub-unit of the Ministry of Foreign Affairs (MFA) or is it an arm's-length agency reporting to its own minister or agency head? Degrees of structural autonomy fill the continuum between these two extremes. This chapter argues that if a donor agency is less autonomous, its policy objectives and aid priorities are more likely to be motivated by national interests of the donor rather than broader humanitarian concerns of development. Conversely, the more autonomous the donor agency, the more likely its motivations and priorities are to be motivated by more altruistic humanitarian interests. This opposition of these two motivations was present in discussing the security issue with many of the study's respondents and reflects the decades-old debate in the literature pitting self-interest against humanitarianism as the competing motivations of aid. It stands to reason, therefore that autonomy from the rest of government can fluctuate depending on the policy issue: the more altruistic the issue, the greater the autonomy of the aid agency; the more politically sensitive or pertinent to national interests an issue, the less the autonomy of the donor agency. The degree of autonomy is constantly under negotiation and in flux depending on the topic at hand, and underlines the frequently referred to conflict that tends to exist between aid agencies and MFAs or other government departments reported in many countries. In the event that a world cultural model aligns more closely with national interest of the state/society rather than global humanitarian aims, the degree of autonomy from the rest of government will influence the tightness of coupling of implementation of the model to the model specifications. This process of donors exercising varying levels of autonomy can explain the more tightly coupled implementation seen in the Sida and USAID cases, as well as account for the apparent decoupling evident in the case of CIDA.

When respondents were asked about the relationship between the donor agency and the respective foreign ministry regarding security and development issues, respondents highlighted the delicate balance that existed in managing the relationship. When asked about USAID's relationship to the State Department on this issue, one respondent stated:

> I think there are times where the development agency and the ministry of foreign affairs are closer together and farther apart and that tends to be cyclical and we are at the point in the cycle where we are much closer together and in fact, all foreign assistance now is being reorganized via our Administrator who is now dual-hatted as the Deputy Secretary of State. [...] At the moment, there's quite a bit of collaboration.
>
> [March 27, 2007]

This closer collaboration and the dual role for the USAID administrator were all relatively recent developments. The respondent continued:

> This is a tricky topic because the way the US security assistance in is generally delivered in a way that creates operational partners to advance US interests. Security Sector Reform and security programming from a development perspective is interested in operational capability but really more so in developing host nation capacity to make decisions about their own security. So those two things are sometimes at odds and sometimes they are complementary. What our approach has been to point out that more often than not, they are complementary and that all of the operational training you can give, won't be sustainable unless it's done in line with the host nation's requirement and needs.
>
> [March 27, 2007]

These competing approaches highlight the tendency of the donor to approach security sector reform from the perspective of advancing recipient country interests, while broader security interests of the US government may or may not be complementary.

These competing motivations highlight the tensions surrounding donor autonomy from the rest of government in the security and development area. Indeed, in the US case, the lack of donor agency autonomy from the State Department leads to implementation of a security and development approach which is at the basic level vested with US national security interests. When questioned about which of these competing interests usually dominated, the same respondent suggested:

> I guess national security interests always win. I suppose that it does come down to a case-by-case basis, but you know, given the legislative limitations and the different mandates of the actors on the donor side, responsible for providing related programming, you can have programmes going on at the same time. I mean what we're working towards in our programme is taking a comprehensive approach, you know, [starting] at the assessment through programme design and delivery through monitoring and evaluation, but that's a long way off. In the military parlance of crawl, walk, run … we're crawling.
>
> [March 27, 2007]

This comprehensive approach the respondent addresses is a reference to the whole-of-government type of approach that is espoused in the world polity models discussed earlier in this chapter. The USAID approach to security and development is therefore very heavily influenced by the State Department, the Department of Defense, and other interests in the US government, and within such influence, very closely reflects the world model expectations set for donors. The relative lack of autonomy of USAID from the State Department, in this case, ensures adherence to a world polity model that very closely aligns with US national security interests.

The autonomy of the donor agency is also raised by a Swedish respondent, suggesting that it is the nature of the Swedish system to have the decisions made by the MFA while expecting Sida to dutifully implement them:

> In a context like the Swedish where you have a Ministry of Foreign Affairs dealing with sort of policy issues and implementation should in theory be carried out by a government office such as Sida, there is also that divide. There's been a lot of cooperation in this field, but there's also been some disconnects sometimes. That can sometimes explain why it takes some time to implement policies. The logic in the Swedish system is rather complex, it goes back a couple hundred years, about the theory that the ministry should be small and focus on instructions for the implementing agencies, who should then carry out, and they should be quite

independent. But in the role of Sida, it's been slightly complicated sometimes. I don't want to overemphasize this, but in an area like this [secu-
rity] and human rights, it's very hard to draw the line what's clear foreign
policy and its implementation.

[September 13, 2006]

As the implementing agency, Sida is deemed by this respondent to be quite
independent, but rather than creating it s own policy and priorities, it is a
policy-receiving organization much like USAID. In this respect, the MFA
plays an important role in the Swedish system to help set policy for the development assistance agency. This same respondent highlighted this close relationship in discussing the first Sida policy on conflict and development:

[T]he first policy was also sort of a platform for the cooperation between
Ministry of Foreign Affairs and Sida in this field. It provided input to
what the Ministry then picked up as the policy area which they took forward into the DAC when [it] set up the first task force [on Conflict, Peace,
and Development Cooperation] …

[September 13, 2006]

In the Swedish case, therefore, the role of the MFA in setting policy had
a major influence on the nature of the Sida policy on conflict. Indeed, the
main Swedish representative at the time on the DAC Conflict, Peace, and
Development Cooperation was an officer of the MFA and not a Sida representative – highlighting the important role of the MFA in contributing to
policy development in this area. This relationship still exists in the Swedish
case, and Sida's Peace and Security group view their policy mandate as stemming not only from the Sida policy on those issues, but also more broadly
with how the security and development issue have been framed in the 2003
Policy for Global Development.

A Canadian respondent echoed the importance of CIDA's autonomy from
the Department of Foreign Affairs in shaping the response to security and
development:

… I think the difference was that human security came through as more
of a Foreign Affairs, purely diplomatic initiative, it wasn't viewed as
responding to development issues, it was viewed as an external view from
a Foreign Affairs type of perspective on sort of what needed to be done,
but it wasn't bottom up, participatory, democratic, developmentally oriented etc. For the security stuff, because there is a broader discussion, and
it wasn't so much of a unilateral push, there were a lot more pieces that
came into it. And the question in my view as they were going through it
was: 'OK, we need to do more on security. The question is how incremen-
tal we need to be in what we're doing? We need to tie it to development
because we know that even if we do all this conflict prevention stuff it's

got to be tied to long-term development to be sustainable. Our sustain-ability requires the conflict prevention, and basically the peace is a pre-cursor to continuing.' Anyway, so I think there was a lot more interest, and some of that was just the international discussions that were going on, and some of the failures of states in the 1990s that you started to see a little bit better example that unless you had the two together you were not going to make progress.

[April 11, 2006]

According to this respondent, in the Canadian case the relative autonomy CIDA has from the Department of Foreign Affairs and International Trade (Pratt, 1994) allowed the organization to sidestep the human security agenda to some extent because it was perceived as not having a developmental orienta-tion. At the same time, when the move to address more conventional security issues rose to prominence on the international agenda, this evolution of secu-rity and development concerns had greater appeal to certain groups within CIDA as it was not branded as a Foreign Affairs initiative in the early stages.

Another respondent highlighted how the divergent and competing inter-ests of different government departments influenced Canadian participation in the international discussions at the DAC on security, development, and ODA (Official Development Assistance):

You know, you had the development view and then you had a foreign pol-icy view – DND [Department of National Defence] weren't real players, but there were parts of Foreign Affairs who definitely wanted to see ODA opened up so that some of these peacekeeping/peacebuilding activities would be affordable. And so you have the spectrum and it took a while. [...] It was a compromise and we were certainly in an awkward position because [Canada] was chairing and so [Canada] had to remain somewhat neutral, but then we had Canadians at the flag and we had that dynamic between CIDA and Foreign Affairs and CIDA had the lead on Foreign Affairs. So there was a bit of an internal pushing and shoving about com-ing up with a Canadian position. But it was a healthy debate and I think we ended up with a common position because of it.

[January 30, 2007]

These divergent views and the 'pushing and shoving' involved in coming up with a Canadian position, demonstrate the relative autonomy of CIDA on these issues in contrast to USAID and Sida. That CIDA is at liberty to have a different viewpoint than DFAIT and DND illustrates that its autonomy from the rest of government in this case has actually enabled it to adopt a position which, in fact, demonstrates a diminished level of implementa-tion of the security and development model outlined earlier in this chapter. Without DFAIT pushing CIDA to adopt a strong system to implement the SSR agenda and other conflict and development issues, CIDA has instead

taken an approach to the issue which is only loosely coupled to the principles they agreed to in the donor statement from the 2004 DAC High Level
Meeting. One respondent suggested that CIDA had not taken these issues
very seriously, and attributed this partially to the absence of DFAIT or other
government department leadership on the issue, as well as the general lack of
coordination between departments at the more senior level:

> In sum, I don't believe that we've taken the DAC guidance in this area
> very seriously even though we've participated in its development and
> a lot of that – some of that – may be to do internally. It also has to
> do with the fact that other government departments really don't have a
> strong sense of what this DAC guidance is all about. I don't think the
> Department of Foreign Affairs fully, you know, [there's] a lot of rotation
> through there. You don't have a lot of continuity and certainly I don't
> believe the central agencies are fully up to speed on what the content of
> some of this stuff is and there's only so many hours in the day. I've tried
> to kind of reach out and talk to people a little bit more, but the fora for
> these kind of things – it happens at the very senior levels of government,
> at the deputy minister level, maybe even occasionally at the DG level. It
> doesn't actually happen and it's difficult to spontaneously get it going at
> the analyst level and it's because we're tasked by other people to do other
> things. Also, we don't really have the authority to convene anything that
> has any kind of weight.
>
> [February 6, 2007]

Identifying the frustrations that can face the donor agency analyst who does
not feel senior management is leading on an issue, this respondent highlights the difficulties of managing the relationship with other government
departments. This respondent's frustrations with the inability to achieve
something that 'has any kind of weight' in the security and development
area at CIDA is reflective of CIDA's indifferent treatment of the issue at the
corporate level and the subsequent decoupling of CIDA's implementation
from the intent of the SSR model. Indeed, in Canada, DFAIT can arguably be seen to lead activity on the security and development issue – especially the SSR issue – through newly formed funds and organizational units
within that Department. In this sense, CIDA's relative autonomy from the
rest of government and DFAIT has allowed its senior management to avoid
implementation of a rigorous approach to security and development at the
same time that DFAIT has been very active in SSR as a means of furthering
Canadian interests. In light of this autonomy, it is only in the very pressing or high profile country-by-country cases where CIDA's autonomy from
DFAIT is diminished and a more comprehensive approach to security and
development issues is taken – something demonstrated in recent research on
CIDA's experience with programming in Afghanistan (Brown, 2008). Where
CIDA's autonomy is reduced, the implementation of the model becomes

more closely coupled to the global norms and expectations of the donor community around the SSR priority.

Another respondent suggested reluctance by CIDA to enter into the SSR programming in an integrated fashion, as there is a perception that it runs contrary to CIDA's culture of developmentalism, and as such, much of the work on this in the Canadian system has fallen to DFAIT:

> In terms of Canada, security system reform is very much right now on the Foreign Affairs side of things and they have responsibility for advancing that area with the creation of START and the Global Peace and Security Fund. It has not, as I said, traditionally been part of the CIDA culture and so often when they [CIDA] talk about security, they talk about justice. [...] We've done those kinds of things, but we haven't we haven't, as I said, integrated this.
>
> [February 6, 2007]

From this perspective, CIDA has had the latitude to not integrate SSR concerns intensively into its programming and policy, and from a broader Canadian perspective this has been sufficient to meet international expectations on Canada, as DFAIT has undertaken SSR work in a more formal manner. CIDA's autonomy from DFAIT in this regard has contributed to the decoupling of Canadian positions at the DAC from the actual implementation of work in the same area.

Autonomy from the rest of government, and the respective ministries of foreign affairs, appears to have played a significant role in all three cases in determining the extent of the implementation – or degree of decoupling – of a recognizable world polity security and development model in each country. The lesser autonomy of the donor agency in both Sweden and the United States yielded a more effective and tightly coupled application of the security and development model set forth in the DAC guidelines on the subject, whereas CIDA's relative autonomy from DFAIT and the rest of the Canadian government allowed CIDA to proceed with a much less intensive, less comprehensive, and decoupled treatment of the issue within its overall policy and programming frameworks. The ability to exercise greater autonomy from the rest of government on these issues in the Canadian case effectively encouraged a decoupling of policy from practice. Canada did support and agree to the international declarations made at the DAC and contributed to the guidelines that subsequently followed, yet CIDA has not taken a strong stance on these issues internally. DFAIT has instead taken the lead on SSR issues and, despite not being a traditional aid implementing agency, is funding most Canadian programming in this area.

Greater autonomy from the MFA and rest of government appears in the cases examined here permit a donor agency to deviate from a world polity model of development assistance that may be more in line with national interests rather than developmental or humanitarian concerns.[4] This suggests the need to examine this process in the context of other priorities that are fundamentally more humanitarian in nature and less directly linked to national interests. If, for instance, we consider the priority of gender and development examined in the previous chapters, this process of asserting autonomy might also be seen to function as expected. CIDA's greater autonomy allows for a more liberal application of gender and development models, whereas USAID's lesser autonomy inhibits its approaches to gender. Sida, in contrast, is encouraged to pursue the gender and development specifically because of its lesser autonomy and the key place of gender equality values in Swedish public policy. This suggests that a more thorough exploration of how these processes work is merited in future research.

Security sector reform, aid, and micro-level processes

This chapter's comparative case study of security and development models shows that there are common social processes which account for the striking similarities in the application of these models in each donor agency. Simultaneously, these processes can account for the distinct differences demonstrated among the three donors. Both the catalytic policy processes inspired by international activities within the DAC and the process of asserting agency autonomy from national governments shape how specific donors have taken up the recent move towards security sector reform and mainstreaming a security and development approach in development assistance. Like the previous chapter, the case study above highlights important micro-level processes which explain the international influences of the World Society on nation-state institutional and policy models – especially in the aid sector. The presence of catalytic events and declarations or the mediating process of the internal autonomy of nation-state actors from the rest of government both become significant explanatory processes to consider when discerning the influence of world polity models on independent states.

The processes identified in this chapter in combination with those found in Chapter 5, are significant additions to world polity explanations of the spread and adoption of common policies and institutional frameworks among nation-states. Though not exhaustive in their explanation of the phenomenon of policy isomorphism among aid donors, these processes play a key role in the interface of world society and the nation-state leading to greater uniformity among states. The processes identified arguably have the potential to apply beyond the aid sector to more broadly explain homogeneity of nation-state policies and institutions in other sectors – a matter for future research into this area. Within this broader context, future researchers might address whether some countries more easily influenced via these processes than others, examining the permeability of various countries to world society influence. In addition, these processes raise concerns about the nature of the relationship between world society and the nation-state. This relationship is not as clearly demarcated as past research might suggest. Indeed, delineating between world society and nation-state becomes increasingly difficult when one considers inter-governmental bodies and their role in the World Society. The OECD DAC under consideration in this study is a prime example where disentangling what is world society and what is nation-state agency becomes difficult, and requires further investigation. Extending research on the world polity in these directions would surely unearth other social processes implicated in how world society influences the nation-state, organizations, and individuals, and perhaps provide more insight into how nation-states, organizations, and individuals iteratively influence world society. In Part III of the book these issues are investigated in greater depth, outlining the implications of the findings from Part II for both the understanding of world society influence on states and the nature of the globalization of foreign aid.

Notes

1 Some might be surprised that it was not the United States who instigated the adoption of the SSR agenda, especially given the context of the Bush Doctrine and the rise of the post-2001 'Global War on Terror'. Instead, the research literature refers to the critical role played by the UK in placing SSR on the donor agenda. An influential and innovative donor, the UK's DFID was seen as the agency spearheading donor convergence around SSR. Although the United States was the largest donor by volume of aid dollars and had a longer history of engagement on security programming than some other donors, they were not perceived by the donor community as the prime movers behind this shift in the global aid policy agenda.
2 The summaries that follow highlight the situation as of early 2008 for each donor.
3 See the interview schedule in the book's Methodological Appendix.
4 An interesting contradiction to this finding that must be acknowledged here is that in the case of the United Kingdom's Department for International Development (DFID), its general autonomy was likely responsible for the UK taking a vanguard role in pioneering the integration of SSR into British aid programming. In this respect, the relative autonomy of DFID would appear to enable innovation around engaging on an issue that, at the time, was unconventional for aid donors to address and more closely reflected national security interests.

References

Andersen, R. (2000). How Multilateral Development Assistance Triggered the Conflict in Rwanda. *Third World Quarterly*, 21(3), 441–456.

Babb, S. L. (2001). *Managing Mexico: Economists from Nationalism to Neoliberalism*. Princeton, NJ: Princeton University Press.

Ball, N., & Hendrickson, D. (2009). *Trends in Security Sector Reform (SSR): Policy, Practice and Research.*, CSDG Papers, No.20, London: King's College London.

Beckfield, J. (2003). Inequality in the World Polity: The Structure of International Organization. *American Sociological Review*, 68(3), 401–424.

Boli, J., & Thomas, G. M. (1999). *Constructing World Culture: International Nongovernmental Organizations Since 1875*. Stanford, CA: Stanford University Press.

Brown, S. (2008). CIDA Under the Gun. In J. Daudelin & D. Schwanen (Eds.), *Canada Among Nations 2007: What Room to Manoeuvre?* (pp. 91–107). Montreal: McGill-Queen's University Press.

Brown, S., & Grävingholt, J. (2016). Security, Development and the Securitization of Foreign Aid. In S. Brown & J. Grävingholt (Eds.), *The Securitization of Foreign Aid* (pp. 1–17). Basingstoke: Palgrave Macmillan.

Brzoska, M. (2003). *Development Donors and the Concept of Security Sector Reform*: Geneva Centre for the Democratic Control of Armed Forces.

DFAIT. (2007, December 10, 2007). The Global Peace and Security Program (GPSP). Retrieved from www.dfait-maeci.gc.ca/foreign_policy/start/start_GPSP-en.asp

Duffield, M. (2001). *Global Governance and the New Wars: The Merging of Development and Security*. New York: Zed Books.

Duffield, M. (2007). *Development, Security and Unending War: Governing the World of Peoples*. Cambridge: Polity.

Finnemore, M. (1996). Norms, Culture, and World Politics: Insights from Sociology's Institutionalism. *International Organization*, 50(2), 325–347.

Government of Sweden. 2003. Shared Responsibility: Sweden's Policy for Global Development, Gov. Bill 2002/03: 122 (2003).

Haas, P. M. (1992). Introduction: Epistemic Communities and International Policy Coordination. *International Organization*, 46(01), 1–35.

Holsti, K. J. (1996). *The State, War, and the State of War*. Cambridge; New York, N.Y.: Cambridge University Press.

Jackson, R., & Rosberg, C. (1982). Why Africa's Weak States Persist. *World Politics*, 35(1), 1–24.

Jean, S. (2005). Security-Sector Reform and Development: An African Perspective. *Security Dialogue*, 36(2), 249–253. doi:10.1177/0967010605054652

Jepperson, R. L., Wendt, A., & Katzenstein, P. J. (1996). Norms, Identity, and Culture in National Security. In P. J. Katzenstein (Ed.), *The Culture of National Security: Norms and Identity in World Politics* (pp. 33–75). New York: Columbia University Press.

Keck, M. E., & Sikkink, K. (1998). *Activists Beyond Borders: Advocacy Networks in International Politics*. Ithaca, N.Y.: Cornell University Press.

Kim, Y. S., Jang, Y. S., & Hwang, H. (2002). Structural Expansion and the Cost of Global Isomorphism: A Cross-National Study of Ministerial Structure, 1950–1990. *International Sociology*, 17(4), 481–503.

King, G., & Murray, C. J. L. (2002). Rethinking Human Security. *Political Science Quarterly*, 116(4), 585–610.

Kogut, B., & Macpherson, J. M. (2008). The Decision to Privatize: Economists and the Constructions of Ideas and Policies. In B. A. Simmons, F. Dobbin, & G. Garrett (Eds.), *The Global Diffusion of Markets and Democracy* (pp. 104–140). Cambridge: Cambridge University Press.

Lechner, F. J., & Boli, J. (2005). *World Culture: Origins and Consequences*. London: Blackwell.

Maloney, S. M. (2005). From Kabul to Konduz: Lessons for Canadian Reconstruction of Afghanistan. *Policy Options* (May 2005), 57–62.

McAdam, D., Tarrow, S. G., & Tilly, C. (2001). *Dynamics of Contention*. Cambridge, U.K.; New York: Cambridge University Press.

Meyer, J. W. (2007). Globalization: Theory and Trends. *International Journal of Comparative Sociology*, 48(4), 261–273. doi:10.1177/0020715207079529

Meyer, J. W., Boli, J., Thomas, G. M., & Ramirez, F. O. (1997). World Society and the Nation-state. *The American Journal of Sociology*, 103(1), 144–181.

Migdal, J. S. (1988). *Strong Societies and Weak States: State-society Relations and State Capabilities in the Third World*. Princeton, N.J.: Princeton University Press.

Nef, J. (1999). *Human Security and Mutual Vulnerability: The Global Political Economy of Development and Underdevelopment*. Ottawa: International Development Research Centre.

OECD. (2004a). Development Assistance Committee High Level Meeting: 15–16 April 2004. Retrieved from www.oecd.org/document/9/0,2340,en_2649_34567_31540297_1_1_1_1,00.html

OECD. (2004b). Security System Reform and Governance: Policy and Good Practice. Retrieved from www.oecd.org/dataoecd/40/58/31526562.pdf

OECD. (2004c). Policy Brief: Security Sector Reform and Governance – Policy and Good Practice. *OECD Observer*. Retrieved from www.oecd.org/dataoecd/20/47/31642508.pdf

OECD. (2005). *Security Sector Reform and Governance*. Retrieved from Paris: www.oecd.org/dataoecd/8/39/31785288.pdf

OECD. (2005). *Security Sector Reform and Governance*. Retrieved from Paris: www.oecd.org/dataoecd/8/39/31785288.pdf

OECD. (2017) *Query Wizard for International Development Statistics*. https://stats.oecd.org/qwids/

Paris, R. (2001). Human Security: Paradigm Shift or Hot Air? *International Security*, 26(2), 87–102.

Pratt, C. (1994). Canadian Development Assistance: A Profile. In C. Pratt (Ed.), *Canadian International Development Assistance Policies: An Appraisal* (pp. 3–24). Montreal: McGill-Queen's University Press.

Sida. (2005). *Promoting Peace and Security Through Development Cooperation*. Sida.

Smith, C. (2001). Security-sector Reform: Development Breakthrough or Institutional Engineering? *Conflict, Security & Development*, 1(1), 5–20.

Spear, J. (2016). The Militarization of United States Foreign Aid. In S. Brown & J. Grävingholt (Eds.), *The Securitization of Foreign Aid* (pp. 18–41). Basingstoke, UK: Palgrave Macmillan.

Swiss, L. (2016). Space for Gender Equality in the Security and Development Agenda? Insights from Three Donors. In S. Brown & J. Grävingholt (Eds.), *The Securitization of Foreign Aid* (pp. 188–211). Basingstoke, UK: Palgrave Macmillan.

Thibault, P. (2003). CIDA's Approach to Peacebuilding. Retrieved from www.humansecurity.info/sites/cchs/files/pdfs/Consultation%20Papers/thibault_-_pdf.pdf

UNDP, United Nations Development Programme. (1994). *Human Development Report 1994: New Dimensions of Human Security*. Retrieved from New York City:

UNDP, United Nations Development Programme. (2005). *Human Development Report 2005: International Cooperation at a Crossroads: Aid, Trade and Security in an Unequal World*. Retrieved from New York City:

United States Government. (2006). *National Security Strategy*. United States Government.

USAID. (2002). *Foreign Aid in the National Interest: Promoting Freedom, Security, and Opportunity*.

USAID. (2005). *Conflict Mitigation and Management Policy*.

USAID. (2009). *Security Sector Reform*. Retrieved from www.state.gov/documents/organization/115810.pdf

USAID & State Department. (2007). *Strategic Plan Fiscal Years 2007–2012: Transformational Diplomacy*.

Uvin, P. (1998). *Aiding Violence: The Development Enterprise in Rwanda*. London: Kumarian Press.

Uvin, P. (1999). Development Aid and Structural Violence: The Case of Rwanda. *Development*, 42(3), 49–56.

Part III
Globalization's influence on aid agencies

6 Processes of globalization
Linking micro and macro

So far, I have identified five main processes of globalization and the many mechanisms of which they consist. The cases examined in the previous section clearly illustrate these micro-level social processes at work in mediating the interface of the nation-state with world society and facilitating the transfer of development assistance policy models to donor agencies. These processes are implicated in each of the case study countries considered, but to varying degrees. In this respect, the processes identified as factors in shaping world polity model adoption are neither exclusive nor exhaustive explanations of how world society influences the nation-state at the micro-level. Instead, they each serve key functions in translating world polity models into domestic agendas and, this chapter will contend, make significant progress in filling the gaps identified in Chapter 2's discussion of world polity explanations of globalization. These processes explain why aid donors from diverse domestic contexts settle on relatively similar policies and institutions, and arguably can be expected to operate in a similar manner when examined in other cases of policy isomorphism. This chapter aims to examine these processes more closely in the context of the gender and security case studies from Part II of the book, identify the mechanisms that compose them, and compare how they operated in each of the three case study countries and in the context of their development assistance sectors. From this examination, this chapter builds towards generalizing about the function of these – and other – micro-level social processes as the missing component in world polity/world society explanations of the diffusion of policy models which promote globalization and uniformity among nation-states.

Gaps in world society explanations of diffusion and uniformity

Many of the shortcomings of world polity theory research stem from a lack of depth in the explanation of how world society affects its constituent states, organizations, and individuals. This rests in part on the tendency in the literature to opt for macro-level cross-national quantitative analysis as the method of choice. In this way, a great amount of evidence illustrates the correlation between policy and institutional model adoption and a number of world society factors, including membership in international organizations, the timing of international conferences, and the actions of other nation-states (Berkovitch 1999a; Boli and Thomas 1997; Boli and Thomas 1999; Cole 2005, 2013; Drori 2007; Drori, Meyer, and Hwang 2006; Frank, Hironaka, and Schofer 2000; Frank, Longhofer, and Schofer 2007; Hironaka 2002; Jang 2003; Meyer 2007; Meyer, Frank, et al. 1997; Ramirez and McEneaney 1997; Ramirez, Soysal, and Shanahan 1997; Swiss 2009, 2012). What is missing in the existing explanations of world polity influence on diffusion and global uniformity is therefore a deeper understanding of how this influence occurs. The lack of focus on the individual agency and experience of the persons involved in these governments and organizations overlooks the active agency of the individual and groups on the adoption of these world polity models.

The premise of this book is that to expand the explanatory power of world polity theory we must examine micro-level processes in tandem with the conventional macro-level explanations. The theoretical innovation forwarded by this book is that this linking of macro and micro can most easily be achieved by taking inspiration from literature on the social processes and mechanisms at work in the contentious politics of social movements (McAdam, Tarrow, and Tilly 2001; Tarrow 2005). Though criticized for being overly simplistic and descriptive rather than explanatory (Welskopp 2004; Simeon 2004; Rule 2004; Kjeldstadli 2004), the present study demonstrates that this approach can add depth to the explanations of globalization and isomorphism of institutions and policies among nation-states in recent years. Indeed, the qualitative case studies in Part II identified several processes that explain the phenomenon of homogeneity and apparent consensus among donors to test the theoretical innovation of synthesizing from the literature on contentious politics to fill these gaps in the world polity literature.

Micro-level social processes of world polity influence

This chapter revisits the five primary social processes identified in Part II of the book. By looking at their applicability in both cases, one can begin generalizing more broadly from the present case studies to many cases of world polity influence on the nation-state. As mentioned at the close of Chapter 2, this generalizability is one of the most compelling features of the analytic framework employed throughout the book. Because the world society research literature has widely established the extent of international influence on isomorphism at the macro level and that the processes of globalization identified earlier are at their theoretical core intended to be swappable into a multitude of contexts, it stands to reason that the processes derived here are applicable far beyond the aid sector. This next section begins to examine how we can view these processes as a key micro-level feature of the globalization of policies and norms more generally. Before casting the net that widely; however, re can begin to generalize about the role of these processes by examining each in the opposite case study to that in which they were identified in the previous chapters. Accordingly, in the next few pages it is worthwhile to examine internalization and certification, embeddedness with civil society, and bureaucrat activism in the context of the security and development case, and conversely examine catalytic policy drivers and autonomy from rest of government in terms of the gender case.

Internalization and certification

The process of internalization and certification was evident in the gender and development case discussed in Chapter 5. Through this process, donors could adopt an externally generated model that was validated as legitimate within world society and therefore legitimate for application in their domestic context. Three mechanisms coincided to varying extents to compose this process: standards setting/policing, appeal to outside authority, and mimicry. In this respect, the process of internalization and certification depends on both internal and external actors to facilitate policy model adoption and refinement. International organizations like the DAC and the UN act as venues for standards setting and they then follow up on these standards by policing them through peer review and annual status reports on treaty and other obligations. Donor agency officials actively participate in activating the latter two mechanisms both by referring to outside sources of legitimacy to justify policy decisions and by copying approaches and techniques used elsewhere and deemed 'best practices' for achieving their aims.

The process of internalization and certification appears in both case studies considered here, though it was dealt with primarily in the chapter on women and gender. If we look at the security and development issue, all three donors demonstrate experience of a process of internalization and certification with all three mechanisms of standards setting/policing, appealing to outside authority, and mimicry at work to varying degrees.

Again, the DAC had a role to play in standards setting in the security area, with the creation of DAC guidelines on Security Sector Reform (SSR), the DAC created a set of expectations on its donor members to address SSR issues in their work and detailed how this work could best be achieved (OECD 2004a, 2004b, 2004c, 2005b). One respondent who had worked with the DAC also highlighted the DAC role of beginning to police these standards by stating that all the most recent DAC peer review reports had made certain to include a security and conflict component in their assessment of donor members. Indeed, examination of peer review reports for all three of the case study countries reveals a prominent focus on conflict and security in each (OECD 2005a, 2006c, 2007). In this respect, all three donors were subject to expectations that they meet DAC standards on the security and conflict issue, and were already being assessed on their compliance and success at meeting these standards only a short number of years after the model rose to prominence on the DAC agenda. Like in the gender case, the DAC role in setting and policing standards appears to have had the same effect on donors in the security case. Internalization of the security and development model begins with the standards set by the DAC and the later pressure that follow-up through the DAC peer review process exerts on each donor to show it is doing something in the security and development area.

The appeal to outside authority was a less-evident mechanism at work in the security and development case; however, this can be explained because the security issue can be more closely linked to national interests and therefore requires less external validation or certification to be accepted within agencies. Respondents in all three cases referred to the DAC guidelines and to other work on the issue in the international community at the UN level and in academic circles, but these outside referents were used mostly as guidance for directions that would be taken in the agency, rather than as a means of validating or legitimizing security and development approaches. In the case of a policy model more closely tied to national interests, it appears less likely that the mechanism of appealing to outside authorities is required to certify the model within the nation-state government structures.

Finally, evidence of mimicry – or the intention of mimicry – exists in the security and development case as respondents in all three case study countries emphasized the work of Great Britain's development assistance donor, the Department for International Development (DFID) on the security issue, and the fact that it had worked to shape their approaches to security. The unanimous recognition of DFID as a leader in the security and development field was voiced by all respondents on the security and development issue. Indeed, DFID's leadership in this field caused other donors to look to them for examples of best practices in how to programme on security and how to incorporate a conflict/security policy into their work. Notably, DFID's creation of Conflict Prevention Pools (CPPs) – a funding tool to coordinate British efforts to prevent conflict and assist in post-conflict situations – for Africa and for the rest of the developing world in 2001 was held up as the primary example for donors to follow in the security and development sector (DFID 2004). Indeed, the whole-of-government approach taken by DFID and the rest of the UK government in managing the CPPs has been emulated in both Canada and the United States as an approach to security, conflict and development. Canada's Global Peace and Security Fund (GPSF) is an example of a development assistance apparatus that takes inspiration from the DFID CPPs, even though the GPSF is administered in Canada by the Department of Foreign Affairs and International Trade (DFAIT) rather than CIDA. By adopting approaches that are perceived as successful elsewhere and emulating the policies and programmes of other donors on security and development issues, the three donors in this case study all demonstrate some level of mimicry involved in internalizing and certifying their own approaches to the issue.

The process of internalization and certification features in the security and development case in a similar, although not as central, fashion as seen in the gender case study. This process of internalization and certification appears to be a key component of nation-state entities integrating world polity policy and institutional models into their systems and operations. Not only limited to influencing the mobilization and framing of contentious politics as demonstrated in the social movement literature (McAdam, Tarrow, and Tilly 2001; Tarrow 2005), internalization and certification is a micro-level process which helps clarify the influence of world society on the nation-state. In the case of development assistance, bilateral donors internalize and certify models promulgated on the international stage, leading to greater uniformity and even consensus on policy priorities. The function of this process requires individual agency within donor organizations. It necessitates an outward-looking viewpoint that examines and then chooses to integrate new approaches into the day-to-day operations and policy agendas of donors. It is this active micro-level agency by donor officials and others involved in the development assistance sector that is one of the missing components in most world polity explanations of institutional and policy isomorphism. These policy and institutional models cannot be internalized and certified within an organization without the active hand of individuals making decisions to adopt, institutionalize, and refine new approaches to their work.

Embeddedness in civil society

The nature of donor relationships with civil society, particularly the process of a donor being embedded in the development-related civil society in its domestic constituency, emerged from the interview evidence as another micro-level social process that accounts for some of the influence of world society on the nation-state to promote greater uniformity of development assistance policy. In contrast to the process of internalization and certification however, the embeddedness of a donor in civil society does not emerge from both case studies. Indeed, respondents queried about civil society and the security and development agenda were uniform in their denial of much civil society influence on the approach taken to security and development issues. This is not to suggest that civil society were not interested in or engaged on the issues, as each country case provided evidence from civil society respondents who had strong views on the issue. NGO respondents in all three countries in fact discussed certain levels of discomfort with recent donor moves to incorporate security sector reform into their operations. Still, this discomfort evident in all the civil society respondents did not appear to directly impact the approaches adopted by CIDA, Sida, and USAID.

In contrast to the gender and development case in Chapter 5, where embeddedness in civil society appeared to contribute to the fuller acceptance of the model, the security and development case shows no such relationship. If anything, given the views of resistance expressed by civil society respondents in each country, we would expect to find the opposite relationship if donors had strong ties to civil society on the security issue. In this respect, embeddedness with civil society should impact world polity model acceptance dependent on the point of view taken on that specific issue by civil society. In the aid sector, this varies depending on the relationship of a policy model to motivations of either humanitarian internationalism or national interest. It is no surprise that civil society is more broadly in favour of the humanitarian-inspired issue of gender equality and perhaps less enthused about the enmeshing of development assistance with conventional security concerns. Still, the evidence here indicates that embeddedness with civil society can be very selective on the donors' part, as many civil society respondents were more vocal in their positions on security than on gender equality, but their influence seemed limited to the adoption of the gender model in the American and Swedish cases.

This selective influence via close ties to civil society is therefore a process which can only explain the adoption of certain world polity models. If the model is more instrumental to national interests or less controversial to society at large, then it is less likely to be as susceptible to civil society involvement with the nation-state than an issue that has a broader humanitarian motivation and appeal. Further research to validate this assertion is necessary to be able to generalize further about this relationship. It does suggest, however, that not all world polity institutional and policy models are equal in the eyes of the nation-state. Some tie more directly to national self-interest than others, while others can have a much more universal humanitarian appeal. Where the nation-state chooses to engage closely with civil society, consulting with them for advice and direction or working jointly with civil society to derive a new approach to an issue, the politics surrounding the policy model appear more likely to be detached from obvious national self-interest. This would explain the inability of civil society in the security case to effectively influence donors, whereas the influence of embeddedness in civil society networks was obvious in gender case in both Sweden and the United States.

Bureaucratic activism

Individual agency mediating the interface of world society and the nation-state is nowhere more evident in this book's case studies than the process of bureaucratic activism. Here, donor officials directly affect the type of world polity models that donors take on, refine, and integrate in their policies and programmes. The mechanisms identified in the gender and development case included: champions, guerrillas, entrepreneurs, and person exchange. These four features of bureaucratic activism were evident in the gender case, and arguably two of the four can be seen in the security case based on the interview data for that case. The two mechanisms which did not appear in the security case were the champion and the bureaucrat guerrilla. This may be because – for the most part – there is not much management resistance within the three agencies studied to the concept of addressing insecurity and conflict through development assistance. Even CIDA's lacklustre adoption of the security and development issue does not on the surface appear to be due to management resistance, but instead can be blamed on a lack of strategy for integrating the issue more fully into CIDA's policies and programming and a broader government of Canada decision to situate security and development programming at DFAIT. As such, the need for security champions or for unconventional 'guerrilla' approaches to expanding the security and development issue within these agencies is not there in the same way it appears in the gender case. This underlines the fact that not all social mechanisms involved in these processes are necessarily implicated in the process at all times, something illustrated elsewhere in the literature on contentious politics (McAdam, Tarrow, and Tilly 2001; Tarrow 1998).

The mechanisms of person exchange and bureaucratic entrepreneurialism are, however, evident in the security case. For example, several of the individuals interviewed who were tasked with the security and development portfolio were brought into the donor agencies from outside positions of experience in military and security work elsewhere with private firms, other government departments, and international organizations. This previous work enables these security specialists to bring their experiences into the donor agency and then use it to promote new directions on the security and development issue. All respondents except one working directly on this file in each of the three countries studied meet this profile. It appears that with the recent turn towards expanded action on security and development within the bilateral donors that many of them turned to people with this outside expertise internalized them, and tasked them with pushing the agenda on the issue within the organization to meet international expectations. It is at this level that the bureaucratic entrepreneurs emerge, as the people working on the security and development issue initially within these agencies appear to have to craft much of the momentum on the issue from their own energies. Indeed, the distinction between the success of pushing these models forward at Sida and at USAID and the relative failure to achieve a concrete position on the issue at CIDA appears to stem at least somewhat from ineffectual bureaucratic entrepreneurialism and partly from the decision of DFAIT to take the lead on these issues in the Canadian context.

In this respect, bureaucratic activism, the process of individual nation-state officials working actively to promote, expand, or institutionalize a policy agenda within their department or agency, appears also to be a key process in explaining how it is that nation-states come to adopt common models of the world polity. Although not as central to the security and development case as it appeared in the gender case, several of the bureaucrat activist mechanisms do appear in both instances, and arguably should be apparent in myriad other examples of world polity influence on the nation-state.

Catalytic policy drivers

The catalytic policy driver was very evident in the security and development case. An issue being placed on the international agenda at a meeting of donors or at a broader international conference can catalyze a response to a new issue among donors who have not yet addressed the issue sufficiently within their organization. The catalytic policy driver also has the ability push a donor to revise and refine its approaches to take part in a new international effort on the issue. In this sense, it is less the actual meeting or conference that spurs policy model adoption and refinement, and more due to the actual participation of the nation-state in preparing for the international event. This preparation forces the government body to adopt a position where they may not have held one previously, or to revise a previous held policy to meet with ever-shifting international expectations. In the security and development case study this process was evident in that none of the three donors studied had a position on security sector reform before the issue came to prominence on the DAC agenda soon after 2001.

In the gender and development case, the catalytic policy process was also described in several instances by respondents when they discussed the influence of participation in the 1995 United Nations conference on women in Beijing and its two follow-up conferences in 2000 and 2005. Donor officials who took part in their countries' delegations to these conferences were required to take a fresh look at their existing gender policies and apply new directions in response to new expectations prior to participation in the conferences. In this respect, the influence of these conferences closely mirrors the process of standards setting and policing described earlier, but the main difference is that the process occurs in preparation for and during the participation in an international event. Still, the catalytic policy driver is not as influential in the gender case as in the security case because much of work on gender had already occurred in recent years.

Still, this process can be held to have an important role to play in the spread and development of new world polity models in the development assistance sector – particularly in cases where very few or perhaps even no donors have an existing position on a subject. The recent push towards donor harmonization and aid effectiveness in preparation for the Paris Declaration provides a good example of this. Little to no work had been done previously on serious coordination amongst donors, yet participation in the international process of defining and refining aid effectiveness and harmonization forced donors to adopt policies and that reflected these 'new' principles of development assistance. Indeed, both the Swedish Policy for Global Development and CIDA's Strengthening Aid Effectiveness policy statement are outcomes of the catalytic policy drivers behind the aid effectiveness and harmonization agendas (CIDA 2002b; Sweden 2003).

Autonomy from rest of government/Ministry of Foreign Affairs

Not to be confused with the feature of agency structure identified earlier in the book, the actual process of asserting autonomy from the rest of government or, in the case of development assistance donors, from the Ministry of

Foreign Affairs, played a role in both the security and the gender cases. In the security case, CIDA, the lone donor that could assert their autonomy adopted a security and development approach that did not meet as closely with the international expectations in this field. In contrast, Sida and USAID were both less autonomous in this matter and their approaches to security and development more closely mirrored the international expectations which arguably were very near to national self-interest of their governments.

In the gender case, this process functions in a more complex manner, as greater autonomy asserted by CIDA permits a fuller adoption of current gender and development trends, while lesser autonomy on the part of Sida and USAID have mixed outcomes. Sida, even though it does not exert much effort to distance itself from the Swedish Ministry of Foreign Affairs, has the gender policy and approach which most clearly mirrors the world polity model delineated in Chapter 5. In contrast, USAID's close ties to the State Department appear to limit the extent of gender and development implementation at the corporate level within the agency. This contrast again falls along lines of underlying motivations for the policy model involved. The gender and development model is something primarily motivated by more humanitarian or altruistic concerns. In this sense, gender equality is not fundamentally central to the foreign policy interests of most states. Indeed, it is this distance from overriding national self-interest that arguably makes the gender and development model something that is de-prioritized by USAID and its relative lack of autonomy from the State Department. Sida, on the other hand, is very active on the gender and development front expressly because the gender equality issue is perceived as a central concern of the Swedish government both domestically and in its foreign policy. For the Swedes, the gender and development model is central to national self-interests because of its humanitarian appeal. Sida is therefore pushed by its lack of autonomy from the Swedish MFA and the rest of the Swedish government to actively promote gender equality and adopt a progressive gender and development policy in keeping with Swedish domestic priorities.

This finding suggests that the results of the process of exerting autonomy from the rest-of-government or from the Ministry of Foreign Affairs in the case of development assistance donors are contingent on the nature of the policy or institutional model under consideration. If we categorize these models according to their centrality to national-self-interest, it appears that more autonomy will enable fuller adoption of those models which are at greater distance from national interests and will permit lower levels of compliance with models that are more tightly linked to national interests. When national interest and humanitarianism overlap in development assistance, as occurs in the case of Sweden and the gender and development model, then the lack of autonomy can in fact encourage the adoption of a more humanitarian aim for self-interested reasons.

The five processes illustrated in Table 6.1 are implicated in facilitating the spread of common development assistance policies among bilateral donors,

Table 6.1 Summary of processes emerging from qualitative case studies

Policy model Case study	Country	Micro-level processes				
		Internalization & certification	Embeddedness in civil society	Bureaucratic activism	Catalytic policy drivers	Autonomy asserted from MFA
	Canada	Yes	No	Yes	Yes	Yes
Gender	Sweden	Yes	Yes	Yes	No	No
	USA	Yes	Yes	Yes	Yes	No
	Canada	Yes	No	Yes	Yes	Yes
Security	Sweden	Yes	No	Yes	Yes	No
	USA	Yes	No	Yes	Yes	No

leading to a uniformity of policy on both the gender and security issues. This chapter demonstrates that the processes are not implicated equally in each policy model instance. Dependent on the nature of the policy model and its centrality to the national self-interest of the nation-states implicated, the five processes identified will be present in varying degrees to mediate the adoption and refinement of world polity models within the aid sector. Table 6.1 above indicates whether a process is implicated in each country's experience of the two policy models included in the study. No country has all five of the processes implicated simultaneously, but each process emerged at one point during the qualitative analysis of the interview data collected for each of the three countries.

Making macro–micro linkages

Collectively, the processes emerging from the cases of gender and security addressed in this book are necessary additions to world polity explanations of the spread and adoption of common policies and institutional frameworks among nation-states. The explanatory power of frequently cited macro-level correlations between model adoption/diffusion and international organization membership, treaty ratification, global conferences, contagion effects/model density, and civil society influence is expanded substantially by pairing these macro-level influences with micro-level processes of globalization. Figure 6.1 visually illustrates these linkages in a basic fashion, acknowledging that many of these micro-level processes can be linked to many plausible macro-level correlations. Even those processes which appear to only better explain a limited number of macro-level relationships have more than one linkage, reflecting that social processes are malleable and can operate similarly in different contexts to achieve similar outcomes. Though not exhaustive in their explanation of the phenomenon of policy isomorphism among aid donors, these micro-level processes are clearly implicated in the interface of world society and the nation-state leading to greater uniformity among states. The five processes at the core of this book's findings arguably can be

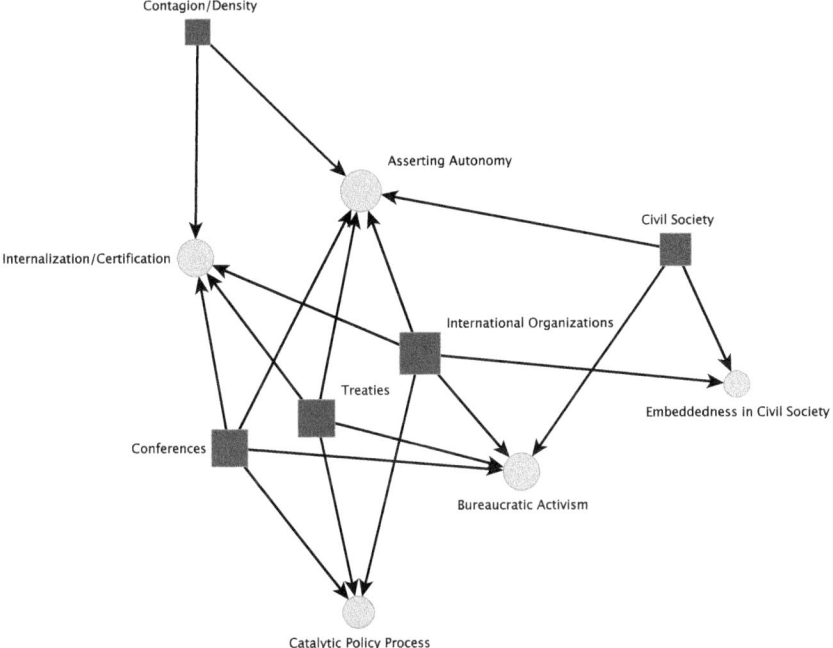

Figure 6.1 Macro–micro linkages of world society influence*

* Dark squares = macro correlations; light circles = micro-level social processes. Nodes sized by number of ties.

considered beyond the scope of the development assistance sector to more broadly explain homogeneity of nation-state policies and institutions in other sectors. Indeed, extending research on the world polity in these directions would surely unearth other social processes implicated in how world society influences the nation-state, organizations, and individuals, and perhaps provide greater insight into how nation-states, organizations, and individuals iteratively and recursively influence world society. This question of the next steps for research on this topic is the focus in the closing chapter of the book.

References

Berkovitch, N. (1999). The Emergence and Transformation of the International Women's Movement. In J. Boli & G. M. Thomas (Eds.), *Constructing World Culture: International Nongovernmental Organizations Since 1875* (pp. 100–126). Stanford, CA: Stanford University Press.

Boli, J., & Thomas, G. M. (1997). World Culture in the World Polity: A Century of International Non-governmental Organization. *American Sociological Review*, 62(2), 171–190.

Boli, J., & Thomas, G. M. (1999). *Constructing World Culture: International Nongovernmental Organizations Since 1875*. Stanford, CA: Stanford University Press.

CIDA, Canadian International Development Agency. (2002). *Strengthening Aid Effectiveness*. Gatineau: CIDA.

Cole, W. M. (2005). Sovereignty Relinquished? Explaining Commitment to the International Human Rights Covenants, 1966–1999. *American Sociological Review*, 70(3), 472–495.

Cole, W. M. (2013). Government Respect for Gendered Rights: The Effect of the Convention on the Elimination of Discrimination against Women on Women's Rights Outcomes, 1981–2004. *International Studies Quarterly*, 57(2), 233–249.

DFID. (2004, September 2004). The Africa Conflict Prevention Pool: A Joint UK Government Approach to Preventing and Reducing Conflict in Sub-Saharan Africa. Retrieved from www.fco.gov.uk/Files/kfile/ACPP%20Information%20 Doc%20-%20final,0.pdf

Drori, G. S. (2007). Information Society as a Global Policy Agenda: What Does It Tell Us About the Age of Globalization? *International Journal of Comparative Sociology*, 48(4), 297–316. doi:10.1177/0020715207079532

Drori, G. S., Meyer, J. W., & Hwang, H. (2006). *Globalization and Organization: World Society and Organizational Change*. New York: Oxford University Press.

Frank, D. J., Hironaka, A., & Schofer, E. (2000). The Nation-state and the Natural Environment over the Twentieth Century. *American Sociological Review*, 65(1), 96.

Frank, D. J., Longhofer, W., & Schofer, E. (2007). World Society, NGOs and Environmental Policy Reform in Asia. *International Journal of Comparative Sociology*, 48(4), 275–295. doi:10.1177/0020715207079530

Hironaka, A. (2002). The Globalization of Environmental Protection: The Case of Environmental Impact Assessment. *International Journal of Comparative Sociology*, 43(1), 65–78.

Jang, Y. S. (2003). The Global Diffusion of Ministries of Science and Technology. In G. S. Drori, J. W. Meyer, F. O. Ramirez, & E. Schofer (Eds.), *Science in the Modern World Polity: Institutionalization and Globalization* (pp. 120–135). Stanford, Calif.: Stanford University Press.

Kjeldstadli, K. (2004). Mechanisms, Processes, and Contexts. *International Review of Social History*, 49(01), 104–114.

McAdam, D., Tarrow, S. G., & Tilly, C. (2001). *Dynamics of Contention*. Cambridge, U.K.; New York: Cambridge University Press.

Meyer, J. W. (2007). Globalization: Theory and Trends. *International Journal of Comparative Sociology*, 48(4), 261–273. doi:10.1177/0020715207079529

Meyer, J. W., Frank, D. J., Hironaka, A., Schofer, E., & Tuma, N. B. (1997). The Structuring of a World Environmental Regime, 1870–1990. *International Organization*, 51(4), 623.

OECD. (2004a). Development Assistance Committee High Level Meeting: 15–16 April 2004. Retrieved from www.oecd.org/document/9/0,2340,en_2649_34567_31540297_ 1_1_1_1,00.html

OECD. (2004b). Security System Reform and Governance: Policy and Good Practice. Retrieved from www.oecd.org/dataoecd/40/58/31526562.pdf

OECD. (2004c). Policy Brief: Security Sector Reform and Governance – Policy and Good Practice. *OECD Observer*. Retrieved from www.oecd.org/dataoecd/20/47/ 31642508.pdf

OECD. (2005a). *DAC Peer Review: Sweden*. Retrieved from Paris: www.oecd.org/dac/peer-reviews/35268515.pdf

OECD. (2005b). *Security Sector Reform and Governance*. Retrieved from Paris: www.oecd.org/dataoecd/8/39/31785288.pdf

OECD. (2006). *The United States: Development Assistance Committee Peer Review*. Retrieved from Paris: www.oecd-ilibrary.org/development/part-ii-dac-peer-review-of-the-united-states_journal_dev-v7-art41-en

OECD. (2007). *Canada: Development Assistance Committee Peer Review*. Retrieved from Paris: www.oecd.org/development/peer-reviews/39515510.pdf

Ramirez, F. O., & McEneaney, E. H. (1997). From Women's Suffrage to Reproduction Rights? Cross-national Considerations. *International Journal of Comparative Sociology*, 38(1–2), 6.

Ramirez, F. O., Soysal, Y., & Shanahan, S. (1997). The Changing Logic of Political Citizenship: Cross-national Acquisition of Women's Suffrage Rights, 1890 to 1990. *American Sociological Review*, 62(5), 735.

Rule, J. (2004). Review Essay: McTheory. *Sociological Forum*, 19(1), 151–162.

Simeon, D. (2004). A Unified Field Theory for Contention? *International Review of Social History*, 49(01), 115–121.

Shared Responsibility: Sweden's Policy for Global Development, Gov. Bill 2002/03: 122 (2003).

Swiss, L. (2009). Decoupling Values from Action: An Event-History Analysis of the Election of Women to Parliament in the Developing World, 1945–90. *International Journal of Comparative Sociology*, 50(1), 69–95.

Swiss, L. (2012). The Adoption of Women and Gender as Development Assistance Priorities: An Event History Analysis of World Polity Effects. *International Sociology*, 27(1), 96–119.

Tarrow, S. G. (1998). *Power in Movement: Social Movements and Contentious Politics* (2nd Edition). Cambridge, U.K.; New York: Cambridge University Press.

Tarrow, S. G. (2005). *The New Transnational Activism*. New York: Cambridge University Press.

Welskopp, T. (2004). Crossing the Boundaries? Dynamics of Contention Viewed from the Angle of a Comparative Historian. *International Review of Social History*, 49(01), 122–131.

7 The globalization of aid
Conclusions on consensus

With more than 142 billion USD of official development assistance in 2016, and many billions more in private aid transfers and remittances transferring from developed to developing societies on an annual basis for development, it is undeniable that this assistance plays a significant role in shaping the relationship between North and South. The politics of aid are intertwined with trade, geo-political, and even cultural relationships between nation-states and undoubtedly have the potential to influence the lives of billions of people in developing societies. For this reason, movement towards a more uniform set of aid policy objectives has a bearing on the development of recipient societies and needs to be better understood. Donor rhetoric about 'emerging consensus' over recent years required unpacking, and the actual processes and pressures of globalization at work among donor agencies needed to be examined. What has caused the striking similarity in approaches to development assistance among donor states? As one of the first efforts to take up this question, this book has applied multi-methods analysis centred in the world society approach and has elucidated several of the social processes of globalization at work in the bilateral aid sector. Through both a macro-level quantitative lens and two in-depth comparative case studies at the micro level this book has revealed several processes which account for the increasing uniformity among bilateral donor agencies and the globalization of aid.

At the macro or global level, the analysis of the adoption of a gender and development model among the full set of Western donor nations shows the direct influence of international conferences, organizations, and treaties on donor adoption of common approaches to aid. These findings confirm that world society influence on the institution of development assistance can clearly be identified even at the granularity of specific policy priorities. This macro-level framework of world society influences set the stage for my qualitative investigation of micro-level social processes of globalization at work in the three countries and two policy areas. This qualitative analysis of data from Canada, Sweden, and the United States showed the presence of five micro-level processes shared to varying degrees across these donors that reinforce their adoption of common approaches to both gender and security in their foreign aid policy and programmes. Evidence from both priority areas allows for generalization to other aid policy issues, as they each represent important instances of a common donor agenda on the international stage. These processes of globalization have not previously been identified in either the world society or foreign aid literatures and are arguably one of the unique contributions of this book. By identifying specific processes that account for policy isomorphism in the aid sector, we can see that nation-state enactment of world society models is due in large part to the individual agency and interactions often obscured in previous world polity research. Greater understanding of these and other similar processes permits a fuller understanding of world society and its globalizing influence on not only the development assistance sector, but indeed the entire universe of nation-state institutions.

This chapter summarizes the book's main arguments and contributions to research on globalization and development assistance and reflects on the broader implications of its core argument. The chapter first revisits the central questions guiding this study in light of my collective findings. Next, it discusses the innovative contributions of this study to the various academic and policy research literatures engaged. Finally, the chapter closes with a discussion of potential directions for future research prompted by the study of the globalization of aid policy.

Consensus revisited

This book began with three central questions that shaped its inquiry into globalization in the aid sector. Through responding to these questions, the book provides a clearer picture of how the interface of world society and the nation-state is mediated by social processes of globalization. It is worthwhile to revisit each question and the answers provided it by this book's primary arguments:

1. How does world society affect nation-state institutions and what are the processes that promote consensus or uniformity of policy and priorities among foreign aid donors?

The question of how world society influences nation-state institutions and what processes are entailed in the globalization of policy in the aid sector was central to this research. Both the quantitative and qualitative findings discussed throughout this book suggest that world polity explanations effectively explain globalization in the foreign aid sector. Indeed, the influence of other donors, international organizations, international conferences, and international treaties all appear to constitute this world society influence. At the macro level, this influence is suggested by the correlations of policy priority adoption with the timing of international conferences, and with the influence of the actions of other donor agencies. At the micro level, Part II of this book indicates that several key social processes are at work in promoting common approaches to both gender and security.

Processes of internalization/certification, embeddedness with civil society, bureaucratic activism, catalytic policy drivers, and the assertion of autonomy from the rest of government were all shown to play a role in the adoption of more or less uniform approaches to development assistance. These processes and the related mechanisms of which they are composed mediate the relationships between nation-state and world society and revolve largely around the actions and perceptions of individual donor agency personnel. In this sense, the processes of globalization that account for increased consensus and homogeneity of aid policy can be seen to function through the individuals that make up the institutions and organizations that compose the nation-state and world society. That these common processes and related mechanisms are relevant and responsible for the adoption of similar policy in divergent national contexts suggests their broader applicability in explaining processes of globalization even outside of the foreign aid sector.

2. What role does individual agency play in mediating the interface of world society and the nation-state?

The processes and mechanisms identified in the preceding chapters act upon the state institutions to promote adherence to globally developed policy models, encourage the refinement of those models, and provide feedback to world society in the form of these refinements. A range of actors are implicated in these social processes of globalization, including not only nation-state actors and international organizations, but also academic experts, consultants, private firms, and civil society groups. At the root of each, however, is some focus on the individual and the actions of individuals to facilitate each process. In this respect, the response to this second central question highlights the critical role for individuals within these organizations to act collectively to achieve adoption, institutionalization, and refinement of these models. This focus on individual agency has not, previously, been a strong focus of the primarily macro-level perspective on globalization adopted by world polity researchers. Indeed, this reduction of world polity influence to the level of individual agency contradicts the tendency of institutional theory to reject reductionism (Schneiberg and Clemens 2006). Arguably, this focus on individual agency helps elaborate the mechanisms and processes through which world society influence and the enactment of global models occurs. This nuances our understanding of the cultural influence of world polity models by identifying agency among the people that comprise world society that is often absent in this literature.

3. What role does civil society play in the spread of world polity models of development assistance?

Finally, although this book argues that civil society can play a role in the spread of common policy models – more specifically, the degree of embeddedness or closeness between state institutions and civil society groups appears to mediate the adoption of certain policy models – the influence of civil society was not as direct as a wide reading of the aid and world society literatures might have predicted it to be. Active lobbying or advocacy directed towards aid donors by civil society groups appeared to have little reported effect on the policy decisions taken by donors. In this sense, the role of civil society in spreading the common models of development assistance was less than some of the literature on non-governmental organizations and the world polity suggests it should be (Boli and Thomas 1997, 1999; Chabbott 1999). This surprising finding suggests that in the aid sector the influence of civil society is less one of direct lobbying and advocacy and more likely to be one of individual networking and loose ties between donor officials and civil society representatives. Recalling the processes identified earlier, such informal ties would include the influence of, for instance, frequent personnel exchange between civil society groups and donor agencies.

On the whole, the findings detailed here respond to all three of the central questions guiding this study. In sum, this research points to the need to privilege both macro- and micro-level explanations of globalization if we are to better understand the influence of world society on the state and other organizations. This finding raises several implications both for the research community and the foreign aid policy and programming community. These implications are discussed in the next two sections.

Implications for research

This book makes unique contributions to each of the research literatures with which it engages. It reveals key social processes of globalization that function through the interface of nation-state institutions and world society. By demonstrating how the development assistance sector has moved towards greater uniformity of policy objectives in the gender and security areas, this study unearths the processes and mechanisms through which globalizing pressures are applied to the state. In this way, this book makes several important contributions to the literatures on world polity theory, development assistance, and globalization.

World polity and the nation-state

This book contributes to research on the world polity in several ways. First, the world polity literature has not frequently examined foreign aid as one of the institutional models implemented by nation-states. Aside from some research which examined the role of development INGOs (Chabbott 1999), my recent work on aid and world society embeddedness (Swiss 2016a; 2016b; 2017; Swiss and Longofer 2016) and other research on the issue of state planning (Hwang 2006), the world polity literature has for the most part overlooked the issue of development as a manifestation of world society models. This book's novel contribution is in part demonstrating that the foreign aid process is yet another manifestation of world polity influence on the nation-state and other organizations. Indeed, all the evidence discussed here suggests the aid sector reflects world polity policy models in both gender and security areas. Extending this important conclusion, it can be argued that, indeed, the entire development assistance sector can equally be seen to be subject to the institutional and policy pressures of world society to conform to a uniform approach to providing aid to the developing world.

This highlights the book's second contribution to the world society literature, the contention that, apart from simply spreading similar institutional forms and structures among nation-states, world society is also responsible for the high degree of isomorphism of policy objectives within those institutions. This focus on policy similarity is something identified in some of the world polity literature previously (Barrett and Frank 1999; Hafner-Burton and Pollack 2002; Schofer and Hironaka 2005); however, this book has elaborated on the issue of policy isomorphism by showing the direct connection between the proliferation of policy models by world society actors at the macro level and the role of individual agency by nation-state representatives in the adoption of common policy agendas by nation-states at the micro level. Part II of the book's focus on the micro-level processes and mechanisms of globalization, many of which revolved around individual actions and relationships, adds another layer of depth to the understanding of policy isomorphism and world society's influence on the nation-state. The argument that threads throughout this study is that the influence of world society on the nation-state is palpable and real, but in effect is borne out by the actions of individual representatives of state institutions and their actual participation in relationships with individual representatives of other states and international organizations.

Development assistance motivations

The second main contribution I make here is to the somewhat limited literature on bilateral foreign aid – on the motivations which underlie the provision of foreign aid by well-off countries. The literature on aid has long established two polar opposites of motivation for donors: national interest and humanitarianism. The post-development perspective on development as an exploitative discourse can – in some sense – be grouped in with the latter. The processes of globalization and the mechanisms of which they are composed affect policy priorities distinctly when alternate motivations for assistance are at work, and that these global policy models can be at once motivated by both national and humanitarian interests. In this respect, the polar opposition of humanitarian and self-interest needs to be nuanced to allow for development objectives which can encompass both impulses. The case studies here show clearly that, in the case of Swedish development assistance policy, the gender and development approach appealed both to a humanitarian agenda and a national interest in gender equality which permeates Swedish society. In this respect, the different motivations for providing aid can be seen to vary widely even within a single country context or within a specific policy model. Although countries can be classified as being predominantly either nationally self-interested or humanitarian, in fact, these motivations need mostly to be considered as both/and, rather than either/or propositions. It is for this reason that different processes of globalization identified in this research can interact differently on the same policy model, as donor countries possess various motivations for a given objective. For instance, exerting autonomy from the rest of government in one case, may lead to the same globalizing effect as failing to do so in another.

Social processes and the politics of globalization

The final contribution pertains to expanding the research literature on the world polity to account for social processes of globalization at the micro level. By adopting an approach like that found in the study of contentious politics of social movements (McAdam, Tarrow, and Tilly 2001; Tarrow 1998, 2005), one can identify several social processes and mechanisms of globalization that operate to promote uniformity and homogenization of policy models across states. These processes consist of several interrelated social mechanisms which link to form an identifiable process. This deepens the understanding of world polity influence and globalization from simply a matter of macro-level correlations with organization membership, international conference participation, and the actions of other states to include micro-level effects through individual agency within the organizations and institutions of the nation-state. By showing that several common processes and mechanisms are identifiable in diverse country contexts and on different policy issues, it becomes clear that these social processes of globalization are a key component in explaining world society influence on the nation-state, and more specifically, can account for increased uniformity and homogenization of nation-state policy priorities in areas like the foreign aid sector. The case studies on gender and on security illustrate how these processes may function differently on issues of national interest as opposed to issues of international humanitarian appeal. This finding is significant, as it helps to deepen the explanatory power of world society perspectives on the politics of globalization.

Implications for foreign aid actors

Given bilateral foreign aid is a process involving multiple actors; this investigation of the globalization of aid policy has implications for many stakeholders in the aid sector. At this point, it is worth considering the implications for three main groups: donors, civil society, and recipient governments.

Implications for donor agencies

The primary implications of this research for donor agencies are twofold. First, we should consider the conclusion that individuals within donor agencies matter when it comes to adopting, institutionalizing, and refining donor policy. This is an important consideration if donor officials wish to see reform or effect change within their organizations. Rather than being solely dependent on foreign policy concerns or the dictates of some distant intergovernmental body like the DAC or the UN, bureaucratic activism is a key means through which individuals can promote change within agencies. The second implication for donors is the need to re-evaluate how their relationships with civil society work to structure policy priorities. Instead of counting on civil society activism and interest groups to lobby and advocate through conventional means like letter-writing and lobbying of elected officials, this book suggests that civil society influence is much more likely to transfer through informal ties and networks involving aid officials and NGO representatives. Donor officials wishing to more effectively integrate civil society perspectives into their policy development processes would be wise to expand on such ties and networks where possible to affect greater embeddedness in civil society.

Implications for donor-country civil society

Perhaps the greatest surprise offered by this book is reserved for the development-oriented civil society community regarding donor perceptions of their influence. Without a representative random sample of aid officials, it is a stretch to conclude that direct advocacy and lobbying is as ineffectual as donor officials make it out to be. Still, the conclusions drawn here regarding the significance of informal ties and networks between donors and civil society need to be considered by NGOs and community groups alike. If the aim of an organization is to reshape donor approaches to a specific aid policy issue, the value of cultivating informal ties with aid officials tasked with those areas of responsibility should not be underestimated. Indeed, where donors are open to and encouraging of engagement with civil society, it appears it is most likely through the informal networking channel that the bulk of civil society influence can be wielded.

Implications for governments and civil society in recipient countries

One admitted weakness of this book is its relative silence on the role played by recipient country governments and civil society groups within the process of the globalization of foreign aid. This limitation arises mostly out of the need to narrow the scope of research to sufficiently examine the globalization of bilateral aid efficiently in this volume. Still, the results of this work yield some interesting implications for these actors. Two specific aspects seem particularly salient to government and civil society actors in recipient countries. First, if aiming to influence donors, an additional means through which to do so is by attempting to influence the so-called 'rationalized others' of world society through active involvement in international and intergovernmental organizations. By working to shape the agenda on these stages, recipients of Official Development Assistance would be better able to assert an increased influence over the donors with which they deal. Second, civil society and recipient government officials would do well to strike up and engage in informal networks with aid agency officials responsible for the bilateral aid programme directed to their country. If processes of civil society embeddedness can be extended beyond the scope of donor country civil society, it would imply that NGOs and community groups that receive aid in recipient countries might also be able to exert influence over donor policy agendas and adoption of specific world society models of development through these ties to donors.

Further inquiry into 'emerging global consensus'

This examination of the globalization of aid policy fills some of the gaps in the explanatory power of world polity theory, but also raises other questions that warrant further investigation. There are undoubtedly numerous directions in which this research could delve further into the globalization of aid, but three would appear central to any future research on this subject: (1) expanding the present case studies to include information from other donor countries to validate the present findings; (2) examining the actual impact of this globalization of development assistance policy on the development options of recipient countries; and (3) examination of the same processes of globalization described here in other institutional and policy contexts. These final few pages briefly explore each of these possible research directions.

Additional donors to validate qualitative findings

One of the potential shortcomings of this study could be perceived bias in the limited sample for the qualitative cases. The findings would undoubtedly be strengthened with the addition of one or two more donor countries to complement the existing three. This would permit comparison between an even broader spectrum of donor country contexts and allow for the integration of case study countries that represent different geographical regions. Indeed, the inclusion of the United Kingdom would be a valuable addition to this study. Respondents in all three of the existing donor cases frequently referred to the United Kingdom's Department for International Development (DFID) as the donor they most often looked to emulate. This perceived role of DFID as a cutting-edge leader in the donor community would make the organization a valued addition to the data. Other contexts to be explored through the addition of additional donors would include how the globalization processes identified function differently in freshly minted donor agencies of recent acceded European Union members like Poland and the Czech Republic, or even in the case of the so-called 'non-DAC' or emerging donors like China, India, Brazil, or Saudi Arabia (Gulrajani and Swiss 2017). Corroboration of the book's findings in alternate contexts would provide a deeper understanding of how the micro-level processes of globalization revealed here function beyond this book's limited purview.

The globalization of development assistance policy: impact on the developing world

Globalization's impact on the developing world is often regarded in light of trade, employment, and cultural considerations, but this research shows that the potential for globalization to alter the aid agenda is also a concern for development worldwide. The primary rationale for studying the globalization of development assistance policy indeed rests in its potential impact on development in recipient countries. The notion that a narrower international agenda of what makes 'good' development could potentially limit the development options and alternatives for billions of people in the developing world requires further investigation.

In the past, donors have been known to set strict conditions on aid that had a similar effect on development in recipient countries. Indeed, the Washington Consensus of the 1980s and its focus on macro-economic structural adjustment as the driver of development has already been shown to have negatively impacted countless lives throughout the developing world (Bradshaw et al. 1993; Sparr 1994; Desai 2002). More recently, the so-called good governance agenda of donors has imposed new conditionalities on recipients and the aid effectiveness agenda has promoted a reduction in the overall number of countries to which donors provide aid in the name of focus (Munro 2005). The impact of these donor trends on development and the lives of people in many recipient country societies remains to be widely studied and merits further investigation.

Social processes of globalization in the world society / nation-state relationship

The arguments proposed in this book would benefit from additional research to confirm the role and function of the micro-level social processes of globalization identified here in other sectors of world society/nation-state interaction. The cases examined in the foreign aid sector in the preceding chapters provide two examples of how these processes and their related mechanisms work to shape policy and institutional structure. Investigation of other institutions and policy frameworks to identify the same or similar mechanisms and processes at work would help to deepen the understanding of these processes of globalization. This would complement this book's main findings in several ways. Research that looks at an even more widely adopted policy framework or institution – something that not only wealthy states, but most nation-states possess – like central banks, internet regulations, national women's machineries, or health systems would help to demonstrate how processes found in the aid sector could be extended to form a clearer picture of the common social processes at work in all aspects of the nation-state relationship with world society.

Conclusions on consensus

At the beginning of this book, I raised questions about the apparent globalization of policy priorities in the aid sector – what is it that prompts emerging consensus among donors? World polity explanations of globalization and institutional isomorphism among nation-states offered a theoretical base upon which for me to begin to investigate this question. My investigation integrated influences from both the development assistance and social movement literatures and the use of a multi-methods and multi-level approach to research to examine the processes of globalization in the aid sector at both the macro cross-national and micro-comparative case study levels. My results make a strong case for the influence of world society on the nation-state to adopt the institutions and common policy frameworks of foreign aid. The macro-level influence of world society actors, treaties, and conferences, pairs with the micro-level processes of globalization which promote and reinforce the emerging consensus of approaches to both the gender and security issues in the aid sector. These macro and micro explanations of globalization were found in diverse country contexts of three different major donors, and are illustrative of the wider functioning of the interface between world society and the nation-state. There is emerging consensus – a form of globalization – happening in the global foreign aid sector. Rather than deriving purely from donor interests or altruistic humanitarian aims, this convergence around sets of aid priorities are directly attributable to the influence of world society functioning at multiple levels.

World society as a global level and abstract concept seems more concrete when viewed through the agency of individual officials and the relationships they maintain between their organizations and others. The processes revealed here hinge on this active agency and underpin the influence of world society which has already been ably established in the political sociology literature. Although development assistance may be an arm of the foreign policy of all major donor countries, it does not occur in a vacuum away from international influences. Indeed, the common approaches adopted by donors are encouraged by the international development assistance community in an active manner and integrated into donor agencies by the actions of development workers in a very real way. Common micro-level processes of globalization push donors to adopt similar approaches to gender, security, and a multitude of other policy models. In the end, the influence of world society on the nation-state and the corresponding phenomenon of a globalized foreign aid agenda are strongly reinforced by the active participation of donors in this world society and the impact of common processes at work which encourage growing uniformity of development aims for them all.

References

Barrett, D., & Frank, D. J. (1999). Population Control for National Development: From World Discourse to National Policies. In J. Boli & G. M. Thomas (Eds.), *Constructing World Culture: International Nongovernmental Organizations Since 1875* (pp. 198–221). Stanford, CA: Stanford University Press.

Boli, J., & Thomas, G. M. (1997). World Culture in the World Polity: A Century of International Non-governmental Organization. *American Sociological Review*, 62(2), 171–190.

Boli, J., & Thomas, G. M. (1999). INGOs and the Organization of World Culture. In J. Boli & G. M. Thomas (Eds.), *Constructing World Culture: International Nongovernmental Organizations Since 1875* (pp. 13–49). Stanford, CA: Stanford University Press.

Bradshaw, Y. W., Noonan, R., Gash, L., & Sershen, C. B. (1993). Borrowing against the Future: Children and Third World Indebtedness. *Social Forces*, 71(3), 629–656.

Chabbott, C. (1999). Development INGOs. In J. Boli & G. M. Thomas (Eds.), *Constructing World Culture: International Nongovernmental Organizations Since 1875* (pp. 222–248). Stanford, CA: Stanford University Press.

Desai, M. (2002). Transnational Solidarity: Women's Agency, Structural Adjustment, and Globalization. In N. A. Naples & M. Desai (Eds.), *Women's Activism and Globalization: Linking Local Struggles and Transnational Politics* (pp. 15–33). London: Routledge.

Gulrajani, N., & Swiss, L. (2017). *Why Do Countries become Donors? Assessing the Drivers and Implications of Donor Proliferation.* London: Overseas Development Institute. Retrieved from: www.odi.org/publications/10747-why-do-countries-become-donors-assessing-drivers-and-implications-donor-proliferation:

Hafner-Burton, E., & Pollack, M. A. (2002). Mainstreaming Gender in Global Governance. *European Journal of International Relations*, 8(3), 339–373.

Hwang, H. (2006). Planning Development: Globalization and the Shifting Locus of Planning. In G. S. Drori, J. W. Meyer, & H. Hwang (Eds.), *Globalization and Organization: World Society and Organizational Change* (pp. 69–89). New York: Oxford University Press.

McAdam, D., Tarrow, S. G., & Tilly, C. (2001). *Dynamics of Contention.* Cambridge, U.K.; New York: Cambridge University Press.

Munro, L. T. (2005). Focus-Pocus? Thinking Critically about Whether Aid Organizations Should Do Fewer Things in Fewer Countries. *Development and Change*, 36(3), 425–447.

Schneiberg, M., & Clemens, E. S. (2006). The Typical Tools for the Job: Research Strategies in Institutional Analysis. *Sociological Theory*, 24(3), 195–227.

Schofer, E., & Hironaka, A. (2005). The Effects of World Society on Environmental Protection Outcomes. *Social Forces*, 84(1), 25–47.

Sparr, P. (1994). Feminist Critique of Structural Adjustment. In P. Sparr (Ed.), *Mortgaging Women's Lives: Feminist Critiques of Structural Adjustment* (pp. 13–39). London: Zed Books.

Swiss, L. (2016). A Sociology of Foreign Aid and the World Society. *Sociology Compass*, 10(1), 65–73.

Swiss, L. (2016). World Society and the Global Foreign Aid Network. *Sociology of Development*, 2(4), 342–374.

Swiss, L. (2017). Foreign Aid Allocation from a Network Perspective: The Effect of Global Ties. *Social Science Research*, 63, 111–123.

Swiss, L., & Longhofer, W. (2016). Membership has its Privileges: Shared International Organizational Affiliation and Foreign Aid Flows, 1978–2010. *Social Forces*, 94(4), 1769–1793.

Tarrow, S. G. (1998). *Power in Movement: Social Movements and Contentious Politics* (2nd Edition). Cambridge, U.K.; New York: Cambridge University Press.

Tarrow, S. G. (2005). *The New Transnational Activism*. New York: Cambridge University Press.

Methodological appendix

Given that some readers are rightly more interested in research methodology than others, this methodological appendix succinctly outlines in greater detail the methodological approaches that underpin the book's mixed-methods approach. First, the appendix outlines the quantitative analysis that comprises the macro-level analysis in Chapter 2. Then, the appendix discusses the methodological outline of the qualitative case studies discussed in Chapters 4 and 5.

Methodological notes for quantitative analysis (Chapter 2)

This part of the appendix details the quantitative analysis and methodology that underpins the findings summarized in Chapter 3. For presentation of this analysis in its fullest form, please see Swiss (2012). Table A.3 at the end of this appendix details the coding of the country-level data that was used to create the analysis.

Method

Event history modelling techniques have been widely used in earlier world polity research (Frank, Longhofer, & Schofer, 2007; Hironaka, 2002; Ramirez et al., 1997; Wotipka & Ramirez, 2008; Swiss 2009; Swiss and Fallon 2017). Furthermore, this approach enables the efficient cross-national study of political phenomena over time (Box-Steffensmeier and Jones, 1997). The analysis summarized in Chapter 3 employs a constant rate event history model to explain the rate at which a donor country is likely to adopt a WID/gender policy or unit. With this approach, the rate of transition from no policy to policy adoption is assumed to be time-independent and dependent on only the vector of related covariates (Ramirez et al., 1997). The model appears as:

$$\log[r(t)] = B'X$$

In this case, r represents a country's transition rate from having no gender policy or unit to the destination state of having either a gender policy or unit within the donor agency; X represents the vector of covariates, and B the vector of related coefficients. If we exponentiate each side of the equation we show the time to transition (r) and the influence on this time of each covariate ($\exp(B)$) (Ramirez et al., 1997). Model results demonstrate the effect of each independent variable on the time between a country entering the risk-set in 1968 after the advent of the first gender unit in Sweden (or at the year of the onset of aid provision for five later donors) and the adoption in each country of their own WID/GAD policy or unit.[1] The year 1968 was selected for the beginning of the risk-set for existing donors at that time, because it was felt that it was only reasonable to assume countries were at risk of developing their own WID/GAD policy or unit after the advent of the first WID/GAD unit.

The analysis proceeds in two stages. First, the effects of the various world polity measures are examined independent of domestic donor characteristics. Next, the measures of donor autonomy and generosity are included in the models to examine the extent to which the institutions of each country's development assistance sector shape world polity influence.

Data

The dataset used for Chapter 2's analysis consists of event timing, donor structure, international organization membership, and domestic context variables for twenty-two member countries of the OECD DAC, as well as yearly time series of ODA disbursement levels for each country (Paxton et al., 2006; Roodman, 2005). The risk-set includes twenty-two countries, twenty experiences of transition, and a total time at risk of 418.5 country years.

The dependent variable in the analysis is the rate of transition for a donor country from the origin of the first donor WID/GAD unit in 1968 (Sweden) to its adoption of either a WID/GAD policy or the creation of the WID/GAD unit in its organization. This information was compiled for each country using available information from current gender policy documents, evaluation reports, and OECD DAC Peer Review reports. Examples of these events are typified by the passing of the Percy Amendment by the US Congress in 1973 requiring American aid to address WID issues or Canada's adoption of its first policy guidelines on WID in 1976.[2] The rate is measured by taking the duration in years between entry into the risk-set and the creation of a unit or establishment of a policy and then matching it with a dummy variable to indicate occurrence of the WID/GAD event – countries which have yet to experience the event are coded with a zero for those years prior to adoption. In the year a donor adopts a WID/GAD policy or creates a unit, the dummy is set to one and they exit the risk-set. Countries never experiencing a transition are right-censored and exit the risk-set in 2003.

In the first stage of the analysis, several covariates are included to test the effects of world polity factors on the adoption of gender policy that reflect influence stemming from the demonstration effect of mimicry of other donors donor embeddedness in international organizations, and the influence of a global agenda perpetuated by international treaties and conferences.

The possibility of donor mimicry is examined through a measure of the overall density of the policy model on the global scale by a count of donors who have already adopted a WID/GAD policy or unit. This count variable is time-varying by year.

International influences of treaties and conferences are measured through two variables. The first is a timing variable that accounts for the year in which each donor country ratified the Convention on the Elimination of all forms of Discrimination Against Women (CEDAW). This is a time-varying dummy variable with a reference category reflecting those countries not yet ratifying the treaty in any given year following the creation of the CEDAW in 1980.[3] The second variable accounts for the timing of significant international conferences. More specifically, it is a categorical variable that splits the risk-set into two time periods that correspond with the two most recent United Nations World Conferences on Women (Nairobi 1985, and Beijing 1995). This variable includes two categories: the post-Nairobi/Beijing period after 1985 and a reference category pre-1985, prior to the Nairobi conference.[4]

The final world polity variable is a measure of embeddedness in the world polity as indicated by the presence of a country's residents holding membership in a select sample of women's international non-governmental organizations (WINGOs) (Paxton et al., 2006). Countries in the dataset range in the number of memberships for their citizens from 2 to 24. This is a time-varying covariate with data collected in select years. Following Paxton and her co-authors, the missing values for years falling between these collection points are interpolated in the dataset (2006).[5]

In the second stage of the analysis, two measures are included in the models to account for factors relating to the differing characteristics of each country's development assistance programmes. First, a measure of donor structure is included in the models, specifically the autonomy of the donor body from the ministry of foreign affairs in each donor country. This is a dummy variable, with autonomous donors coded as one, and setting integrated donors as the reference category. Donor autonomy was coded to reflect the institutional setup of each country's donor agency over the majority of the time they are included in the risk-set. Coding of this variable is shown in Data Appendix. Second, a measure of overall donor generosity is incorporated in the analysis by including a time-varying covariate of ODA as a percentage of Gross National Income (GNI) in constant 2004 USD (Roodman, 2005). In the models this variable is logged to reduce skewness.

Results

Results from the first stage of exploratory event history analysis of the rate of WID/GAD policy adoption are shown in Table A.1 below. Results are

Table A.1 Bivariate exponential models of rate of WID/GAD policy adoption, 1968–2003

	Model 1	Model 2	Model 3	Model 4
WID/GAD count	0.13** (0.05)			
WINGOs membership		0.14*** (0.04)		
CEDAW ratification			0.73^ (0.41)	
World conferences on women (pre-1985)				
Post Nairobi & Beijing, 1985 onwards				1.12*
				(0.48)
Constant	−4.06*** (0.51)	−4.88*** (0.57)	−3.41*** (0.32)	−3.68*** (0.42)
Log Likelihood	−23.60	−24.16	−26.54	−24.92
Number of events	20	20	20	20
Number of countries	22	22	22	22
Country-years at risk	418.5	418.5	418.5	418.5

Robust standard errors in parentheses. Reference categories in brackets.
Notes: ^ significant at $p<0.1$; * significant at $p<0.05$; ** significant at $p<0.01$; *** significant at $p<0.001$.

provided in four models which each test a specific world polity variable of interest to test the hypothesized relationships outlined earlier in Chapter 2.

Model One includes the density measure count of WID/GAD policy adoptions or unit creation. The significant coefficient for the density measure indicates an increased rate of adoption for countries as the global count of WID/GAD policies increases. This decreased time means an increased rate of adoption, and confirms support for the hypothesized effects of density on policy adoption. The influence of WID/GAD policy density is significant at the $p<0.01$ level.

The influence of WINGO memberships is tested in Model Two. The WINGOs measure is significant at the $p<0.001$ level and is associated with an increased rate of policy adoption. The greater the number of WINGO memberships held by a donor state's citizens, the more quickly it is likely to adopt a WID/GAD gender policy within its development assistance donor.

Model Three includes the CEDAW ratification variable which fails to meet the typical $p<0.05$ threshold for significance, but does have a p value of less than 0.1. This marginal significance suggests that support for a hypothesized effect of treaties and conferences, is not confirmed in this model. The direction of the coefficient and the marginal significance suggest that countries ratifying CEDAW are quicker to adopt a WID/GAD policy than those that have not, but this relationship merits further exploration in stage two of the analysis.

Model Four includes the conference variable and shows that in the period from 1985 onwards, encompassing the conferences in Nairobi and Beijing, countries experienced a faster rate of WID/GAD policy adoption than in the pre-1985 era. This finding is significant at the *p<0.05* level and confirms the role of conferences outlined in Chapter 2.

Table A.1 does not include a full model incorporating all four of the main world polity influence variables in a single model, due to problems of multicollinearity between the measures. A typical solution to this problem would be to drop one or more of the variables from the analysis; however, because the chapter takes a specific exploratory focus on these factors in particular, a decision was taken to maintain the models as presented. Because the variables are count and time-period based dummies, there is significant correlation between the measures. This multicollinearity could not be reduced through transformation of the covariates, and yielded distorted coefficients for some of the measures. This collinearity does not affect the results as presented in this, and is a regrettable side effect of working with count data and a small N dataset over time.[6]

Table A.2 Multivariate exponential models of rate of WID/GAD policy adoption, 1968–2003

	Model 1	*Model 2*	*Model 3*	*Model 4*	*Model 5*
Donor autonomy	0.16	0.19	0.00	0.14	0.17
	(0.27)	(0.39)	(0.40)	(0.33)	(0.33)
Donor generosity (Logged ODA % of GNI)	0.61^	1.03*	0.56	0.73^	0.78^
	(0.33)	(0.48)	(0.39)	(0.38)	(0.42)
WID/GAD count		0.16**			
		(0.05)			
WINGOs membership			0.14***		
			(0.04)		
CEDAW ratification (No)				0.84*	
				(0.37)	
World conferences on women (pre-1985					
Post Nairobi & Beijing, 1985 onwards					1.22**
					(0.47)
Constant	0.38	1.51	–1.63	0.64	0.67
	(1.85)	(2.49)	(2.18)	(2.13)	(2.33)
Log Likelihood	–26.51	–21.01	–23.32	–24.82	–23.11
Number of events	20	20	20	20	20
Number of countries	22	22	22	22	22
Country-years at risk	418.5	418.5	418.5	418.5	418.5

Robust standard errors in parentheses. Reference categories in brackets.
Notes: ^ significant at *p<0.1;* * significant at *p<0.05;* ** significant at *p<0.01;* *** signify cant at *p<0.001.*

Testing for the hypotheses related to donor structure and generosity is illustrated in Table A.2. The five models in this table incorporate the measures for donor autonomy and generosity, first on their own in Model One, and then alongside each of the world polity measures in Models Two through Five. Although the direction of the coefficients for each variable is consistent with the predictions in Chapter 2, neither is statistically significant throughout. These results fail to confirm the hypotheses regarding donor structure and autonomy; however, some support is shown for the notion that donor generosity affects the diffusion of aid policy models. In Model Two the significant coefficient for donor generosity demonstrates that more generous donors are more quickly going to adopt WID/GAD policy scripts. The significance of this measure does not meet the $p<0.05$ threshold in other models, but is marginally significant at $p<0.1$ in Models One, Four, and Five.

Table A.2 also shows that all four of the world polity measures are significant and confirm the hypothesized relationships outlined in Chapter 2 when donor structure and generosity are controlled for. Indeed, Model Four shows that CEDAW ratification is now acceptably significant at the $p<0.05$ level, confirming the role of treaties in shaping WID/GAD policy adoption.

Table A.3 Data appendix – Chapter 2 variable coding

Country	Formation of donor agency/ unit	Gender unit/ policy	CEDAW ratification	Donor autonomy
Australia	1974	1976	1983	Autonomous
Austria	1974	1995	1982	Integrated
Belgium	1962	1981	1985	Integrated
Canada	1968	1976	1981	Autonomous
Denmark	1971	1987	1983	Integrated
Finland	1972	1995	1986	Integrated
France	1992	2000	1983	Autonomous
Germany	1975	2001	1985	Autonomous
Greece	1999	2002	1983	Integrated
Ireland	1974	1996	1985	Integrated
Italy	1987	1998	1985	Integrated
Japan	1974	1992	1985	Autonomous
Luxembourg	1985	1997	1989	Autonomous
Netherlands	1965	1986	1991	Integrated
New Zealand	2002	2001	1985	Autonomous
Norway	1968	1975	1981	Integrated
Portugal	2003	–	1980	Integrated
Spain	1988	–	1984	Integrated
Sweden	1965	1968	1980	Autonomous
Switzerland	1977	1993	1997	Integrated
United Kingdom	1961	1988	1986	Autonomous
United States	1961	1973	–	Autonomous

Overall, these quantitative results paint a picture of world polity influence on donor agencies at the macro level. Further, some evidence supports the claim that this diffusion can be conditioned by various features of the domestic development assistance context. Having identified and confirmed these relationships at the macro level, these findings set the stage for the micro-level investigation of the same influences in the qualitative cases presented in Part II of this book.

Methodological notes for qualitative cases (Chapters 4 and 5)

Chapters 4 and 5 discuss the qualitative case studies based on document content analysis and data collected from in-depth interviews with forty-one individual respondents working in the development assistance sector in the three countries in 2006 and 2007. These interviews were semi-structured but relatively open-ended with a base interview schedule that expanded or contracted where necessary through the use of informal probes to follow-up on earlier responses (Berg 2004; Gorden 1998). A sample interview schedule is included at the end of this section. Building on the quantitative, macro-level results discussed in Chapter 2, the interview questions focused on individual and institutional experiences in the development assistance sector, the relationships between people and institutions, and the various forms of international collaboration that occur in the development assistance community, related to the two policy issue areas of gender and security. Respondents were asked questions about the roles played by specific international organizations and other donor agencies, as well as the influence of domestic governments and activists. Interviews about individual experience within development agencies and organizations helped to reveal the social mechanisms and relationships at work in policy making – aspects that cannot be fully understood simply from analysis of policy documents. The interview schedule was developed following several preliminary interviews with key informants (Gorden 1998). In addition, the issues raised in the interviews were also informed by the outcomes of the macro-level quantitative analysis. All interviews were conducted in English, recorded to digital file format, and fully transcribed. In each case respondents were recruited for interviews via a snowball sample approach, beginning with key gatekeepers in specific institutions and more broadly in the development assistance community. Interviews continued in each setting until an acceptable level of theoretical saturation was reached and respondents were mostly echoing and reinforcing the themes that had already been identified in previous interviews. Respondents were recruited directly via telephone and e-mail communication to arrange for interviews that tended to take place either in the respondents' workplace or an acceptable alternate location, or over the telephone. Some interviews instead took the form of small group discussions when an individual felt the interview would benefit from hearing from one or more of their colleagues (Berg 2004). These group sessions were recorded and transcribed in the same manner as the interviews. Respondents received no compensation for participation in the study, but many requested to be informed of the research results upon completion.

The data collected from these interviews was coded and analysed using a qualitative analysis programme (ATLAS.ti) to examine causal relationships and emerging themes within the three country cases and within the overall study. Seventy-eight codes were identified. These codes were grouped into broader emerging themes which came to represent the features of domestic context and the mechanisms and social processes identified in Chapters 4 and 5. Major mechanisms revealed in the coding process were explored in more detail in memos to assist in the analysis and better understanding of the relationships between various codes and emergent themes and issues. These codes and themes were compared and contrasted among the three countries and both within and between the two case study topics of gender and security.

Sample interview schedule

Interview Schedule – Version 1.7 – October 4, 2006

CIDA – Gender equality

POLICY

> CIDA's Policy on Gender Equality has been in place since 1999. How well has it been accepted within the agency? How do you think it is being implemented? Is it achieving its purpose?
>
> What do you feel the future holds for CIDA's gender policy? Is a new policy in the works?
>
> If so, can you describe the policy development process?

Gender at CIDA

> What challenges does promoting gender equality at CIDA face?
>
> Are sufficient resources being dedicated to gender at CIDA?
>
> What have been the affects of gender mainstreaming at CIDA?
>
> How far has CIDA moved from a WID and Gender Equity perspective to a true Gender Equality approach?
>
> Has there been any successful examples of broader approaches to gender incorporating men/boys and masculinities into GE policy/programming at CIDA? Why or why not?

Outside influences

> How influential do you feel other donors have been on CIDA's gender policies?
>
> How is gender equality policy & programming at CIDA influenced by international organizations? DAC, UN, etc.

How is gender equality policy & programming at CIDA influenced by
civil society?

How is gender equality policy & programming at CIDA influenced by
outside experts/consultants? academic research?

CIDA's influence

How influential has CIDA been among other donors on GE issues and
policies? On civil society?

Notes

1 Event history analysis 'risk-sets' are the group of observations, in this case countries,
counted as 'at risk' for the event to take place. When the event takes place, event
history analysis acknowledges a 'transition' from 'origin' to 'destination state'. Five
donors who began providing aid later than the rest of the DAC enter the risk-set at
later dates: Ireland, 1974; Luxembourg, Portugal, Spain, 1980; Greece, 1996.
2 Please see Table A.3 later in this appendix for a full list of coding of the dependent
and other explanatory variables.
3 For further information, see the year of CEDAW ratification listed for each country in Appendix 1.
4 Other models including a categorical variable that accounts for all four of the
World Conferences on Women post-1975 yields similar results to this, showing
that the dichotomy of pre- and post-1985 is the salient marker for the timing of
these conferences. This is consistent with the literature on how gender and development became more central to the international women's rights agenda post-
Nairobi (Moser & Moser, 2005).
5 The WINGOs data was collected and coded by Paxton and her co-authors (2006)
and examines a select sample of thirty WINGOs over the time period from 1930
to 2003 in 196 countries. Though thirty WINGOs is a low number in the context
of the wide array of WINGO actors involved in the international women's movement, it can be argued that the variable accurately reflects the extent of embeddedness of a society in the international women's movement. As an alternative
measure of embeddedness, alternate models controlling for the formation of a
national-level chapter of Oxfam in each donor country to proxy national embeddedness in development-related civil society were also run. The results showed
significance when the Oxfam variable was included on its own in a model, but
the *p*-values dropped below the acceptable threshold of significance when donor
autonomy and structure variables were included. Given that the WINGOs membership is more closely linked to discourse on women's rights and gender equality,
it was more sensible to proceed with only this measure of embeddedness.
6 Results for this model are available upon request.

References

Berg, B. L. (2004). *Qualitative Research Methods for the Social Sciences* (5th Edition).
Boston; London: Pearson/Allyn and Bacon.

Box-Steffensmeier, J. M., & Jones, B. S. (1997). Time is of the Essence: Event History Models in Political Science. *American Journal of Political Science*, 1414–1461.

Frank, D. J., Longhofer, W., & Schofer, E. (2007). World Society, NGOs and Environmental Policy Reform in Asia. *International Journal of Comparative Sociology*, 48(4), 275–295.

Gorden, R. L. (1998). *Basic Interviewing Skills*. Prospect Heights, Ill.: Waveland Press.

Hironaka, A. (2002). The Globalization of Environmental Protection: The Case of Environmental Impact Assessment. *International Journal of Comparative Sociology*, 43(1), 65–78.

Moser, C., & Moser, A. (2005). Gender Mainstreaming Since Beijing: A Review of Success and Limitations in International Institutions. *Gender and Development*, 13(2), 11–22.

Paxton, P., Hughes, M. M., & Green, J. L. (2006). The International Women's Movement and Women's Political Representation, 1893–2003. *American Sociological Review*, 71, 898–920.

Ramirez, F. O., Soysal, Y., & Shanahan, S. (1997). The Changing Logic of Political Citizenship: Cross-national Acquisition of Women's Suffrage Rights, 1890 to 1990. *American Sociological Review*, 62(5), 735.

Roodman, D. (2005). *An Index of Donor Performance*. Center for Global Development. Working Paper Number 67. Retrieved from: www.cgdev.org/files/3646_file_WP_67_Revised.pdf

Swiss, L. (2009). Decoupling Values from Action: An Event-History Analysis of the Election of Women to Parliament in the Developing World, 1945–90. *International Journal of Comparative Sociology*, 50(1), 69–95.

Swiss, L., & Fallon, K. M. (2017). Women's Transnational Activism, Norm Cascades, and Quota Adoption in the Developing World. *Politics & Gender* 13(3), 458–487.

Wotipka, C. M., & Ramirez, F. O. (2008). World Society and Human Rights: An Event History Analysis of the Convention on the Elimination of All Forms of Discrimination Against Women. In B. A. Simmons, F. Dobbin, & G. Garrett (Eds.), *The Global Diffusion of Markets and Democracy* (pp. 303–343). Cambridge: Cambridge University Press.

Index

Index to *The Globalization of Foreign Aid: Developing Consensus* by Liam Swiss
Page numbers in italics refer to figures in the text